A Tortuous Path

A Tortuous Path

Atonement and Reinvention in a Broken System

Christopher E. Pelloski, MD

Author's Note:

Some names have been changed or omitted to protect the person's privacy. Also, for the sake of brevity, some conversations have been combined or condensed.

ISBN-13: 978-1726303316
ISBN-10: 1726303314

Printed in the United States

To the nonviolent prisoners of politics and convenience and all others who live under misinformed, draconian social policies.

"Child pornography possession cases on the docket of a United States district judge will include men of all ages ranging from late adolescence to old age. They will include students, teachers, administrators, physicians, lawyers, executives, church leaders, and others from all walks of life. Most lead otherwise normal and productive lives. They are good husbands, good fathers, good employees, good students, good friends. Few if any have prior criminal records. When they are caught, the consequences are enormous. Reputations are shattered; careers are ended, and families are destroyed. Suicides are not uncommon. The human costs are staggering, certainly equal to those in the most serious cases of drug addiction and in a population that is usually otherwise healthy."

—The Honorable James L. Graham, Southern District of Ohio
United States of America v. Christopher E. Pelloski

Table of Contents

Preface

"Tortuous /tôrCH(ōō)əs/ adjective: 1. full of twists and turns; 2. excessively lengthy and complex."

—MERRIAM WEBSTER'S COLLEGIATE DICTIONARY, 11TH EDITION

THE SENTENCE FOR accession with an attempt to view child pornography (to which I pleaded guilty) was handed down on July 11, 2014. After that, I remained in legal limbo for two more months before I would self-surrender at the Federal Correctional Institution, Elkton. This brought my total time under house arrest to fourteen months. The manner in which most of the local news entities handled the sentencing hearing was predictable. It cast me in the worst light possible, portraying me as a habitual abuser of children (hands-on implied), while suggesting the judge took it easy on me. This only served to stoke the already roaring Troll Fires, rather than informing the public of what really happened and why.

But I ignored all of that and focused on being with my children for as long as I could. I finished the primary writing for my first book while mentally preparing to go to prison. Those were the only constants I had before me. The other questions—*How long would I really be gone? What would I do and where would I go when I got out?* and *What will happen to my marriage and suspended medical license?*—those were all uncertainties.

I also had a false sense of accomplishment then, when it came to my mental health and overall outlook on life. I thought I had it all wrapped up and tied in a bow. It made perfect sense to me at the time. I had finally received the correct diagnosis of PTSD with dissociative features. Through counseling, I had addressed the difficult moments of my childhood that triggered the illness. I saw how my offense was a direct symptom of these experiences. Of course, I was criticized by some (including several friends and colleagues) for making excuses. Apparently, somewhere along the way, the definitions of *explanation* and *excuse* had become interchangeable for some. Or most likely the term *excuse* was applied to an explanation that people didn't want to hear or believe.

I just wanted to put it all behind me and move on.

Because of this mindset, I viewed going to prison and its aftermath as part of the obligatory formality, the after-the-fact punishment. There were certainly equal measures of arrogance (narcissism, some would say), naivety, and denial that went into this assessment. However, I would soon figure out that the journey is never really over. Closure is not only an elusive luxury but it's very relative. And there is always something new to learn—often from the most unexpected sources.

Acknowledgments

I WOULD LIKE TO THANK Julie Sommerfeld for making this book happen. Without you, my voice and many others' stories would go unheard. I would also like to thank Laura Gay Loskarn, for being in my corner since my journey began and for bravely permitting me to reprint her son Ryan's last letter to the world.

I would be remiss if I did not recognize the incredible work of journalists, Jacob Sullum and Elizabeth Nolan Brown, of the magazine, *Reason*. Their unflinching articles have been an invaluable resource for conducting the research required for this book.

Lastly, thank you to all who unconditionally loved and supported me and gave me a chance at redemption and recovery.

PART I

Camp

Chapter 1

"The degree of civilization in a society can be judged by entering its prisons."

—FYODOR DOSTOYEVSKY

MY BROTHER GAVE me the rules of prison, based on his experience:

- *Don't look anyone in the eyes for too long, without saying a quick what's up?* Direct eye contact without qualifying input is a challenge.
- *Do not tell anyone why you are there.* Especially with my charge.
- *Do not tell anyone how long you will be there, especially if you are a short-timer.* Someone who had nothing to lose would take a swing at you and fuck up your early out date—in order to graciously spread the misery around.
- *Don't tell anyone where you are from.* Things can get back to hurt family members.
- *Never put yourself in a position where you owe someone.*

These were the thoughts going through my mind as we put miles behind us on the way to my self-surrender at the Federal Correctional Institution, Elkton, with an annoyingly itchy left ankle. It was an overcast Ohio day: September 16, 2014.

The facility, when we arrived, was surreally normal. The room we entered was like the lobby of a doctor's office or library, with a large reception desk. Another guy was checking in, too. Just a kid. When he gave his birthday to the receiving guy, the year was 1992, the year I finished high school. He was young and earnest. "I just have five-and-a-half months." *WTF?* I looked over my shoulder at him. *What are you talking about? Don't say that out loud. That violates the code! Jesus, rookie.* Like I knew what the hell I was talking about.

He hugged his father goodbye. "I love you son, and take care." The father, a farmer from rural Ohio, was worried but proud to already know his boy would make it. There was that twinge of rebellion in his twang that comes with people who do not live in cities, no matter where you find yourself in the U.S. He had the rough skin and accelerated aging brought on by nicotine and direct sunlight, but his body wiry-strong beneath. "Love you too, Pop," the young man said.

I'd decided long before that there was no way my dad was taking me to prison. All of the crap he'd endured with my brother had shut him down. And my wife, Susan, had had enough of me by then, too. And even if she hadn't, her hands were full. She had to get the kids to and from school as usual on that big day. It was my father-in-law who was the obvious choice. Only he could do it. And he volunteered before anyone had to ask.

The goodbye with him and my mother-in-law was, like the room we stood in, eerily familiar and businesslike. I'd said this goodbye before: Off to summer camp. Off to college. Off to marriage. Off to medical school. Off to residency. It was just another life change that came with uncertainty and risk—except this time, maybe the danger was real.

After they left, things got down to brass tacks. I'd purposely worn the same clothes I wore to my arraignment in July 2013. I wanted them burned. And so they came off of my body, to go to the incinerator. "Damn son, did you get in a fight with a cat?" the processing officer said, pointing at my left ankle, which was evidently rejecting its new barrenness. It had developed red, scabbed-over crisscross scratch marks. For fourteen months, an electronic tether that ensured I remained inside during my house arrest had been tightly wrapped around it. I'd kept my secret safe from the kids, all that time, despite wrestling and running around with them.

Stripping down completely was followed by lifting up my scrotum, turning around and spreading my buttocks while artificially coughing, opening my mouth and rolling my tongue around, and showing the soles of my bare feet. I would eventually learn that this would also be the toll I paid for visiting with people from the outside world. Whenever a prisoner has contact with the outside, this is the routine—all in the name of prison safety. I might have been carrying a hacksaw or a packet of heroin in my lower GI tract—or worse, an acetylene torch tucked between my cheek and gum.

The perfunctory look on the officer's face told me this process was nothing new for him. He was used to repeating instructions for awkward, suddenly naked first timers. For me, it was somewhat unnerving. But I couldn't complain too much. I had seen worse, done worse. During my radiation oncology residency, I'd extracted from women's reproductive organs metal implants placed there to deliver radiation to their cervical cancers. So I knew about the awkwardness of an utter lack of modesty in the company of strangers. But this time I was on the other end of the probe.

I was issued dark brown boxers, green pants, tube socks, and a brown T-shirt. The clothes had black markings all over them, as if they'd passed out at a party and woke the next morning covered in Sharpied graffiti. The messages were difficult to make out. Some might have indicated the size of the garments or that they were temporary issue, but others were clearly profanities. Then there were the shoes. Slippers. Purposely loose cloth over a rubber slab of a sole. They made walking without rolling an ankle difficult.

"Are these…?" I asked.

"Yes. They are the right size," the guard replied while thinking about a hundred other things and looking elsewhere. He handed me a net laundry bag full of bedding, towels, and extra clothing.

The young kid and I were moved to a holding tank in a hallway. He wore the same clothes I did. In the adjacent holding tank were guys in all beige outfits. One of them was called out, and he and several officers went through his belongings. Food, clothing, toiletries, paperwork in cardboard boxes. Looked like he was checking out. I was still trying to determine the significance of our color coding. It had to mean something.

"Pelloski," a face poked in the room, I looked up and nodded. "Go to that room at the end of the hall to your left. That is Psych Intake." As I walked away, I overheard him giving his instructions to my tank-mate: "You, Newhouse, you follow him and go to the room on the right. That is General Intake."

The Psych nurse was a matronly middle-aged woman, with large glasses that were popular in the eighties, as was her puffed-up hair style. I couldn't criticize. Most people adopt a style they like and keep it over time. I still rocked my *Beverly Hills 90210*–inspired sideburns (something that was cool almost thirty years ago) even though mine were now violated with gray, as if I were dipped up to my ears in peroxide.

The nurse was very sweet, while being businesslike. "So I am going over your paperwork, and you have ADD or depression or PTSD? It is kind of confusing," she said apologetically.

"That's OK. It *is* confusing." I reassured her, and we both had a chuckle. "For a long time people thought I had ADD, so I took Ritalin for years. Then it was thought I also had anxiety disorder, too. So Effexor got added to the mix." She wrote this down in the margins of her printed report. "Eventually, when all of this came out," I said pointing to my new prison garb, "I was diagnosed with PTSD. So I stopped the Ritalin and Effexor and was started on Zoloft."

"OK," she said jotting a few more things down. She looked through her papers a bit more. I knew what was coming. "But it says you are not taking any meds. You are not on Zoloft?"

"No."

"When was that discontinued?"

"About a week ago."

"Who discontinued that?"

"I did."

"You decided to stop taking psych medicine a week before you come to prison?"

"I know it seems—"

"What did your psychiatrist think about that?"

"He doesn't know. I have not seen him in almost six months."

She was very perplexed, almost upset, "Were you seeing anyone?"

"Yes. My therapist. The social worker who correctly diagnosed me." She looked skeptical. "I know this seems odd, like I am self-managing. And yes, I am to an extent. But please realize that for most of my adult life I have been on medication that I did not need. PTSD is not something that needs meds all the time. I was on Zoloft for over a year and it was time to stop. Look, if prison is going to be sad or scary, I want to feel it for once, and not have it dulled by medication."

"Why did you stop seeing your psychiatrist?"

"That is complicated, too. Let's just say he did not steer me in the right direction—and he was not going to stand by me in the long run."

"But, making this change, on your own, right now. Prison is a difficult adjustment—" she looked more concerned at that moment. "We can resume here—"

"How about this? If I notice that I am having trouble or want to hurt myself or others, I will come to you guys as soon as possible. I really do not think I need this medication—and I am sure you have heard this before, but I need to start feeling what I am supposed to feel. I got through with Zoloft, I don't see the point now."

"OK," she relented with reluctance. "We will keep a close eye on you, too."

We had an accord. After some signatures and paperwork, I switched rooms with my co-admittee.

The General Intake guy was a little more gruff, a skinny, black-haired white man with blue stubble already showing under the smooth, shaved skin of his pale, thin face. He looked like he derived all his nutrition from coffee and cigarettes. Still, he had a good sense of humor about his job and the boxes he needed to check.

"Do you have any reason to think that your personal safety will be threatened if you are in the general prison population? Any family who are cops or in politics or gangs?"

"No." I thought for a bit more. "Well, I heard guys with my charge—"

"Guys with your charge *are* the general population here." And he quickly made his check and moved on.

"Do you want to kill yourself?"

"No."

"Are you fearful of coming to prison?"

"No."

"Good. Because where you are going, down the hill, is one step above the Boy Scouts."

I was going to the FSL, a victory, a huge one for me. Federal correctional institutions (FCIs) like the one I currently sat in, are medium- and low-security facilities with strengthened perimeters (often double fences with electronic detection systems) and mostly cell-type housing. Federal satellite low (FSL) facilities are low security, often adjacent to an FCI or other higher security facility. They have dormitory housing, a relatively low staff-to-inmate ratio, and limited perimeter fencing with unrestricted inmate movement. At Elkton, the FSL was called "down the hill," due to its topographical relationship to the corresponding FCI. Sex offenders—even nonviolent/noncontact, computer-based offenders like myself—were not permitted to serve their time in true federal "prison camps" (a.k.a. Club Fed), which have no fences, due to the inmates' perceived lack of security threat. Apparently, all intake for the center was done at the FCI.

A View of Elkton, Courtesy of Google Earth

They took my picture and made an ID card for me. My new name was 71491-061.

For the transfer to the FSL, the kid and I were put into four-point shackles, which reduced our steps in our unstable slippers to about ten inches for each pace, marched across the four hundred–foot FCI yard, past the twelve coils of razor wire that hugged the bases and tops of the perimeter fences, and into a van escorted by two guards with loaded shotguns. Despite being terrified that a stumble or wrong move would result in a hole being blasted in me, I still found it a bit odd that less than three hours before I'd stopped at a McDonald's with my in-laws and eaten a Sausage McMuffin. How had the act of self-surrender instantly made me a security threat that necessitated all of this?

Down the hill. More razor wire, more buzzing of doors being remotely unlocked. More paperwork. And finally, I was admitted into Elkton FSL, or "camp," as Susan and I had named it for the kids. A camp where I would learn how to make better choices and avoid any more bad consequences.

One of the guards asked an inmate standing nearby to take me to my cube. My new address: G-A-24C.

If my life were a movie at that moment, walking through the G-A unit towered over by my escort, a gigantic red-headed, red-bearded guy nicknamed Vanilla, it would have been directed by Terry Gilliam. It was simultaneously overwhelming and a more pathetic display of humanity than I had ever seen. It looked like the barracks of an army that was *badly* losing a war being fought on its own soil—one that was running out of soldiers fit for combat. The sound was a surreal cacophony of laughing, yelling, and swearing—men living on top of one another. This human warehouse was about a hundred yards long and contained, under a thirty-foot raftered ceiling, about 55 twelve-by-ten-foot cubicles. The cubicle walls stood five feet tall, and each cube held two or three beds, most with double-decker bunks. About half of the cubes paralleled the bulletproof windows. The other half occupied the middle of the space, in two rows with aisles on either side.

Everywhere I looked, I was confronted with things I never would have expected: very young guys, who elsewhere would have been identified as high-school nerds, sitting cross-legged on the floor and playing (double take) yes, Dungeons and Dragons. Old men bent ninety degrees over their walkers, shuffling along singing to themselves. Every few bunks, to my right or left, lay the motionless heap of a body, completely covered from head to toe, as if blankets could block the fluorescent glare and incessant noise, even yelling coming from just inches away. The mounds never flinched or woke in protest. I was also struck by the whiteness of the place. African Americans make up 40 percent of the U.S. prisoner population (despite comprising only 13 percent of the general population). Yet, I saw none as I walked through the unit.

I have no idea how I got to my cubicle. The entry to the cube just appeared before me, and so I entered, carrying my sack of belongings over my shoulder.

"That's yours, buddy," my temporary guide said, pointing to the top bunk. "Let me know if you need anything. I am just over there in 42." I had no idea what he'd just told me, so I just silently nodded and he walked off. I saw a long pair of inert legs on the lower bunk, so I put my net bag on the top one quietly, as if any of my movements could have been heard over the din. But my cube-mate had already been awakened by my guide.

"Hey, man," he greeted me. He was puffy around the eyes, wakened from his nap. "I didn't think you would get here before four o'clock count." I shook his hand, which was dry and cracked. He had rosacea across the cheekbones of his youthful face, and a pustular infection to go along with it. He noticed me noticing and answered my thoughts:

"I work pots and pans in the kitchen and I keep getting skin infections. The damned rosacea doesn't help either," he said smiling. He was older than me but looked like a little boy in the face.

"How do you—How do any of you sleep through this?" I asked, waving my hands around to both break the ice and get off the subject of dermatological ailments.

"I get up before five a.m. I am so tired, I can sleep through anything," he said, after pivoting to a seated position in his bottom bunk. "Plus, after going through boot camp, I learned to sleep standing up." He stood up and surveyed the unit with me, as if he were seeing it for the first time too—or maybe just reminding himself of the bewilderment just over the divider walls. "But some guys—like that guy over there," he said, pointing to a heap, "some guys have decided to sleep away their time." He scanned for another motionless, covered corpse and pointed again, this time far across the unit, "But some guys—like him over there—they wake up, go to pill line, take whatever the hell they are given, come back, and are just snowed. Every day. I have watched guys come here and gain a hundred pounds. Lots of over-medication here. Sad."

Just then, someone returned to their cube, slammed their locker, exclaimed "Fuck!" and walked back out of the unit. "And some maybe need more meds," my cube mate said with a smile. "You have no idea how lucky you are to have landed in this cube." He smiled again and gave me a pair of earplugs in an unopened wrapper. Seeing his hands again with this exchange reminded me of my own skin issue. My ankle had stopped itching; it had already forgotten its former tether.

Then the welcoming committee came out of nowhere. Like individual fish who broke off from a school of fish that otherwise moved and darted in unison. It was as if these guys materialized out of this dizzying and arbitrary pattern of movement just to greet me. Faces, smiling and warm.

"OK, you need to get those damned slippers off!" a large visage suddenly exclaimed from the background. A huge man, maybe 350 pounds, buzz cut head and square—he reminded me of Curly or Joe from the Three Stooges a bit. He handed me rubber shower shoes, a few razor blades, soap, toothpaste, and a toothbrush. "You will turn an ankle wearing those motherfuckers!"

I looked at my feet and accepted his kind offerings, "Yeah, man. I can barely walk in them. Thank you."

"Oh! they make you wear those damned things so you don't run off and twist an ankle if you try to get away. Like you was going to try to get away, right? Sweet Jesus." I laughed a bit and he looked at me closer.

"You a self-surrender, ain't you?"

"Yes."

"I can tell. You guys all look so rested and calm when you get here. And your face is full—not all thin and tired-looking. Well, I ain't thin now, look!" He laughed, smacking his immense belly with pride. "They call me Jelly Roll. I make sure the new guys get all set when they arrive." His smile was infectious—another boyish face that had seen a lot of living and aging. He then got a little more serious. "Look here. I don't give a shit what you did to get here or who you were before you got here, but we all need to help each other out and do our time and get the hell out of here. So anything that makes it better for you is better for all—and is better for me. So if you need anything, just ask ol' Jelly Roll, and I can help." I nodded. And he continued, "Make sure you get outside and get fresh air too. Don't live in this piece of shit. I spent eighteen months in county jails before I got here in damn near middle of winter, and you bet your ass I was out walking in the snow and being outside. I didn't care if it was five below, my ass was outside walking, and people thought I was crazy! Ha ha ha!"

The thought of walking out in the open sounded amazing to me. House arrest had limited my movement to within five feet of doorways and trips to court and appointments with shrinks for fourteen months.

Jelly Roll abruptly parted with me. "OK, man. You take care here!" and with that, his large body disappeared back into the ocean.

"He got sixteen years," my cube mate informed me.

"Jesus."

"And he did not self-surrender. He bounced around the system while his case went on."

"For what?" I asked, forgetting my brother's pointers, "The Prison Code," before catching myself. "Never mind," I said softly.

"Dude," he chuckled, "I am pretty sure you are here for the same reason as me. And the same reason as him." I looked at my cube mate, petrified. "You are a SO, a sex offender. Not a toucher, though. CP charges. Some of the guys read about your case and knew you were coming. It's OK. We were—"

A new face appeared, this one offering a stained mug. "You like coffee, I bet?" He was a young guy, bald/shaved head and goatee. Indeed I did. I was up to about a pot a day during my house arrest, while I was writing my first book. I feared a massive caffeine withdrawal headache coming on that day.

"Oh, yes."

"Here, take this spare mug of mine. It may smell like mustard—I stored my mustard in it for a while. But after a few brews, it should be good." He handed it to me and then disappeared into the environment.

Then another thin man, in his fifties with heavy frame glasses, showed up at the entry to the cube. "Here, I don't get that Maxwell House sludge. I get the *prima* Columbian," he said in a faux-aristocrat voice. "OK, OK. Either way, it is instant and crappy, but the Columbian is just a touch better. And it may say to add two teaspoons in the instructions, but damn it, I'm a rebel, and will put in the third scoop just because!" he defiantly announced as he handed me a packet of instant coffee. I suspected the deflated look on my face had betrayed my thoughts on the matter when he said, "Look, this isn't the freshly ground Starbucks Sumatra Blend but it will get the job done." And once again, a random appearance quickly dissolved into the current.

I returned to putting my things away and making my bunk.

"I'm Leonard, by the way," my cube mate said.

"I'm Chris."

At that moment, our other cube mate appeared. "You the new cellie?" (We may have lived in cubicles, but *cubie* just didn't sound right.)

"Yes."

"I'm George."

George had a lot of features that reminded me of my Austrian grandmother. Dark, thick hair, olive complexion, perfect white teeth—European, but definitely darkened by the Moors' 711 AD invasion. He had returned from his afternoon run: four miles just about every day,

I learned later. "I'm going to hit the shower, but we will catch up." He pointed to my locker, which was the size of a minifridge. Since I was the new guy to the cube, my locker was the one closest to the entry way and aisle, the least favorable position, just like my top bunk. "This one is yours. You can start getting all your stuff squared away in there," he explained as he walked off with a towel. I started nesting.

"Hey, I didn't mean to pry or freak you out," Leonard said, after reseating himself on his bunk to make room for me to move around in the six-by-four-foot open area intended for three grown men. "A lot of guys here read up on the laws and follow cases. Yours was one they followed closely. How much time did you get? I know it was short."

The rules were still in the back of my mind, so I hesitated.

"It was a year, wasn't it?" He answered his own question.

"Yeah. Plus a day."

"Well, that is good. That will give you good time and shave off your sentence by a couple of months. And if you get to a halfway house, you will get out even sooner."

Under federal law, prisoners serving more than one year in prison get fifty-four days per year of "good time" on the anniversary of each year they serve, plus prorated good time applied to a partial year served at the end of their sentence. This encourages good behavior during incarceration, as it can be revoked for rule infractions. This rule was the reason for my twelve-months-and-a-day sentence: The extra day qualified me for good time.

"He won't get halfway house," a third voice chimed in from above. In the adjacent cube's top bunk sat a guy in his early thirties with a completely buzzed head. He was heavyset but looked as if his weight gain was recent and sudden and his skin was still catching up to his extra volume, stretching and appearing bloated. He looked as if his entire body were under an uncomfortable internal pressure. "He won't be here long enough to get all of the paperwork done. My god, it took them over a year to get things right for my halfway house—even though I ended up declining it."

Those words sent shivers down my spine. I was expecting to be out soon, working again and keeping Susan and the kids in the house they were living in. It would really mess things up if there were delays. The look on my face was noticed by the neighbor, who was looking down at me as if presiding over our cube and the lockers below him. His bare foot rested on the top of the divider wall, complete with a big toe the size of a doorknob and nearly as spherical. He changed the course of his address.

"A lot of the newer guys coming in here the last few months are getting these one- and two-year sentences," he said half to me and himself. "I used to get pissed when I heard about this. I was like, *What the fuck—these guys did what I did, and I get four years?*" His thoughts seemed to be pulled toward himself no matter what tack he took. "I used to get mad, and then I realized, I probably needed that time, to really figure things out. I had no connection with my feelings. I had so much anger. And I really didn't realize that what I was doing was so wrong. The first few years, I just wasn't getting it. And when I got kicked out of the program the first time, because they found porn in my locker—that was my wake-up call." *He needed* another *wake-up call?* I thought.

"I just had no boundaries, you know?" he continued, as I put away prison-issued socks and towels and occasionally nodded to let him know that someone was listening to him talk to himself. "I mean, first my uncle rapes me when I am like four or five—and I was told that was normal by him. He wasn't violent or scary about it, so I didn't know any better. Then my older cousin and I fooled around a lot when I was nine or so. I am not gay, but, you know, we did gay things together. Then my hot sixteen-year-old babysitter is showing me her pussy and making me play with her tits when I am like eleven. Of course I liked it—what am I supposed to do?"

I stopped what I was doing and stared at him in disbelief. Here I was, not a few hours into prison, and I was hearing this guy's detailed sexual history—when I had been instructed to remain mute about myself. This guy was dumping all this information onto a complete stranger, openly and freely and so matter-of-factly. I caught myself staring and resumed nesting, or resumed the pretense, at least, not to be rude. There wasn't all that much to stow away.

He was still talking when George returned from his shower. "My adoptive parents think other things happened to me when I was even younger. They got me when I was four. My foster mom said I was terrified of men and so angry all the time. Like total crazy tantrums. They didn't know what to do with me." I noticed George shooting a look at

Leonard, and they shared a familiar smile and eyeroll. "But I just had no boundaries, you know. They found something like a million-and-a-half porn files on my computer, and I was like, *Whoa, that's a lot of porn, you know? Like maybe I do have a problem with it?* I didn't know. I thought porn and weird sex stuff was normal. Even stuff with kids in it. Because like it all started with me when I was a kid, you know. But this program is helping. I am glad they let me back in. I am getting it now."

He looked around at the three of us, "That is why I declined the halfway house time. I wanted to spend those six months here and finish the program. My folks were upset, because they wanted me out of here, but I think I did the right thing." After a moment he looked back at me. "Well, either way, I don't think you will get halfway house time." Then he went back to reading his magazine, *Popular Mechanics,* a magazine I had not seen in the flesh since my eighth-grade physical science class. And that was my introduction to the horrifically broken and perpetually mending soul of Crazy Curtis.

At four thirty came the afternoon stand-up count. It was the first moment of silence I had heard since arriving. During the count, several correctional officers (COs) would walk up one side of the unit, getting a headcount from all the cells on each side, loop around and come down the other end. The headcount was then combined with the counts from all the other places where inmates would be (units or kitchen only, at that time of day) and once the numbers added up correctly, there was an all-clear. If the count was off, there would be a recount. The main purpose of these counts was to detect escapees.

Anyone who was sleeping during the count got their asses chewed out. Everyone had to stand. In the 1980s, there was a prisoner who was murdered and covered in blankets to make it look like he was sleeping. For several days, his corpse was duly counted, until the smell of decay grew pervasive, and the officers realized they had a dead inmate. Inmate deaths are generally to be avoided as much as possible. It's bad publicity. Making us stand was one way to ensure we were still breathing, a sign that we continued to exist and mattered, at least within those walls.

There was another count: the nine thirty before lights-out. Then the exhausting day was over with nothing having gone as I expected. Whatever value my brother's code might have had elsewhere, it did not apply to this place.

Chapter 2

"The first person you meet is the worst person you'll meet."

—AN OLD PRISONERS' ADAGE

FOR SOME REASON, I always remember the first night spent in a new station in life with exceptional clarity. I remember looking at the springs of the upper bunk above my head during my first night in college, repeatedly telling myself, *You're in* college *now. You are in the dorm of your college—right now*. Or the first night of medical school, a few months after I got married: *You are a medical student now. You have a wife. You are in your very own apartment in Chicago—right by Wrigley Field, you lucky bastard! The wood beams you are looking at support the roof of the apartment that you are living in—with your wife—and you are going to medical school*. In those instances, I was almost alarmed, surprised that I made it that far. As if I couldn't believe in those moment's realizations.

That first night at Elkton, I looked up at the rafters from my top bunk as people walked past my head. My bunk sat a few inches higher than the height of the cubicle wall, so all the scurrying and scuttling that went on after lights-out, scurried and scuttled just a few inches from where I was to sleep. There was no silent moment for reflection, but I managed anyway: *You are in* prison *right now. Federal. Fucking. Prison. This is your first night, and it is about time you got here*.

This time, I had no problem believing my luck. I had always lived my life as if some calamity was just around the corner. Finally, it had arrived. I'd lost my career. I had an inkling that I was going to lose my wife. And I was worried sick that some horrific accident would happen to my kids. One that would have been entirely preventable had I been with them instead of being a complete loser who couldn't keep it together enough to avoid going to *prison*—even though he'd had the world in the palm of his hand. But I'd known this day was coming, not just since my sentencing, but ever since I saw that first clip online, so many years before.

I knew then there was no escape. I knew there would be a knock at the door one day. And when it came, I wasn't even there. Susan and the kids had to endure that humiliation, and the search that followed, while I drank beer in Colorado and rubbed elbows with smart people. Lying in that bunk, looking at that ceiling and replaying all that had happened, I took it in stride. It was like I'd already known what all of this would feel like. And for the first time in twenty years, I did not have Ritalin, Effexor, or Zoloft to mask my feelings and emotions. I was going to take this all in, without the help of Pfizer or Novartis. So I drifted off to sleep to the incessant buzz of prison.

A few of those in nearby cubes marveled out loud at the way I'd slept through my first night in prison. I felt a bit awkward about being singled out, so I asked George where I could go to sit and start writing letters. (This was another, less-stressed pointer from my brother "Get yourself some paper, stamps, and envelopes as soon as you can," he said, "and let people know where you are and how to reach you.") George directed me to the main TV room, after lending me a pen, paper, envelopes, and stamps.

The room was about a hundred feet long by thirty wide and had six wall-mounted widescreen TVs distributed around it showing CNN, ESPN, Telemundo, and the History channel. There were about twenty tables with four chairs each mounted to them, and all were vacant that early in the morning. The room was empty. At some seats, towels or books or cups served as territorial markings. I went to the closest unmarked table, just to my left, under the Telemundo TV, and set up shop. I pulled out a folded piece of paper and wrote a quick letter to Susan, letting her know I'd arrived OK and was actually at the camp. I was about to start one to my parents when I realized someone was standing across the table from me, arms folded.

He was a very serious-looking Latino man, in his early thirties maybe, with a completely shaved caramel-colored head, which sat upon a neck that was flanked by well-developed trapezius muscles. These in turn sat upon well-developed shoulders and tattooed arms that emerged from his sleeveless undershirt. "Hey man," he said in a calm, cool voice, "I know you are new here. I know you do not know all the rules yet. So things are cool, man. You can sit here now. I will let my boys know that." He then put his hands on the table and spoke in an even more subdued tone. "It's just that, well, we don't want the wrong kind of people sitting here." He explained, as if almost apologizing, with an agonized look on his face, like Robert De Niro delivering a tough line in a movie. "And, if we let one guy sit here, even if we may like *that* guy, other guys may think they can sit wherever they want. Do you know what I am saying?"

"Yeah man. No problem. I can just move over there," I offered, being as diplomatic as I could.

"No, no, man. I insist. You are good at this table right now. You already got all of your shit out," he said pointing at my papers. "But just remember next time. Cool?"

"Yeah," I nodded blankly. "OK." And he walked out.

As soon as he was out of sight, I gathered all of my stuff, and moved to a more neutral, unclaimed location. I felt like a scared suburban white boy, completely forgetting that I'd gone to a socioeconomically mixed high school that already had metal detectors in the late eighties or early nineties—long before Columbine. We'd had an entirely pregnant homecoming court my junior year, and some students had been killed or killed others during their enrollment. Now, twenty-five years later, everything was different. I'd chucked my "hood card" a long time ago, so like a weak bitch, I went and took a safe chair rather than stand my ground. But I was not about to make waves. I would do what I needed to do and get out of there. That was not my world anymore.

Not long after I reestablished my mobile office, I encountered the first person that I really *met* at Elkton: Jon. His appearance was confusing, and he proved to be a tough read. He looked like an amalgam of Jerry Garcia, a walrus, and the caricature of a Jewish man in an old Nazi propaganda poster. There were conflicts about him everywhere. He was balding on top yet had long dark hair that he put in a pony-tail—the quintessential aging hippy look. He had a swagger and confidence, as if he were a chiseled lifeguard on a beach, yet he dwelled within a fat, hirsute middle-aged body. Most striking, though, was his outlandish handlebar mustache. For someone I assumed was also here on a sex offense, this was a horrible look. He looked like a villain. All he was missing was a black cape and top hat and a damsel-in-distress he could wrap up in rope and place on the railroad tracks in the path of an oncoming steam locomotive.

I found his sudden appearance, so close on the heels of my encounter with the Latino strong-safety, to be a calculated move—like he was waiting for me to be alone again. My suspicion was confirmed when he quickly sat down and immediately started talking to me, as if taking advantage of a limited window of opportunity to divulge whatever he was about to say.

"Ah, at long last we have the good doctor," he opened. I smiled and looked back down at my empty sheet of paper, hoping to convey that I wanted to write some more. That I was adapting to my new surroundings. That I might possibly want to be by myself and correspond with some people on the outside. No dice. He continued, "I see you've gotten your introduction to TV room politics—it's a big deal in prison, you know," he said, laughing. "For a lot of these guys, a chair in the TV room is the only thing of worth they ever owned."

He stopped laughing for a bit. "Yes. Racism is alive and well in prison. You'll soon notice that a third of this TV room is black." He pointed to the opposite side of the room. "The TV over there is always ESPN, and the one across from it is usually BET. There are also three more black TV rooms—one of them is just for one *particular* black guy! Three out of the six potential TV rooms, and two out of the six common room TVs, are claimed by blacks." He laughed again, twisting the points of his handlebar mustache villainously. "I did the math one day. There are about fifteen black guys in our unit—or 10 percent of the population—yet they claim 42 percent of all of the available TVs. Is this part of the slavery reparations they have been talking about?"

I could tell he had practiced his shtick. The rate at which he spoke made me think he was practicing the same circular breathing technique that enabled woodwind and brass musicians to play notes that outlasted the normal respiration cycle. There were no natural pauses in his speech, either.

He pointed to his right. "And you are familiar with the Telemundo TV. That is the Spanish sixth of the common room. They also have one of the TV rooms. And there are *five* of them. Five Spanish inmates, total. Meaning there are five TVs available for the remaining one hundred plus white guys here. Well, four, if you discount the Haters' TV room—those guys are technically white, but not like the *normal* white sex offenders here." Before I could ask about "Haters," he returned to his main theme—bashing the black inmates. "Which is really fine by us actually. It is annoying though, if you think about it too hard, but in the grand scheme, it serves a purpose. While they account for less than 15 percent of the population, here they account for 90 percent of the noise, so it is good to have them in their own places where they can yell, hoot, and holler, and have all that fucking noise contained in *their* rooms." At that moment, I looked up, having not heard prejudice so coldly come out of someone's mouth with such ease and eloquence in a long time—not since the years at my lily-white private college and the neocons that lurked on its campus.

A VISUAL PRESENTATION OF JON'S NUMBER CRUNCHING

"Oh, I am sorry if I have offended your limousine liberal sensibilities. That's right, you probably came of age during the PC movement—where you talk about it but do nothing. Well, let me tell you something. My parents were these progressive Jewy types that went down to Selma and Birmingham to help out with the Civil Rights movement. One of my five ex-wives is black. So I am all about equality. But what I have seen in my nearly five years in the prison system has changed me. I have seen these guys yell around the clock all night, never stopping, screaming about inane bullshit, like who is better, LeBron or Jordan, when all I wanted to do was fucking sleep. I watched them shit in their hands and throw it at the guards as they climbed up cell bars—like fucking monkeys would do—and beat each other to a pulp." He paused to change his tone, slightly. "I know. I know. They are the by-product of a defunct and failed society and culture, and part of that package happens to be the black skin they are covered in—but I really don't give a shit anymore. They bother me. And the sight of them disgusts me. Which is why I don't mind that they take up half the TV rooms. Then I don't have to hear them. The real criminals are contained while the rest of us can enjoy some quiet and get on with our time. This is the only place," he said, pointing down at the table (but pointing at Elkton, really), "in the five prisons and jails I have been in, where this is possible."

He continued after his first audible inhale, as if he had never spoken to another human being before. "Yes. I said it. *They* are the criminals. *We* are not. We looked at something. Those pieces of shit sold drugs and guns. They didn't watch a video of someone selling drugs and guns. They actually *sold* drugs and guns. We are the fastest growing federal prisoner demographic. White guys who have something to offer society who are filling up cells just to even the playing field, so politicians cannot say the federal prison system is inherently racist: See, look—we got white guys too. You walk up and down this unit and you will meet executives, college professors, lawyers, educators, business owners, job creators. The opportunity cost in income tax alone here has got to be astronomical."

Then came the part he had been building to. "I was one of the top realtors in the Vancouver-Seattle area. I raised over a million dollars for cancer research—yeah, *cancer,* Mr. Cancer Doctor. And I knew Lance

Armstrong, personally. I ran my own company and employed over twenty people. And I get ambushed crossing the border from Canada to the U.S. So the headlines got to say that I was part of an international child pornography ring. That is why I was sent to Washington, D.C.—I had no home district. Taken into custody right there. It was an international event. No warning. I spent the next six months in that D.C. county jail and dealt with my wife screaming at me every time I tried to call her and instruct her on what to do with our finances. Of course, she did some stupid things and I lost more money—but it's not like it was ever going to be mine again anyway. Being stuck in that cell was the worst. I would cry myself to sleep every night for the first few months. All because I looked at things, child porn, and sent pictures requested by someone in a chat room who ended up being an FBI agent.

"You have no idea how lucky you are—for the judge you got, for your house arrest, and what you avoided for doing the very same thing I did. And to just land here at Elkton. Self-surrender." I didn't have the heart to point out that what he did *was* a little bit different from what I did. But from my current perspective, sitting there in prison, it would have been like one fly claiming his pile of dog shit was superior to the next fly's.

"The saying here is that Elkton is the home of chomos, homos, bitches, and snitches. That guy you were just talking with, Salazar, he is a crooked cop from Miami. Informants and crooked law enforcement, military types, get sent here for protection. Those are your snitches. If you noticed, there aren't too many scary looking people here. Those are your homos and bitches. Guys who would not last at a normal prison. There is zero tolerance for fighting here. Salazar is here probably because he rolled on someone. I wonder how many people ended up getting killed because of that. Oh, and *we're* the evil ones. The cho-mos."

At this moment he actually stopped and anticipated my next question. I expected him to answer it, but he was almost insistent that I say my line this time: "What is a chomo?" Before I finished enunciating the long *O*, his scripted response started.

"It's prison-speak for *child molester.* A lot of the non–sex offender inmates here assume we molested children. Why else would people get five to ten years, *right*? With a sentence that long, they must have done something really bad. Of course, that's not true. If you are an actual contact offender, you can't even be at the FSL. I verified this with the program staff here. Your security level is too high to be at the camp if you are a contact offender. So you are either up the hill at the FCI or at another institution if you did that. The Elkton FSL is actually a very unique place. Every SO that you meet here will be a noncontact child pornography case only. But if I can't explain to my own family members that I only looked at child pornography and never touched anyone, then how can I explain this concept to the knuckle-dragging, mouth breathers whose only useful skill is stealing cars or blowing up trailer homes trying to cook meth?

"And we are not even at a real camp, technically. A real camp does not have a fence with concertina wire around it. It is open. But since we are sex offenders, we have a higher public safety factor. Yes, these thugs who sold crack and crystal meth to mothers, knowing their kids would rot away and work their way down through the system, or those white-collar assholes who swindled people out of their life savings and ruined families, that have children in them—they get to go to real camps. But not us. Because we are a danger to—*gasp*—the children! The United States is really the only country in the world that puts nonviolent or nondangerous people into prison for long periods of time. In other countries, if you are unsafe, then they keep you away from the public. Well, unless you are a political prisoner. Then you are fucked. Which is why I consider myself a political prisoner. I am here only because it helped someone get reelected for being tough on crime.

"So when you hear that word, *chomo,* they are talking about you. You won't get it much from the black guys or Spanish guys. They prefer not to discuss it and will only pull out that card when cornered. It's the Haters, those fucking redneck, white-supremacist guys. The whole distinction between chomo and non-chomo is their obsession. When you hear that word, just get away. Nothing good will follow."

Just then, someone threw open the door. It was another gigantic, morbidly obese man. This one, in his late twenties or early thirties, had a fiery red, tangled beard that seemed to originate from all parts of his head and neck. He saw us stop talking as he scanned the room. Then he saw what he was looking for, and his ears pinned back, pulling his glasses closer to his face—his head so massive it was noticeable even across the room. He walked in disgust toward the adjacent table, picked up a plastic cup sitting there, and defiantly slammed it down on the table where Jon and I were sitting. The cup bore the engraving "Tiny," his ironic nickname I presumed. "I am so fucking tired of this horseshit!" he exclaimed and stormed out.

It would be months before I would attempt to sit in that TV room again.

If a Civil War–era movie were made at Elkton, the Haters would play either the unkempt Confederate soldiers who had a perverse pleasure in gunning down those uppity Northern aggressors or the grimy cracker farmhands who took a perverse pleasure in whipping the slaves while they toiled in the cotton fields. They were the *South Park*'s "They Took Our Jobs" crowd, specializing in crystal meth, motorcycle gangs, gunrunning, and white supremacy. They were covered in tattoos and wrinkles from hard living, and emanating from these dermal features was pure hatred, down to the "Piss Off" tattoo on one little guy's neck and "White Pride" on the shin of the alpha male of that group.

They were very clannish, or perhaps *Klannish* might be the better word. Like the Borderlanders of old. More than any other Elkton clique, they stuck to themselves. They had their own TV room, and they always made sure they had a man holding the fort at the back of the cafeteria, the tables along the windows. If there was no place else to sit, and those back tables were open, anyone not a Hater who tried to sit there would get his tray flipped over and be yelled at or browbeaten until he moved, while the guards pretended not to notice. The Haters also had their own bleacher section on the yard, even their own softball team—amazingly, the black and Latino inmates would root against them even if they were playing a largely SO team, just because their act got so old. I'm sure they found not just safety but solace in the comradery of the group in what was, from their perspective, the vast ocean of chomos, niggers, and spics that Elkton presented. Despite that, what really pissed all the other inmates off was the way one or another of their lackeys was always brownnosing the guards, making the most of their shared whiteness to curry favor.

I got to know my cube-mate Leonard a bit more on my first full day, after he returned from his kitchen duty. Like most I'd met, he opened up his life story to me. Leonard's resume was impressive, indeed. He served in the first Gulf War in the U.S. Army, Airborne Division, and was part of the first few waves of the ground war in which the Iraqis were entirely overmatched. He had a law degree from Tulane University, was once a traveling/professional puppeteer, had worked at an art house movie theater, and was a practicing Buddhist as well as a recovering pornography addict. His take on the Haters pretty much summed up the kind of person he was.

"You know, those guys are suffering incredibly, too," he would say. Most of them are addicted to heroin or meth. They come from broken homes, no education. There is a lot of pain there. You can see it in their faces. All that shit they do, it's just a macho coping mechanism." Because of his legal background, Leonard had helped a lot of inmates prepare their paperwork for appeals and transfers, and as a result he'd talked with them and got to know them on a different level from most of us, and his "clients" included a few Haters. He was one of the most intelligent, sensitive, patient, and compassionate human beings I have ever met. And, like me, he also had PTSD, officially diagnosed during his pretrial evaluations, and had been sexually abused. He had a young son and daughter, too, and like mine, his wife had stood by him.

"I heard you got your earful from Jon this morning." He smiled. "You will learn that one of the worst things to do in prison is be alone with someone. That is when all the crazy comes out. That is why things are set up so that there is rarely an opportunity to truly be alone with someone else. Sure, you can talk to someone one on one, but it's always out in the open or in common spaces. The shower or shitter stall is about the only time you will truly be by yourself here. The lack of privacy is annoying, but believe me, it beats the alternative. Captivity does weird things to people." He then lowered his head below the cube wall and quietly added, "I should know. I used to be a CO at a maximum-security state prison in Texas. I was a PO, too for a while. That's one of the reasons why I'm here: protection. Even though it's been awhile since I did either. It was just work to keep me afloat until I passed the bar exam." *Corrections officer* and *parole officer? Leonard's resume just kept expanding.*

"Jesus, so you got PTSD, too?" I asked.

"Yeah. I saw a lot of charred Iraqis when we did that sweep, man. It was rough. It was like we were just walking over them. Each guy probably had a wife and kids. And we just walked through and over them, like they were just—garbage." He said solemnly. "And, of course, I have a long line of traumas. My dad and I did not get along. He was a star basketball and baseball player, got a college sports scholarship and all. I was kind of a wimpy kid who could not live up to things. He treated my mom pretty bad. Then they divorced. Sprinkle in some confusing sexual stuff with older kids when I was little and—voila!"

"I have PTSD, too." A third voice came up over the wall. *Good god, Leonard really was not kidding about the privacy part*. It was Crazy Curtis's cube-mate, Jim Russo, a short, older Italian man, with a salt-and-pepper beard and wire-frame glasses. He came around the corner from the adjacent cube. He reminded me of my maternal grandfather a little: short, with very wide shoulders and big arms, even well into his sixties, as this man was. "Yeah, the lady evaluating me says, *You have PTSD,* and I am like, *Get the fuck outta here, I didn't do any combat.* And she tells me, *Nah, nah, that it ain't just with combat. It's any trauma.* So she's going through my life history, and wouldn't ya know it, taking care of my mom all those years fucked me up."

"What do you mean?" I asked.

"She had stomach cancer. Real bad. I mean that shit just ate away at her slowly. It wasn't a quick kind. So every day after school from the time I was about twelve until fourteen, I came home and took care of her. I fed her, changed her clothes, did all the laundry, and cleaned up when she shit and pissed herself as she got worse and couldn't control herself anymore. I just did it, you know. My pop left before this happened. My brother was older and moved out with a family of his own. So it was just me. I had forgotten that tears would roll down my cheeks when I took care of her sometimes. I didn't remember until the lady was talking me through it. She made me go back and remember everything. Like what the bathroom looked like and what the floor looked like. How did the water feel when I bathed my mother?" I could see his eyes getting a bit red. Then he caught himself.

"She was really good you know. She talked me through it and figured it out. Not like the fucks here that call you a goddamned pedophile on the first day you show up. Anyway, she said for a young kid like me to be nursing his dying mother with no other adults is terribly scarring. I didn't know. All I knew is what I knew, you know. And so I guess that is why I drank a lot and have done just about every drug under the sun—never got addicted though. OK, maybe the cigarettes. But coke and heroin were just phases for me." He chuckled a bit, but then got serious. "But not for my daughter. She got hooked on heroin. Tried to kick it, but couldn't. She was doing well, and then one day we got that phone call." His eyes started to well up again. "My wife and I buried her almost six years ago. Man that tore me up."

He thought a bit more. "But I still don't know how that plays into what got me here. 'Cause not long after my daughter died, I come across child stuff on Limewire for the first time, and I was like, *Whoaaa!* What the fuck is this shit? And it was like it just took me away from it, from everything. Like it wasn't real or I wasn't in reality. Don't get me wrong—I knew that shit was wrong. It was fucked up. But, *whooo-waaa,* I can't explain. There was such a draw to it. And you know one thing, I never saw myself as the grown-up in those videos. I always saw myself as the kid, even if it was a little girl in there. Yeah, me, the foul-mouthed dago truck driver, pictures himself as a little girl in there. What in the fuck is that all about? I am *still* trying to figure that one out." As he choked through his words, for me, it was as if the entire unit disappeared.

"You'll probably hear me piss and moan about the four years I had to serve, but I was so relieved when I got caught and was told to stop. You hear that a lot here: the relief. You also hear that guys see themselves as the kid in the pictures and videos, too. It's weird. And all these fucking experts go about it like we wish we were those—like we fantasize about being those sick fucks in those videos, the grown-ups. The adults. They don't know what in the fuck they are talking about.

"The judge I got was cool, actually. Damn prosecutor tried implying that I was going to go on and do those things in real life. She was having none of that and told the prosecutor to shut the fuck up. The prosecutor wanted to give me eight years. You know, they tried getting my twelve-year-old granddaughter to say I was a creep and touched her, but she told them to fuck off, literally, her own words. That was the only time I let her slip with the bad words, you know." He smiled again, but it quickly faded. "But I will never forget how I felt when the judge handed down her sentence to me. She said she added on twelve extra months for one of the videos I watched. It was a horrible one. Poor kid—crying and all tied up. Good god, what did I look at?" He was so earnest. "Anyways, she points at me and says, 'It's people like you, Mr. Russo, that encourage these kind of things to be made.'

"Dear god, I felt so horrible. It was the lowest point of my life, too, because right after I pled guilty, they hauled me off to jail. I bounced around in the lowest shitholes you can imagine. Half the time my wife couldn't get ahold of me. You know. I was making good progress with that psychologist who said I have PTSD, and they rip me right out of everything and make me do diesel therapy for six months before they pulled me in to get sentenced." ("Diesel therapy," I later learned, is a purported form of punishment in which prisoners are shackled and transported for days or weeks on buses or planes to multiple facilities across the country.)

"I was at some shithole county jail in Louisiana—I am from Vermont—so that makes fucking sense, right?" Jim continued, settling into his presentation and slowing his speech a bit, like my grandfather used to do when he told us stories. "I watched this big Arnold Schwarzenegger–looking skinhead motherfucker beat the shit out of this fat young black kid. He killed him. I am serious. I'll never forget that sound, as he smashed his head against the concrete floor over and over and over. It sounded like wet potato chips being crunched. And the blood. Good god. That fucking blood, coming out of his ears and nose."

He became choked up again. This was a story I knew he'd told many times, but each time was like the first for him. No rehearsing could extinguish the fire between his vocal cords. "They let him just lay there for hours. I got pulled out for processing—paperwork stuff—and came back, and he was still there. He wasn't even black anymore. He was—

gray. Big pool of blood around his head. By the time they got to him, they could have just peeled that gelled-up blood off the floor. I didn't know shit like that happened here, in this country.

"So, I go through that shit, get told I am this god-awful monster because of something I am never going to do again. And then I come here, *way* more fucked up than I already was, before all this shit started. It was like the first few years of Elkton was just to unfuck myself from diesel therapy." Some levity returned to his demeanor. "Now, I am not a doctor, Doctor, I am just a lowly truck driver with a high-school diploma, but wouldn't you think that subjecting someone with PTSD to that kind of trauma would be a little, uh, counterproductive?"

"No. No, you are right," I offered. I didn't know whether to cry, vomit, or act tough, so I went the numb and unaffected route.

"You are so lucky you got to stay home and be with your family before you came here, man. Elkton is a fucking cakewalk compared to anything else you could have experienced. I can promise you that."

"I know—Well, I am starting to realize that, at least." I awkwardly stuck my hand out, having nothing of any magnitude or relevance to add. "I'm Chris."

He shook my hand. "Call me, Jim. Hey, I'm just busting your balls about the doctor part. Some doctors are assholes, but I know some good ones. Our family doc checked on me and my mom once a week for the last year of her life. He never sent one bill. Not one fucking bill. God bless that guy's heart. He was a good man, may he rest in peace. And I beat liver cancer. All that drinking and being hep C positive, I got liver cancer. But I got a good doc who saw me through. Man, interferon is a bitch."

"Yes. It's like putting the flu in a syringe," I told him.

He laughed a bit, "You got that right, man." He then looked over his shoulder into his cube. "Just watch out for my cellie, Jon. He gets his nuts all tickled whenever we get a big shot or someone who was a *somebody* on the outside come in here, and he follows them like a puppy dog. Makes him feel better about himself, that 'high-caliber' people did the same thing as him. You—a cancer doctor—I'd say you fit that bill."

"Oh, he already got the Jon introduction—and the Curtis introduction, yesterday," Leonard assured him.

"Ah, so you met Jon and Crazy Curtis already?" he said with exaggerated astonishment. "Yeah, we are quite a colorful fucking bunch here. You got this big-mouth Italian here," he said, pointing to himself, "a Jew who thinks he's a prince, and, uh, I still don't know what the fuck Curtis is, all living here, together. Right next door to you! You should be so lucky." he said with his arms wide apart. He then stepped closer to me, speaking in a low voice but loud enough for Leonard to overhear: "Seriously, though, Doc, you couldn't have landed in a better cube. Leonard and George are great fucking guys. No crazies. They will get you through here. And make you better."

"I heard that!" Leonard shouted.

"Yeah, so? I am being fucking positive. So what?" He lowered his voice again, addressing just the two of us. "Just don't tell nobody. I have a reputation to uphold." He shook my hand again. "Good to meet you, Doc," he said, and returned to his cube.

"Man. Lots of sad stories here. I feel like a schmuck. I have nothing to add. I feel like I skated," I told Leonard.

"No one who is here skates. It's hard for everyone. I can't even imagine what all you have lost. You got hurt in ways a lot of guys can't relate to. So don't sit there and compare what you went through with what they went through."

"True. But I have a feeling a lot of guys here won't give two shits that my name got taken off my own papers that I wrote." We both laughed. "Still. I think I'm just going to shut up and listen. I could probably stand to do that for once."

Chapter 3

"So your argument is that title dictates behavior?"

—KEVIN SMITH, *CLERKS*

DURING MY FIRST few weeks at Elkton I took a crash course in the complex culture of prison life: where to be for the four daily inmate counts; where to get toilet paper; how many dollar-stamps a can of soda costs outside the Commissary (the "general store" of prison—we were assigned one shopping day of the week each quarter); when to wear the greens and when to wear anything else; which TV room and which seats belonged to whom; how the library, email, and mail system worked; who had the laundry hustle (they did other people's laundry for postage stamps); who was an ear hustler (eavesdropper who sold information for stamps); who pulled food out of the cafeteria for food hustles; what the track and weight room hours were; when *up* sometimes meant *down* or even *sideways*.

After I'd been "through the looking glass" for a month, it was time for A&O: Arrival and Orientation, where I was supposed to learn everything about how the institution was run. The majority of the twenty-five or so inmates who filled the white-gray classroom were transfers from up the hill, the FCI, whose good behavior was earning them lower security levels and more day-to-day freedoms. The biggest distinction was that in the FSL unrestricted movement was permissible —as opposed to the FCI. This meant you were free to go to the library or out into the yard as you liked during the day, as most doors were kept open.

In the FCI, doors were opened for ten-minute windows on the hour to allow travel, and then closed, which could turn, say, a quick trip to the library for a book, into thirty or forty minutes of waiting around to leave. Only after lights-out at nine thirty were we restricted to our unit, until lights-on at five forty-five.

George and Leonard prepped me for A&O. "Whatever you do, don't ask any questions. Everyone will hate you for dragging it out." This was because (A) dragging things out interfered with *inmates'* important schedules of doing nothing; (B) dragging things out interfered with the *COs'* important schedules of doing nothing; (C) the real answers to questions could be figured out individually or when an event warranted an explanation; and (D) the answers given at these meetings make your head explode if you really tried to wrap your brain around it. "There is always one guy who asks a shit-ton of questions and tries to hijack the meeting and turn it into a conversation between him and the person presenting. Do *not* be that *one guy,*" was my directive.

I felt a sense of dread when I saw the anesthesiologist in the room. I'd met him a few days earlier, at lunch, shortly after he self-surrendered. He spewed vinegar: He hated his wife, who took all of his money. He hated his partner, who'd committed Medicare fraud in multiple states and pulled him into it. He hated the inmates, who were uncouth savages. He hated the administrators and COs, who he assumed all hated their own lives and were pathetic losers. He pissed and moaned about the eighteen months he'd received (I am sure he rolled on his partner to get such a short sentence, especially in light of Elkton's reputation for housing snitches)—and he did so in front of others at the table who were down for five to twelve *years*—not for defrauding the government but because they looked at the wrong kind of free images online. In short, he'd been in this world for forty-eight hours and had already proven himself to be an annoying blowhard with about as much insight as a turnip.

My money was on him to be the *one guy*. I was sure he hadn't been briefed, as I was. It was unlikely anyone would have ventured to talk to him—or if they did, that he would have listened to them. This skinny, perpetually angry, Conservative Radio–quoting white guy in glasses with his ineffectual gray mustache was going to be the one to torpedo the meeting. Most of the FCI transfers in the room were black or brown, so my whiteness linked me to him in this sea of melanin. Worse, he knew I was a doctor, too. I was sick at the thought he might out me about that in this venue. Shit.

I was right about him being the *one guy*. It was like being the only one who could see two cars on their way to a head-on collision and still being unable to do anything about it.

The A&O was a series of administrators coming in and giving canned presentations on various topics. The first was how job assignments are given, so of course he piped up from behind me with, "Just so you all know, I am a doctor, so I think I should work at Medical—" which was met with a few groans, murmurs, and teeth-sucking sounds and a quick retort: "... Well, medical orderly is really all that is available to inmates, and there is a long waiting list for that. It is not based on your level of medical training—" which was followed by a few snickers. Undaunted, he proceeded to ask lengthy questions when the chaplain came in to talk about the various spiritual and religious services that were available at Elkton, which were met by increasingly loud sneers from the hardened men in the audience.

The laundry CO had his presentation down. He was already talking as he entered the room and walked down the center aisle: "I am Officer X. I run the laundry system here." Then he reached the front of the room, spun 180 degrees, and marched back up the aisle, still talking: "Any questions? No? All right," he said, not pausing for responses. As he hit the doorway, he added, "You guys be good," which was met with a roomful of macho laughter. He was great.

Then came the health and safety presentation, the one I had been dreading. The main health officer came in, looking like she belonged on the control deck of a destroyer, scouting the horizon with binoculars, attired in a navy blue bridge coat, complete with stars and stripes on the shoulder boards. The prison system in the U.S. has some carryovers from the Colonial practice of using unseaworthy vessels to hold prisoners. They were called prison hulks or convict hulks back in the day. A lot of the vocabulary and customs have persisted over the years. For instance, the atrium between the Elkton FSL's two units (A and B), and where we waited before meals, was called a sally port. Before the 1900s, a sally port was a sort of dock where boats picked up or dropped off ship crews from vessels anchored offshore. That meaning is still used in coastal Great Britain. During counts, I heard the proclamation "Officer on deck" a few times. I assumed the uniform was part of that heritage, too.

She went on to give the usual crowded-living-quarters spiel: wash your hands, flu shots, sneeze into your elbow. The whole nine yards.

"What if someone falls unconscious?" the anesthesiologist asked. The gripes became audible again, this time with a few very clear *shits* and *mutha-fuckas*.

"Then you are to notify an officer immediately."

"Well, what if one is not nearby? I heard that someone died up top last month and—"

"There will be an officer present." She cut him off. At this point, had we been in a high school classroom, the good doctor would have been pelted with balls of paper and spit-wads and called a nerd. But instead, it was more *shits* and *mutha-fuckas* and a few *goddamns*. The officer let this go on. The mob was on her side, after all. They could help her silence the *one guy*. But he did not budge.

"I am an anesthesiologist. I am board certified in two different states—" He was cut off again by the officer, who was making it clear this was going to be A&O, not Q&A. I closed my eyes and silently agreed with him. If you ever find yourself or a loved one unconscious, it is an anesthesiologist you'd want standing next to you, more than any other type of physician. Anesthesiologists make people unconscious, control their cardiovascular system, and then miraculously wake them up. They run the code team in hospitals. I was completely on his side on this point, but I stayed quiet and left him to the mob.

"We have a strict policy that inmates are not to put hands on each other—not even in an emergency. That is the responsibility of the guards and corrections officers—"

"But I, of all people, know how to maintain an airway—"

"We know all about those A-B-Cs, too –"

"But I took the Hippocratic Oath—"

"I know you guys take these little oaths on the outside, but I am afraid that they do not apply while you are an inmate under the jurisdiction of the Federal Bureau of Prisons." She then let the angry inmates blast out a few more *shee-its* and *mutha-fuckas*, punctuated by the occasional "*Come the fuck on, man*" to drive her point home to him. For the first time, I looked over my shoulder at him, and I could see he was finally broken. He sat, shoulders slumped, surrounded on all sides by other inmates in their chairs. But he looked alone, as if in a corner, a hundred feet from everyone else. He just stared blankly ahead and then slowly looked down at his useless hands resting on the writing surface. They were open, empty, palms up. He remained silent from that point on.

Something like a smirk crept onto the chief health officer's lips. Satisfied, she continued. "One thing you can do," she offered in a very saccharine voice, "is to encourage your fellow inmates to make healthier choices about what they eat." She said it with such conviction, I initially thought it was purely dry sarcasm. It wasn't. I pictured someone standing over a rotund inmate in the throes of a heart attack and saying, *You, wait here. I will go get some broccoli!*

I was horrified by this latest vacuous statement and scanned the room to see if others shared my ire. But all I saw beneath the cornrows and above the neck tats were faces still angry at the man who was asking permission to potentially save their lives one day—because he was wasting their time and delaying their resumption of the daily jack shit.

The rest of A&O was a blur. When we were dismissed, I stayed in my seat while everyone else got up and left. I did not want to see the anesthesiologist or have to rehash what had transpired. When the room became quiet, I got up to leave, but when I turned around, there he sat. He looked at me in disgust. He didn't have to say it—his eyes told me: *You abandoned me. You didn't back me up*. He didn't move, and I didn't want to prolong the already awkward moment. So I nodded at him and sheepishly started to walk out of the room, looking at the ground. As I passed him, he said, "Well, if that is how those pieces of shit are going to be, then I will have no problem letting them die if I see one of them drop."

I didn't change my pace, nor did I look up. I left the room and made it back to my cube. The anesthesiologist had taken his first real step through to the other side of the looking glass.

About a week after the A&O, it was a typical Thursday night and the day was winding down. The usual fifteen-minute warning for the nine thirty standing count was announced. This was when the three of us tidied up our cube, brushed our teeth, got whatever book we were reading ready on our bunks, along with a reading light, and wrapped up our banter about pop culture, current events, or Elkton gossip. People would come by and return something they'd borrowed or answer a question that was raised earlier. It was not uncommon to get a few drop-ins before the lights were shut off.

"Hey, I am so sorry man—I know you are a doctor or something, and I don't know what else I can do!" an urgent voice interrupted our end-of-day routine. The three of us stopped in our tracks. Standing in our cube's entrance was a guy I'd met while standing in line at the Commissary a few days before. He was not from the G-A unit. He looked terrified, pale, and seemed a bit short of breath, as if he had run there to see me.

"What?" I asked.

"My cellie is on the floor, bleeding from his head. He's not answering us and he's shaking."

"*What?*"

"Yeah, we went to the COs' office on G unit *and* H unit, and none of them are there. We can't find them, and they just called count."

"Are you shitting me?" I asked, already knowing where this was heading.

"No, man. One of our guys has been trying to pull the fire alarms—but they aren't working either!"

"Shit!"

"I know it's p.m. count. But my cellie is out of it, man!" He took in another breath. There were just too many words to say. "He's not just out of it, his eyes are rolled back or something. And he's twitching and not breathing right either!"

I looked at my cellmates for input. They just stared back at me, mouths agape. I looked across my unit and saw everyone returning to their cubes in droves, getting ready for standing count.

"Shit! Is he—are you coming from the other side?" I asked him. G unit was split into A and B, with about 150 guys on each side. I was in A and the unconscious guy was in B. This had bad news written all over it. Not only was I being asked to lay my hands on another inmate, I was being asked to be out of bounds during a standing count. There were many rules at Elkton that were skirted or ignored, but anything dealing with the standing count was nonnegotiable—any infringement against it was verboten.

I wanted to not get involved, keep my head down, and get the hell out of there. I could have no snags. I couldn't go to the SHU (solitary confinement) or have my sentence lengthened or lose good time. I needed to get the hell out of there to get back to my children. But how could I live with myself if I did that when I knew he needed help? What if he died and I did nothing to help? What would my kids think of me if they knew I chickened out to save my own skin? It felt like I pondered this for days, but only seconds passed as all these issues raced through my mind. At the A&O, this had been theoretical, but now the anesthesiologist's questions had hit me square between the eyes. A knot formed in my stomach and I could feel my heart beating against my throat.

"Yes," he answered. "G-B." I looked again at my cell mates. Still the same faces, but I could tell they were doing the same moral arithmetic in their heads that I was. Silence, though, still.

"Fuck this! I'm not gonna just stand here," I said, more to get my own legs moving than anything. "Show me where he is."

We moved quickly through my unit. Just as we passed the empty G unit office, between the A and B subunits at the sally port, someone managed to set off the fire alarm. The alarm strobe lights kicked on at each wall-mounted device like synchronized flashbulbs, and a loud, constant groan like the buzzer at the end of a basketball quarter deafeningly reverberated throughout the entire dormitory. The messenger and I simultaneously, instinctively, broke into a trot in response, as if to run away from the noise.

Once we got into the B subunit, the commotion and chaos were overwhelming. There was a seventy-yard gauntlet of inmates in various stages of undress: old white men with gray hair on their chests, sleek young black torsos, and everything in between, hovering around the opening to their cubes, shouting at each other, arguing, pointing to each other or toward the cube where the unconscious inmate was—and over it all the din of the alarm.

"Everybody back off. Make a hole. This guy is a doctor!" The walkway, previously congested by bodies, aimlessly milling in a Brownian motion of helplessness parted almost instantaneously as my messenger's voice and arms played the role of an icebreaker carving a path for an oil tanker through the Arctic Ocean. I could hear voices at my side as I passed cubes: "That dude's a doc." "Shit, I didn't know that!" and "'Bout time we got someone who knows what the fuck they doin'."

Shit. Now the whole place knew I was a doctor. And now everyone was going to expect that I knew everything about all ailments. I had not done anything remotely doctorlike in fifteen months. So much for keeping a low profile.

As I trotted past the onlookers, I went through my mental checklist of what needs to be done during a code. It was the same mental preparation I did whenever I ran to a fallen person, ever since I was an intern in 2001. *OK. Check for pulse and breathing as soon as you get there. ABCs. If he's OK, then make sure the neck is not injured—wait, what was the ratio of chest compressions to breaths again? They keep changing it. Will I have to give breaths? What if he is bleeding everywhere, what about HIV—shit! There he is!*

He was young, white, lying on his side. Twitching. A small pool of blood, surrounded by little drops. The other cellmate was hovering over him, and trying to keep a rag to his head, which was essentially a moving target, trying to sop up the blood oozing from an inch-and-a-half gash on top of a three-inch bruise forming on the back of his head. All of his limbs were twitching in unison, so I knew his brain and limbs were connected. The spinal cord was probably OK.

"Did you move him into this position?" I asked, as I grabbed the man's wrist to feel the radial pulse.

"Yes, he fell off the chair right there, hit his head, and then he started gurgling." His pulse was strong, probably in the ninety-beats-per-minute range.

"Good," I said to both the cooperative pulse under my fingertips and the cellmate. The unconscious guy looked to be in his early thirties. He had a buzz cut, looked to be in decent shape, and healthy other than his bloody head and seizure. No diabetes, advanced age, obesity, or any stigmata of having a grabber. I pulled his eyelids back and saw saccadic movements of his eyes toward the left, a movement that seemed to coincide with his body's twitching. His face was covered in sweat and his jaw clenched, but there was no blood from his mouth. His tongue seemed unbitten but it was hard to tell if he was breathing OK. "Can you get me a mirror and reading light?" I asked his cellmate. Within seconds they were in my hands.

A flash of condensation formed on the mirror when I put it by his mouth. Then another flash and another, in an orderly manner. He was breathing OK. I flashed the reading light in his eyes and his pupils constricted. No major brain injury.

"Has he ever had seizures before?" I asked.

"Yes."

"Well. Good. He is having one right now." I said, much calmer now. This was not a code blue. He was breathing, with a good pulse, and his nervous system was otherwise OK. "How far did he fall?"

"He was sitting here, the stool shot out from him. Maybe three feet, if that." Good. Probably no skull fracture or torn blood vessels along the brain either. "Will he be OK?"

"Yeah. He is going to feel like shit though. With a bad headache tomorrow. And when he comes to, he is going to be all weird and disoriented. So be ready." There really isn't much you can do for someone having a seizure. Make sure they don't choke, by laying them on their side, and make sure there are no sharp objects around. *Thank god this man is not going to die here among the yelling, screaming, and flatulence,* I thought.

Soon, I heard the booming voice of one of the COs. He was a cool one: the stout African American CO who good-naturedly butchered everyone's name during mail call, which was so endearing that nicknames were created from it. Most importantly for me, he was one who had no quarrel with SOs. "Where is he? What cell?" I could hear him ask frantically down the pathway. "OK, back up, back up." When he arrived at the cube, he stood at the entry. Looked at me, looked at the convulsing inmate, and then looked at me again.

"He is having a seizure," I said quickly. "He will be OK. He is breathing well and has a good pulse. He will be finishing up soon and will be sort of out of it for a bit."With that, the CO came into the cell, got between me and the guy on the floor, and started rifling through his first aid kit. He was shaking. The COs were probably at the main building, just casually walking back to the dorm, only to be jarred into action by the fire alarm. They were late to the scene, and they knew it. By now, a few more officers were making their way over. I could see their heads down the line of cubicles and hear them ask for directions.

It was at this moment that humanity momentarily appeared to warm the cold manufactured air of Elkton. The CO in the cube stood up, looked toward the other officers making their way towards our cube, then back to me. He softly put his hand on my shoulder and said, "You need to get back to where you need to be right now."Then he shot me an extra look and a nod, as if to thank me and say it was OK that I was out of bounds but prompting me to go back. He was letting me return to my cube without any trouble.

After count, after lights-out, and after things calmed down, I made my way back to check up on my patient. I still had some doctoring to do. When I returned to the cube, he was surrounded by about five of his friends who were standing around him as he sat with the Derma-Bond still drying over the cut on his head.

"Wow, you look a lot better than when I last saw you."

"This is the doc I was telling you about who saw you," his friend said in the dimness of lights-out. I extended my hand and the young man shook it.

"Thanks, man."

"Who will be here tonight, with him?" I asked. His two cellies identified themselves. "You will need to wake him up every hour or two and make sure he knows who he is and where he is," I instructed them.

"Do I really have to remember where I am?" the patient asked me. There was some chuckling among the group. I laughed too.

"Well, for tonight at least. Afterwards, you can tell yourself you are in the Bahamas for all I care."There was more laughter, as if they had been waiting for some levity.

"Why do we need to wake him up?"

"It's just a precaution, in case there was a concussion, too. Concussions followed by sleep can turn into comas, especially if there is any bleeding inside the head. So if he is not acting right or not waking up, you get the COs right away and tell them to call an ambulance." They took mental notes, and one of them set an alarm clock.

"Didn't any of the COs tell you guys this?" I asked and was greeted with blank faces and head shakes. "God damn it!" I added, but then caught myself creating undue stress. Both the guy and his friends seemed to get a bit worried, so I reassured them. "I don't think he fell from near high enough to have it be that serious. This is just to be sure, you know." I turned my attention to my patient again, "You are just going to have a nasty headache tomorrow. What triggers your seizures? Were you sick recently?"

"No, the last time I had one, it was when I was working at Home Depot and a door fell off the rack and knocked me in the head."

"Well, shit. You need to stop hitting your head, man!" My patient cracked a smile in agreement. There was some more laughter, and I shook his hand and said my goodbyes.

The following morning, there was a package with all kinds of treats from the commissary sitting on top of my locker—a token of appreciation. I had ingratiated myself with the predominantly gay contingency of the unit. I got a lot of grief about it from my cellmates and neighbors, who called me Florence Nightingale. But it was nice to momentarily feel like a doctor again—or at least useful to someone.

Chapter 4

"Think in the morning. Act in the noon. Eat in the evening. Sleep in the night."

—WILLIAM BLAKE

BY LATE NOVEMBER, I had a routine.

At nine a.m. I would wake up for the morning census count, followed by coffee and reading whatever book I had from the library or gotten in the mail from Qui, a former radiation oncology resident at Ohio State University, where I'd been her program director. She had been in my corner since day one. Her family had escaped from northern Vietnam in 1980, during the Communist oppression that followed the war. Her father, educated as an engineer and having worked for the South, spent two and a half years in a concentration camp due to his previous alliances and political ties. He'd come to my sentencing hearing and was appalled to see how what he felt was a thoughtcrime was handled in the United States. For these reasons, he was sympathetic toward my situation and urged Qui to help me any way she could. To say she was there for me during this time would be a huge understatement.

I never ate breakfast, because six a.m. was just too early. I chose to sleep instead. Only on Fridays, when we got our weekly two rolls of toilet paper (hygiene day!) would I wake up and have my only serving of milk or eggs for the week.

Eleven a.m. was the early lunch. After lunch, I would stroll to the library/educational area to talk with one of the instructors, whom I had befriended. He was a PhD working as a genetic/cancer faculty researcher at my medical school alma mater, Northwestern University (Duke undergrad), when he was arrested for viewing child pornography. He, too, had been sexually abused by multiple adults and was an outstanding athlete—a baseball/softball player. He wrote a monthly newsletter on his experiences in prison and sex offender law issues, and had taken an interest in my first book, which I continued to work on, while at Elkton. So he and I always had a lot to talk about.

From noon to one p.m., I would start getting ready for my day's work out. I had a two-day-on, one-day-off routine. Day 1 was running. I worked my way up to four miles per run. Day 2 was resistance work: four sets of a hundred push-ups, ten pull-ups and a couple hundred walking lunges each, with a walking lap around the track between sets. When I started, I could barely do one pull-up. By the end, I was throwing my chin over the bar forty to fifty times a session. Day 3 was a rest day, but, I would typically shoot baskets, or play in a pick-up basketball game (I developed a three-point shot I'd never had before; guys quickly learned to guard me at the perimeter) or, when the weather was warm, hit some softballs or shag in the outfield.

Every Sunday, I would go to my weigh-in and get my body-fat estimate. I entered Elkton weighing 226 pounds with a 26 percent body fat reading. By March, I was down to about 210 and 15 percent body fat. A few times, like when it was four degrees below zero in February or it was pouring down rain, I was the only guy out in the yard, doing my workout. I could see some of the guys looking out the window, shaking their heads at my stubbornness. But it was one of the few times I could be by myself—I had to do it. Sometimes I would run around the track with tears pouring down my face (prepared to play it off that it was just sweat in my eyes if discovered), reflecting on my life's choices and failures and regrets.

The song "Radioactive," by the Imagine Dragons, was popular on the alternative radio station I listened to while working out at Elkton. Every time I hear that song, I get a burning knot in my throat and goosebumps down my back remembering those cold, rainy days when I was fighting my demons on the track or pulling myself above the bar of the soccer goal on that abandoned activity field—trying to figure out just what in the hell I was going to do when I got out. A verse of that song was especially apropos:

I'm breaking in, shaping up, then checking out on the prison bus
This is it, the apocalypse
I'm waking up, I feel it in my bones
Enough to make my systems blow
Welcome to the new age ...
I'm radioactive

After a few months of this, I was in the best shape of my life since the summer before medical school, when I was running fourteen or fifteen miles per week and weighed 195 to 200 pounds. During the first semester of medical school in Chicago, I ballooned up by 30 pounds thanks to deep-dish pizza and Chinese carryout. At the peak of my downward spiral, as a suffocating, stressed out physician-scientist, I got up to 245 pounds. When I was thirty-one years-old, I looked and felt like I was fifty-one. When I was forty-one, I looked and felt like I was thirty-one. Being a federal prisoner was far healthier for me than being a doctor, it seemed. Go figure.

Around three p.m., I would return from my workout and shower. Then three thirty would be mail call, where I would stand at my place, in front of the bulletin board, across from Angry Buddhist (more about him shortly) and next to George and Russo, still drying off from the post-shower sweats. About every thirty minutes throughout the day, until the system's ten thirty p.m. shutoff, when I wasn't doing something else, I would also check my TRULINCS email, which cost ten cents per minute.

Four p.m. was stand-up count, and then idle time, waiting for dinner, catching up with Leonard (to hear the latest kitchen- or maintenance-crew intrigue) and George (about whatever he'd heard in the yard).

Around five p.m. was dinner.

From after dinner to the nine thirty stand-up count and lights-out was the most unstructured part of the day. I would read, walk the track as the sun was setting, go to the library, and watch some TV or write letters to those who kept in touch with me.

From nine thirty until I went to sleep, which was usually around midnight, I would lie in my top bunk, with earplugs, and read.

Sleep required an antihistamine with Ambien-like powers: chlorphenamine. Good lord, that stuff knocked me out and made Benadryl feel like a cup of strong coffee. The first time I tried it, I was afraid I would fall out of my top bunk and fracture my skull on the cement floor. I could feel the waves of sedation roll over my head and eyes in the twenty or thirty minutes after I ingested the little pill. So I made a ridge of towels and other debris in case I rolled over too aggressively.

The earplugs and the chlor' were the only antidote to the black guys' shouting along to the hip-hop lyrics on their MP3 players, oblivious to the 80 percent of the unit that was trying to sleep. After the TV rooms were shut down, whole long-range conversations complete with raucous laughter would be carried on across the unit at one or two a.m.—like kids communicating between houses after bedtime with walkie-talkies (only without the walkies). I never saw or heard any white guys or Latinos doing this. When I first arrived, yes, my liberal sensibilities *were* offended by the generalized observations about black guys being loud all the time and at inconsiderate moments. I heard about how the noise never stopped up the hill, where the inmate population was 50 percent black, but I dismissed it as provincial prison racism and prejudice from passive-aggressive Rush Limbaugh wannabes who would gripe about "The Darkies" but cower in the presence of blacks and shrink away from open conflict with them.

But I came to realize it was the reality—not all the liberal understanding in the world could make it disappear. African Americans accounted for 10 percent of the FSL population and essentially 100 percent of the noise after midnight. The data were indisputable, complete with background evidence. I could see how, after almost five years, Jon had become a prison racist.

So earplugs and sedatives it was, topped off by a wool cap pulled over my face to protect my eyes from the five forty-five a.m. assault by the overhead lights in the unit. It took a tremendous amount of effort to assure you got the proper amount of sleep in prison. So I took all the necessary measures.

Every Friday night, and sometimes Saturday: poker. I sharpened my game against a lot of great players. And I won a lot of extra toilet paper in the process.

On Saturday and Sunday, I would spend a few hours cleaning the sinks and floor of the G-A unit bathroom. That was my prison job, which paid a whopping seventeen cents per hour, while, mind you, a fifteen-minute phone call cost $3.15. A lot of the guys knew I was a doctor on the outside and, man, would they give me the business: *There's Elkton's best and brightest,* or, *From med school to prison toilets, god bless American education!* or *You missed a spot, Doc,* while pointing to an imaginary blemish on a faucet. This ribbing was oddly welcoming, perhaps due to the comradery of loss that prisoners share. So I would readily laugh it off.

Every Sunday, I called my kids from "camp," timing it so that they wouldn't hear the recorded female voice that said, "This call is from a U.S. Federal Prison" every seven minutes or so during the conversation.

That was my schedule. Simple. I needed to keep my mind occupied at all times, or I would become acutely aware of the complete wastes and asininities of my situation, which would then claw away at my insides, mentally, and I'd feel the suffocation. Even so, sometimes I would slip and think too much.

One day, while shooting baskets on a rest day, I started doing some math. On a random November day of 2012, the federal government made $30 per hour off of me in federal taxes while I ran a full clinic, conducted cutting-edge research in a lab, and trained the next generation of radiation oncologists—all while my children innocently enjoyed a secure financial future and could brag that their dad was a doctor who helped people (even if at home I was "Yelly Daddy"). On a random November day in 2014, as I put up three-pointers and did lay-ups by myself, getting my own rebounds, I calculated that it cost the federal government $5 per hour for me to be there, doing what I used to do at lunchtime when I was in middle school, at an opportunity cost to the U.S. taxpayer of $35 per hour (assuming a 40-hour work week). And that was just the dollars. My ability to treat rare cancers using highly specialized procedures, and the advances that could have resulted from my research—they were gone, too.

My two cellmates and I calculated that, among the three of us, the annual cost of housing us (at $30,000 per person per twelve months), plus the loss of the income taxes we would have paid, amounted to an opportunity cost of over $200,000 per year. Not to mention the twenty-one years of post-secondary education that was currently laying fallow and the six children who were, for all intents and purposes, now fatherless. All because we looked at something that was already there, because we were not well at the time we looked. To think about it too hard would make you crazy.

I read all the books I ever could have ever wanted to while I was at Elkton: classics novels I missed in high school and college, but also contemporary fiction and lots of nonfiction history and humanities. For almost two decades, I'd ignored humanity in an effort to save it from cancer. In almost twenty years, I'd read just two books outside of science and medicine. In seven-and-a-half months at Elkton, I read fifty-four (and published one myself). I have to say, I was pretty happy with my book reading. I think my high school English teacher would be so proud of her student turned doctor turned federal inmate:

FICTION	**NONFICTION**
Catch-22, Joseph Heller	*The Other Side of Normal,* Jordan Smoller
Fahrenheit 451, Ray Bradbury	*Blood Feud,* Lisa Alther
Cutting for Stone, Abraham Verghese	*Don't Know Much About History,* Kenneth C. Davis
The Red Badge of Courage, Stephen Crane	*Days of Infamy,* Michael Coffey and Mike Wallace
The Jungle, Upton Sinclair	*Holidays on Ice,* David Sedaris
The Time Machine, H. G. Wells	*Me Talk Pretty One Day,* David Sedaris
Pygmy, Chuck Palahniuk	*The Cracker Queen,* Lauretta Hannon
The Invisible Man, H. G. Wells	*The Big Necessity,* Rose George
A Prayer for Owen Meany, John Irving	*A Billion Wicked Thoughts,* Ogi Ogas and Sai Gaddam

Slaughterhouse-Five, Kurt Vonnegut
Rabbit Run, John Updike
Brave New World, Aldous Huxley
1984, George Orwell
Tenth of December, George Saunders
Breakfast of Champions, Kurt Vonnegut
One Flew Over the Cuckoo's Nest, Ken Kesey
Choke, Chuck Palahniuk
A Clockwork Orange, Anthony Burgess
Men Without Women, Ernest Hemingway
Survivor, Chuck Palahniuk
To Kill a Mockingbird, Harper Lee
The Cider House Rules, John Irving
For Whom the Bell Tolls, Ernest Hemingway
The Hotel New Hampshire, John Irving
The World According to Garp, John Irving
Being There, Jerzy Kosinski
The Good Earth, Pearl S. Buck
Death of a Salesman, Arthur Miller

Unbroken, Laura Hillenbrand
Perv, Jesse Bering
Guns, Germs, and Steel, Jared M. Diamond
The Removers, Andrew Meredith
The Logic of Failure, Dietrich Dorner
Orange Is the New Black, Piper Kerman
Fingerprints of the Gods, Graham Hancock
From Jailor to Jailed, Bernard B. Kerik
The Narcissist Next Door, Jeffrey Kluger
The Tipping Point, Malcolm Gladwell
Touching a Nerve, Patricia S. Churchland
The Sociopath Next Door, Martha Stout
Gulp, Mary Roach
Mistrial, Mark Geragos and Pat Harris
The Secret History of the War on Cancer, Devra Davis
Handbook of Evidence-Based Radiation Oncology, Eric Hansen and Mack Roach III
Trauma, Shame, and the Power of Love, Christopher Pelloski (me!)

So in many ways, being in prison was like being back in junior high, albeit at federal taxpayers' expense: no responsibility, playing sports, dealing with cliques and immature boys, reading books, and not making much money. But it was also like junior high—especially my seventh-grade year, when I was at the apex of my awkward phase—in that it served up a heaping helping of humility.

I was in prison, cleaning the sinks and floors of the unit's bathroom, making seventeen cents an hour and being teased by career criminals telling me that I missed a spot. I had my case manager calling the lot I was in (the computer-based-only sex offenders with my charge) “monsters.” I had the COs who despised us and would mockingly call over the PA system for Jerry Sandusky to come to the office just to see the looks of shame on many of the guys' faces. I had meth-dealer rednecks calling me chomo, and a whole slew of groups determining where I could and could not be: TV rooms, yard benches, cafeteria tables, etc. Shooting baskets was certainly not the only thing that made me feel like I was back in middle school again. I was broken down into my individual molecules and becoming reconstituted into whatever I now was or at least was supposed to be. The humiliation brought about by my actions was complete in this setting.

Previously, I'd viewed the privilege of being a resident at the top cancer center in the world as something I was entitled to. I was an arrogant prick who probably annoyed the hell out of countless support staff who worked “under me” when I horsed around like a jackass. Now I was about as insignificant as one can be.

I'd completely disrespected the field of medicine with my theatrics—not just with my embarrassing offense, but in how I conducted myself as a doctor. I was drunk with power and prestige, and my disdain for those who chose not to put in the same effort as I would come out when I went on a bender. I had a chip on my shoulder the size of a cinder block, I howled at the moon all too frequently, and my shit did not stink. Now, however, I had no choice but to breathe in the stench of others' shit and farts. Now, I had to be thankful simply not to be harassed by former gangbangers/gunrunners (or gangbangers/gunrunners who were merely on time-out, who would not get caught “next time” or would do things differently to avoid another stretch). I had worked so hard to not end up like a lot of the guys I went to high school with, yet here I was, adding to the storied list of Ferndale felons.

Now, a pint of milk became an earthly treasure to me. Having NPR come in on the radio without too much distortion was a small victory. Finding ice cream in stock at my weekly commissary trip was something to savor. This had become my life in such a short time.

And four months was about all it took for me to get this message loud and clear. When I talked to some of the guys who had been there for a few years—whether on the outside they'd been a lawyer, engineer, teacher, plumber, carpenter, or truck driver—they nearly all said the same thing: "I think I needed prison—well Elkton, at least. I really just needed six months of this. I get it. I did bad and I needed to reassess my life. But everything after six months has been a waste of time. What else is there left to learn? Now it is just trying to avoid boredom."

Our daily schedules of individual appointments were posted in the hallway leading to the sally port the day before. Sometimes they wouldn't go up until almost midnight, so that guys who'd gone to sleep before that wouldn't know they were on the schedule—and would get reamed out for being late or missing their appointments. Fortunately, there were night owls who always kept vigil and would let others know. I rarely was on the schedule, so I rarely really looked after a while. Plus, Jon would always tell me, since that bolstered his sense of self-importance. He was the one who told me when I had A&O and when I had my dental checkup.

"You have your appointment with Dr. Richards at SOMP tomorrow," he giddily announced one day as I was hanging out in the yard with Leonard, George, Russo, and a few others I had not really met yet.

"Richards is a fucking, smug little asshole!" Russo said, waving his hands in disgust.

"What is SOMP?" I asked.

"The Sex Offender Management Program," Leonard explained calmly. "George and I are in it."

"It's just something you have to do," George added. "It's geared for touchers. But they try to make it applicable to us."

"My fucking ass they do!" Russo countered. "On the first fucking day, that blockhead football coach comes in, points at each of us sitting in the circle, and yells at us, calling us fucking pedophiles and child molesters. Three guys just get up and walk out and say they don't need that shit. But I just sit there like a chickenshit and just take it."

"Yeah, but Russo, that was almost two years ago. You gotta admit it's a little better now," George said.

"I know. I am almost done. Thank god. Of course, those bastards will probably make me do it again when I get out of here."

"Football coach?" I asked.

"So there's four people who run it. There's Dr. Richards—he's a psychologist you'll meet with. He used to work at Butner, so you know he toes the party line," Leonard explained. "The Butner study is why we're all screwed."

I nodded. I had learned about the Bureau of Prisons (BOP) study when doing research for my first book. "It was conducted by BOP psychologists who were looking to make the 'science' match the policy. They had these guys busted for child pornography and coerced them into admitting they molested children to make their point. Admitting they did this was rewarded with early completion of treatment. Failure to admit meant they were in there longer and they got punished for it." I listened, but the others had heard it all before. "So the guys in the study started making stuff up to get out of there. The numbers were crazy: something like 90 percent or so who watch child pornography are actual child molesters." Everyone stewed on it. "The thing is, they included guys with previous contact offenses. So it's like they already crossed that line, too. But it fucked all of us here. We are assumed to be them."

"Yeah, I read about that report," I said. "It got shredded by judges and the scientific community. No peer review either," I added, to several listeners' surprise. "I did a lot of research on this while on house arrest. I read this good book called *Justice Perverted* by Charles Patrick Ewing. And there were a few others. The Seto meta-analysis that says the repeat offense rate is like 2 percent. And this report from Endrass said viewing is not a predictor of touching."

"Well, you know your shit then. And you will know why Richards is a dickhead," Russo pointed out.

"Anyway," Leonard continued, "there is Dr. Mason—he is the lead psychologist. He gets it a little better, has seen a lot more and is older. He's a good guy, but probably has marching orders too. Then Mr. Jake, the football coach, and his wife, Ms. Helen. She is a sweetheart—I still don't really know what their credentials are. Maybe they are social workers or something."

George added, "It's like two good cops, two bad cops. Mason and Helen are the good cops. Richards and Jake are the bad cops. But the way I approached it is, this is something I have to do. I'll ignore the crap that doesn't apply to me and get what I can out of it. The whole bad-cop bit is just to break you down."

"Well that may be true. But their shit sticks to you." One of the guys in the group new to me spoke up. His name was Johnny. He was a short, stout, middle-aged man with a gray-flecked goatee. He had a pensive, but cherubic face and was balding on the top of his head. Unlike most of us, he wore his green uniform every day—an indication that he didn't have the money to buy shorts and sweatshirts from the commissary. (Guys who always and only wore greens were cut off, with no outside support or money coming in. They wore their greens threadbare over the year until the annual fresh set was issued to them.) "I finished the program a year ago, which means I started when it was really bad. When that damned Butner study was fresh on the BOP's mind." Everyone got quiet. "My babysitter had me do her doggy-style when I was eleven. It kind of messed me up pretty bad. Of course, at the time I thought it was OK. She was like fourteen or fifteen. But, anyway, during my pretrial, I was sent to a forensic psychologist, who diagnosed me with PTSD and said I looked for sexual pictures of girls that age to kind of make peace with what happened. My dad and mom used to get in all kinds of crazy fights, too—which she said messed me up, too. Anyway. I get diagnosed with PTSD. The psychologist determined that I had PTSD. I took a lie detector that proved I am not into kids—that I didn't hurt anyone." I could tell from the others' faces that they had heard his and others' stories like this many times before.

"So on my first day, they did that," he motioned to Russo. "They got in my face and called me a pedophile. I kept telling them that's not the case. They didn't believe me, of course. I told them about all the evaluations I had. The ones the court accepted. Nowhere in my pretrial paperwork does it say the word *pedophile*—anywhere!" He took a few deep breaths. "But I stick with the program. So I can complete it and be a model prisoner." He said in a tone of mock-cooperation. "And so, what is the first discharge diagnosis they put down on my paperwork from here?" He looked around the group, who already knew the answer. "Pedophilia. That's my diagnosis. That's what I take with me from here. That diagnosis. PTSD never even made the list. Pedophilia and anxiety. That's real fucking great, isn't it? What in the hell am I supposed to do with that on my fucking criminal *and* medical record?" He waited for a response he knew would not come and then muttered, "Fucking bullshit."

We all stewed on that for a bit.

"Well, you probably won't be in the program," Jon said to me, to break the painful silence. "You aren't here long enough, short timer. The program is twenty-four months."

Richards' office was adjacent to the group meeting room in the Elkton's psych department. His PhD diploma, conferred by a university I had never heard of, hung proudly on the wall behind his desk. As he sat there, a smirk on his face, I imagined that being a prison psychologist was the equivalent of being a hospital attorney—another all-hat, no-cowboy situation. He was a clean-cut younger man with puffy cheeks, as if they'd been pushed up by his too-tight collar. His hands were also puffy, gripping the stapled set of papers in his hands as he spoke.

"Well, you are not going to be here long enough to be in the program, but as a sex offender, we still feel it is important to touch base with those with your offense at our institution."

"OK."

"So here is our informational packet regarding the program," he said as he handed the papers to me. "Feel free to read it over. And come back to me if you have any questions." After a pause, he continued. "We are one of three federal facilities that have a SOMP program within the facility itself. That is why there is a higher proportion of sex offenders at Elkton." I nodded. "The FSL is even more unique in that we have Internet-only offenders here. No contact offenders." I continued to nod.

"Now, even though you are not formally in the program, your stay will come under our purview. You will be subjected to random cell and locker searches, at our direction, to determine if you possess any contraband."

"OK. There shouldn't be a problem." I told him.

"Good." He smiled insincerely. "Now, contraband is going to be different for guys like you. It is going to be case-by-case-dependent. For example, if we come across an inmate here on drug crimes and a naked picture or pornography shows up, we would treat that very differently than if it came up in a sex offender's search."

"Makes sense," I concurred, trying to be as cooperative and agreeable as possible.

"But it can include nonsexual things, too." He sat back to pontificate further. "Say a former drug dealer takes up a fancy for art and collects all kinds of colored pencils for his artwork. Well, that's not a problem is it?" he asked me pedantically. "But if you are a sex offender and part of your arousal pattern was to stick pencils up your ass ... Well, if we come across a huge stash of pencils in your locker, that's going to be a problem, isn't it?"

"Yeah." We both hung on that revelation for a while.

"Since you aren't going to be here long enough, that's really all there is to my presentation to you at this point. Just read over the packet and let me know if you have any questions." He then leaned toward me, over his desk. "And if you are having any thoughts that are troubling to you or are, you know, unusual, just let me know."

I could feel my spine tighten with those words. "What kind of thoughts?" I asked, being as outwardly bland as possible.

"You know. About children, or any other bizarre sexual feelings."

"Okaaay?" My face could no longer hide my confusion and irritation.

"Well, you did look at children being sexually exploited, did you not?" He had to get his digs in, apparently. So I dug in, too. Hearing the phrase *did you not?* is the intellectual equivalent of flicking me in the nose and making my eyes water. It's the dumb person's way to dumb down complex things.

"I did." I tried to remain neutral in my tone. Tried. "But, you know, millions of people have watched those ISIS videos, the ones where they cut people's heads off." I thought I would use some of the philosophical arguments I had acquired and sharpened over time, to deflect his Thought Policing.

"What does that have to do with anything?"

"Well, those millions of people watched someone's victimization without their consent, did they not?" I didn't give him much time to answer and continued my one-sided questioning in a rapid fashion, "Did they not encourage ISIS to make more videos because they knew people would watch them? Did they not create a market of decapitation videos by viewing them? Did they not help ISIS achieve their political aims—to have people talking about them, making them relevant?"

He became visibly uncomfortable. I could tell he was connecting the dots I was laying before him. "Again, what does this have to do—"

I quickly cut him off, "It's just that, well, we wouldn't consider those millions of people who watched those videos to be terrorists or murderers or assume they would want to kill people, now would we?" I feigned confusion while shaking my head and shrugging. *Would we?* is *did you not?*'s kissing cousin.

"Well, that is very different, isn't it?"

"Yeah. I guess in those videos, everyone has their clothes on," I said dismissively. I didn't need to say anything more to make my point.

His throat tightened. After he promptly cleared it, there was another awkward silence, which I decided to break. "So, *have* you read Ewing's book *Justice Perverted*? Or the Seto meta-analysis? It's pretty interesting." I learned about making a point without saying it from my father, who was a true artist at that skill.

"No."

"Really? That is interesting."

I let it sit out there that I might be more informed in his own field than he was. I could see him eventually deduce the additional point I was making. And once he did, he motioned to the packet in my hand. "Well, looks like you have plenty more to read now, don't you?"

"I will read it," I said with a forced smile. Being conciliatory is the death blow in this game.

With that, he stood up and motioned toward the door. "As I said, if you have any questions or troublesome thoughts, our door is always open." On that note, I shook his hand and left.

I threw away the packet, in sections, in different garbage cans on my way back to my cube. I was thankful I would not have to participate in this program, just as I would have been thankful to not undergo a surgery by a surgeon who had no idea that bloodletting had fallen out of favor in medical circles centuries ago.

Chapter 5

"'Oh, you can't help that,' said the cat. 'We're all mad here.'"

—LEWIS CARROLL, *ALICE'S ADVENTURES IN WONDERLAND*

I MET A LOT of guys at Elkton. A few stand out.

COMBAT SCRABBLE

There were four phones in the G-A unit. It was a little before nine p.m., and the phones shut off at nine thirty p.m. Each call could only be fifteen minutes long—any longer and it would be automatically cut off—and I needed to call my wife about something. So I got in line. I was fourth, but based on the math, I would be able to connect before nine fifteen, so it was worth the wait.

I preferred to avoid waiting in line at the phones, to shield myself from the anguish that accompanies many phone conversations from prison. Also, when a guy turns around and sees he has an audience, it adds to the humiliation and frustration of the situation. You never want to get pegged as an ear-hustler, either. So I made sure to talk to the guys in line with me, to make it clear I wasn't listening to anyone's conversation. One of the guys on a phone in the middle of the rank was known as Combat Scrabble, so called because of the manner in which he played Scrabble. It was fiery. On a fairly frequent basis, he would goad someone into a game with him, choosing someone who was clearly an inferior player so that he could swear at, berate, and denigrate his opponent at the top of his lungs, making sure the whole unit could hear. He would never challenge the pros, like Staddleman, the former United Airlines executive who spoke seven languages fluently, could fly through a Saturday *New York Times* crossword with a pen, as if he were taking dictation, and was by far the smartest guy in the joint. In fact, he was one of the smartest guys I have ever met.

Combat was in his fifties, and everything about him was prickly and spikey. He had short-cropped hair, a military cut, of similar consistency, color (equal parts faded red, blonde, gray, and white), and length. All the hair on his face and scalp (regions that were largely indiscernible from each other) stood perfectly perpendicular to the plane of the originating follicles. His horn-rim glasses, wide eyes, combustible personality, and pincushion head made Combat Scrabble an explosion personified.

The first time I met him was looking down from my top bunk as I emerged from a rare nap. He stood in our cube, "talking" with George and Leonard. Two sentences after our introduction, this stack of human fire jumped right into the particulars of his case.

"I used to be a defense analyst, god damn it! That was after spending twenty years in the Navy. And now I am here, for this bullshit. Can you believe that?"

"Well—" I was not supposed to answer, but I didn't know that yet, since I had just met him and all.

"After all that service for my country, they lock me up, like a fucking criminal. For what? Because I looked at pictures? Really? Six years? What in the hell am I supposed to do when I get out of here, at fifty-nine years old, with only a career in government work—something I can't do anymore, with my record, with no years in the private sector. And, oh yeah, I am a felon, too."

Always a quick learner, I just nodded my head as he took a breath.

"And it's all arbitrary—you know that, right?" *Keep quiet*, I said in my mind. *Let him rant*. "There are tens, if not hundreds, of thousands of people with that shit on their computers. You do know that? So they pick and choose who they throw away. So they fucking chose me, the bastards." Another breath. "You wanna know something about the Pentagon?"

To this I actually said, "What?" forgetting to keep qu

"Almost 80 percent of their computers had child porr their IT department did a sweep. Eighty fucking percent shit I did. So you know what they did?" I was silent because I was actually taken aback. "They threw out all of their computers and replaced them with new ones, and told their people to stop looking at porn, stop looking at child porn, and put up some firewalls on their servers."

"Wow."

"Yeah. Problem solved, and our entire Defense Department was spared from being gutted by the removal of thousands of employees because of felony convictions—and the public relations nightmare it would have created."

"Damn."

"Yep. I should have just watched this shit at work—not at my home, as a private citizen, like a dumbass! I should have just watched it at work. Not only would I have *not* wound up in this fucking cesspool, I would have gotten a new computer! Oh, and my wife would not have left me, and my family would still be talking to me!"

That was how I met Combat Scrabble. Leonard said he was probably bipolar. I agreed with him.

So I was not surprised that he was very loud on the phone, too, taking no pains to keep his discussion private. Despite the small talk I kept up with my neighbors in line, I couldn't help but hear his piercing voice above the general buzz.

"What do you want me to do?... Sally, listen—" He ran his hands through the spikey red forest on his head. "Sally, I have done everything you wanted me to do... Yes!... No!... Sally, I signed the papers without protest or contest, I—" He looked up at the ceiling in frustration. My heart grew heavy for him. Despair was in his ear, whispering that he was nothing anymore.

A few of the guys ahead of me in line went to phones that opened up. A new one joined me. Murdoch. A fellow PTSDer and war veteran. He was also eyeing the clock. Hoping to get a call started by 9:15. It was 9:08.

"Look, Colby is old enough now—" Combat continued. "Yes, I know ıt has been hard on him too … He's twelve years old now, Sally. I respect your wishes, but … I am not your husband anymore. That's how it is now. I will do whatever—"

It was 9:12 and the last guy ahead of me went to a recently vacated phone. I was next in line. I wanted to be helpful and turned to Murdoch to tell him that I would be the last guy to go before the phones were shut off. "Hey, those other three guys all started their calls after nine. I am just waiting on him," I said pointing at Combat.

"Then we are both screwed," he said.

"What do you mean?"

"He isn't talking to anyone, I bet," he said solemnly.

"Bullshit!" I said, laughing.

"I am not kidding," Murdoch replied. I assumed he was trying to pull one over on the new guy (well, newer—I had been there for a while at this point) so that I would give up and he could jump my spot in line. Murdoch was a clever one. I looked at the clock: 9:19. I'd arrived at 8:55. My amusement abated when I realized that Combat had been on the phone for nearly twenty-five minutes—an impossibility at Elkton. As the penny dropped my inquiry was met with an answer before I could speak. "He has done this before. Someone once saw him on the phone for over an hour. An hour!" I glanced at Murdoch, who looked at Combat with a deep and almost tearily sad reverence. Combat was not a likeable guy by any stretch and Murdoch was equally far from touchy-feely, but he felt for the man. "About six months ago, he gets his divorce papers in the mail here and he—" Murdoch's voice wavered a bit, "He just … cracked, and he's never been the same. He's always been an asshole, but he is definitely different now. Broken. It's really sad, man." His glance came back to mine, as Combat's one-sided conversation hit our ears, as if to twist and squish the moment's cruelty into our minds.

"Well, ask Colby if he wants to see me!"

Murdoch and I just walked away, knowing it was useless to remain in line. Even at nearly nine thirty, right before standing count, I saw Combat gesticulating in exasperation on the phone, with no one on the other end.

DEAF-CON 5

I came up with this nickname. Some of my best prison work, actually. The art of ridicule is part of the prison culture. Which means on some levels, I am not very proud of it. The three-part name, inspired by the U.S. DE-Fense readiness CONdition (DEFCON), hit all the themes: *Deaf* because he was deaf (because his biological mother beat him so badly when he was a toddler that he suffered profound, bilateral hearing loss), *Con* because he was a convict in prison, *5* because he acted like a five-year-old on his best days (despite being over thirty). Like most of us, he was there for noncontact/nonproduction (NP/NC) child pornography charges.

He would take things out of your hand, move cups that you set down, or stand to your right and tap your left shoulder so that you'd look the wrong way, see no one there, and then turn the other to see his shit-eating grin atop an exaggerated goatee, because, you know, that is so hilarious—*every time*. He had the tiniest frame. I think one of my thighs was thicker than his waist. Once, I moved his entire body out of the way with just my forearm when he was playfully blocking the entrance to my cube and I just wasn't in the mood.

He was the guy I feared the most. Not because he was a threat to my safety, but because I was afraid he would catch me on a bad day and I would rip his larynx out with my bare hands and throw it in the garbage, and then slowly climb up to my bunk and wait, with my bloody hands resting upon my chest, for the COs to take me first to the SHU and then to my arraignment on a murder charge. (OK, I would never do that to someone. Let's just say he could be very annoying.)

TOASTER HEAD

Toaster Head was named for the shape of his head, coarse facial features, wide nose, and the frontal bossing (bulging forehead) that comes with untreated, or delayed treatment of, acromegaly. That is when a tumor of the pituitary gland causes bones to continue growing that should have stopped because of excessive growth hormone production. Andre the Giant is a good example of what rampant acromegaly looks like. Toaster was a painful know-it-all.

On the rare occasions I dragged myself to breakfast in the early morning, he often would sit by me at my table and open the spigot of bullshit. Within ninety seconds, there would be blasts about Obama or the Democratic Party. The irony here was that his beloved Republican Party (along with the Democrats) unanimously voted to imprison people with our charge at the severe levels currently mandated. Of course, whenever asked about his offense, being the biggest purveyor of denial in all of Elkton, he summed it up as "high crimes and misdemeanors against the federal government," without elaboration. That story quickly palled with his fellow SOs, especially after someone had a relative on the outside look him up. It turned out he'd had thousands of child pornography images and a pretty extensive trading network set up. But he would continuously deny this fact whenever it was presented to his wide, coarse face. Eventually people stopped bothering and just ignored his drivel when plagued by his presence at a chow hall table.

TWEAK

Tweak was the only real sociopath I knew about at Elkton. There were a few creeps, countable on one hand, but this guy was jacked. Thankfully, I barely had any interaction with him, because shortly after I arrived he was sent to the SHU before being transferred to the Devens Federal Medical Center in Massachusetts, a place where institutionally committed sex offenders go. Tweak got his name from the Tourette's-like twitch he had and because he looked so young, like the character on *South Park*, even though he was twenty-four years old. He was an adopted crack-baby who had an unnatural relationship with his adopted parents, who apparently encouraged and collected his very graphic and accurate drawings of four- to seven-year-old children being raped. I can only imagine what transpired during his upbringing, what was done to him, what boundaries were nonexistent in that household. He had been busted twice for the same kind of drawings while in prison, and had his sentence lengthened as a result of it. It was also why he was sent to Devens. By all accounts, he was brilliant (tested with an extremely high IQ) and could have been an accomplished artist, had his subject matter been different.

Despite weighing about a buck-twenty, Tweak scared the hell out of everyone. There were some big bad dudes at Elkton who could snap my neck, but I never worried that one night I would wake up to one of them eating my entrails directly from my splayed-open abdomen. I worried Tweak would. Even the Haters were uneasy around this guy. Some of them heckled him once at a softball game, when he was at bat: "Pretend it is an eleven-year-old girl and hit it." He stepped out of the batter's box, turned to the group, unphased, and said, "If it is an eleven-year-old, I'm gonna tax that ass." And then stepped back to the plate. They were uncomfortably silent for the rest of the game.

He had the blank doll-like stare of a sociopath, and absolutely no remorse for what he did. This included chatting online with twelve-year-old girls and getting them to send him naked pictures, which he then posted all over online bulletin boards. When confronted with his offense in his first sex offender treatment program session and asked if he thought that could be harmful to young girls, he asked the facilitator, "Why would I give two shits about those bitches?" and then told everyone to go to hell and walked out.

I hated this piece of shit because everyone assumes all SOs with my charge are assholes like him. This in turn helps promote the call for harsh penalties that result in nonviolent people rotting away behind bars for years on end. So, I was glad to see him go and secretly wished him only the worst. Though the irony is not lost on me that I am judging him just as the Haters judged me. I guess there is plenty room for hypocrisy in prison. Even my own.

MR. CLEAN

Every time I went to do laundry—*every* time—there was this same guy there doing his laundry. He was not part of the laundry hustle syndicate. I was sure of that. (That was the realm of Vanilla and Jelly Roll.) At first, I ignored him. Then I came to resent him because he always had one washer and dryer tied up, so on busy days I had to wait longer to get my load done—which would delay my resumption of doing nothing that day. But after a while, I started pretending to read my book and studied him instead. He was a short, well-chiseled Italian guy with a military buzz cut and thick, prison-issued glasses: Chomo 5000s they were called. What made him interesting was that his movements were followed precisely each and every time, like a ritual. I became intrigued.

All lids and knobs were handled with the right hand only, while the left pulled the shirt and pants he was wearing taut, so that no loose-fitting garments would come in contact with any of the machines. When his loads were in the wash and/or dryer and no transitioning was required, he would stand in the middle of the room with both feet firmly planted on the floor, pant legs tucked into his boots, and sway as if on the deck of a gently rocking boat where he was the only passenger.

When it was time to remove his clothes from a machine, he just did not grab them. Each item was removed almost surgically, so as to not touch the sides of the drum. Each was then placed into a washable laundry bag, held high to ensure there would be no contact with the floor. Moving wet clothes from the washer, he shot his full laundry bag into the dryer, the clothes one giant, sodden pellet, to prevent any stray sock or sleeve from brushing against anything but the inside of the machine. Once inside the dryer, he would carefully deposit the bag's contents in the drum.

Despite his exaggerated rituals, you could have a normal conversation with him. The laundry hustlers talked with him all the time, probably because he was a permanent fixture in their area of employ. Topics like weather or sports, jokes, and menu changes in the chow hall flowed from him as he continued his routine without missing a beat. I could see in his face that he was almost apologizing for his antics while talking, as if to say he was sorry but he had no choice: *I know this is ridiculous, but I have to do it*—with a touch of agony, too. Sometimes he would pause his conversation, contort his body in an odd way to maintain his pivot foot on a particular square of tile, check on the status of a load, pivot back and then resume talking as if nothing happened.

Finally, I brought him up to my cube mates. "Dude, I keep seeing this guy doing the laundry, whenever I am in there. I saw him at commissary last week and he spent more on cleaning products than I spend on food for a whole month: hand sanitizers, soaps, detergents. What the fuck?"

"That's Mr. Clean," George informed me. He needed no other descriptors to know who I was talking about. "He washes all of his clothes every day. All. Whether they have been worn or not. He cleans his cube every day at five a.m.—Lysol, mop, dusting, everything. He can't help himself."

"Jesus."

Leonard added, "That's why he is in a cube by himself. No one can live with him. He's a nice guy, and the guys who tried to live with him felt sorry for him, but they couldn't handle the constant cleaning."

"There was one time when someone's muddy boot fell over the edge of the wall, you know, from a neighboring cube. So the boot lands on his locker, right? And kicks dirt everywhere," George recalled, with a gossipy giddiness. "People said he jumped out of his cube like a bomb went off." George's face began to lose its smile, though. "But he didn't yell at anyone. He didn't say anything." George paused for a bit, before finishing the story. "He just spent the next ten hours cleaning his cube. Every square inch of it."

After I became fully aware of him, I could discern his movement pattern in a crowd. He stood out from the noise. Walking down the common areas, he would stop in his tracks and go up against the wall to let people pass him without contact. When I was cleaning the sink and floors in the bathroom (my BOP job), I saw many times his hand-washing technique, which required two or three types of soap and ample application up to his elbows. It would have made the staunchest of surgical scrub nurses proud.

Prison must have been absolute torture for him. To be housed in cramped quarters with hundreds of other germ-harboring and germ-producing organisms that shed hair and dead skin everywhere, that profane the air with intestinal gas and the stench of feces. I felt horrible for him. I wished his judge would spend a day with him and realize that for every day Mr. Clean spent here, it wreaked an emotional toll equivalent to at least ten days for a "normal" person. I learned he'd lost fifty pounds because all his money went to cleaning supplies.

ANGRY BUDDHIST

Angry Buddhist was a shorter white guy, in his early forties, whose baby fat had never melted away, giving him a much younger appearance, almost adolescent. He sported golden blonde skater bangs that stood out against his shaved temples and trendy thin-rimmed glasses. His oversized sweatshirt and baggy shorts were missing only a pair of Airwalk shoes to nail his outfit. His acerbic tone, multilayered humor, and well-developed lexicon betrayed the fact that he held a master's degree in English literature from Ohio State University.

One of the most surreal and hilarious moments of my time at Elkton happened at the weekly Buddhist service, which was every Thursday at seven p.m. in the Recreation Center. Starting in January, my cellie Leonard convinced me to attend the service to learn something new. I had shunned world religion courses in college because the professor that taught them hated overzealous pre-med students and made sure he put a hole in their GPAs to teach them a lesson. To this day, I am not sure what that lesson was. Regardless, I just wasn't up for that kind of risk then. Not coming from a brand-name undergrad school like Yale or Princeton, I couldn't have some humanities class tarnish what needed to be a nearly spotless academic record.

I regretted the omission, though. All religions were a black box for me then, and my ignorance continued well after my "liberal arts education." Ironically, it was house arrest and prison that offered time for me to learn about humanity, not the cutthroat pre-med track, which was predicated on serving and saving humanity. I had finally cracked open the Old and New Testaments and figured out where all the names I had heard before fit into the Christian stories. After that, I figured it would be good for me to learn about another religion—Buddhism—that half a billion or so people practice. So I started going to the weekly service.

I really liked the tenets of letting go of attachments and suffering, seeking inner peace, and treating others with respect and kindness. The Noble Eightfold Path seemed like a great way to live. Mindfulness, not being mean towards others, etc. It was very Christlike in its philosophy. It had a lot of psychological applicability to trauma or enduring life's traumas without getting too bogged down in the details or self-pity. It was good for a PTSDer like myself. But the one thing my constantly running mind could not do was quiet itself. Meditation, a cornerstone of Buddhism, eluded me. Even with all the therapy I'd had and really slowing down my life, I could not calm my churning mind.

I got close only once. Each session closed with ten to fifteen minutes of meditation. It was difficult. Outside the room all kinds of noise was going on: guys playing instruments, pool and ping-pong matches, yelling. It was hard to learn how to meditate with all that just outside the door. I would hear words or sounds and try to figure out who was saying it and why, as if I was a computer that couldn't resist processing incoming data. But one night, I got close. I could hear my heart beat. I controlled my breathing. My body became so relaxed I could not feel the gravity acting on it. I'd arrived at that stillness between consciousness and sleep. For a brief moment, I forgot I was at Elkton. I was actually doing it!

Briefly.

Without warning, the door to the room was kicked open explosively, shattering the peace and dumping the five of us in the group into an immediate groggy, flinching confusion. The room was bright—I'd had my eyes closed for almost ten minutes and my pupils had no time to adjust—and at first I didn't believe what I was seeing was actually happening.

Angry Buddhist stood in the room, shouting at the guy leading the service. "Don't you *ever*, *EVER*, condescend to me like that, you motherfucker!" There was a long pause, then he said, "What the hell is this?" He made a mockingly smug, squinty face and gestured with his hands as if to say, *Keep it down*. The veins in his neck bulged and the redness in his face under his fair skin showed that he was doing everything he could to contain himself. "If you pulled that shit in any other prison—*any* other prison—*SMACK*!" He swung his right hand and smashed it against his left hand, which he held inches away from the other guy's face, with a thunderous clap that reverberated in the room. "Unbelievable!" he added, and then stormed out.

Later, Leonard and I kept laughing and relaughing at the absurdity of it all: one Buddhist yelling at another right at that moment of the sacred meditation. It was comedic gold. The more we thought about it, the harder we laughed. Moments like this helped pass the time. So they were highly valued and often revisited.

A few days later, I ran into Angry Buddhist in the chow hall, "Dude, what in the hell happened the other night?" I asked as we stood in line.

"Oh, fuck Mike," he said, unapologetically. "That dickhead commandeered the damn group a while back, and I just couldn't do it anymore so I quit going. He's not a Buddhist. He just makes the whole thing about himself. He knows I play the guitar at night. I was making no more noise than anyone else. So he comes and singles me out and tells me to keep it quiet." He paused to tell the server he wanted some sweet potatoes and continued. "He pulls that crap on me all the time." He started laughing, "I know you guys were just wrapping up your meditation, and believe me, I am well aware of the irony. Not very Buddhist-like of me. But I just couldn't take it anymore." We sat down. "My apologies. I'm not too proud of that moment. But like a good Buddhist, I will just have to let it go," he said with a smile.

"It's all good. Leonard and I could not stop laughing that night."

"Oh, I'm sure it was quite a treat," he chuckled, but then got serious, as if getting back to his underlying preoccupation. "Ugh!" he said while shaking his head in disgust.

"What?"

"I am getting out of here soon. And there are some snags with where I will go. They want me to go live with my dad in Dayton again when I get out. They are not thrilled about me staying by myself. After, well, after my 'accident.'"

"Accident?" I asked.

He stuck his wrists out towards me, so his sleeves rode up, showing his scars. "I 'accidently' tried to kill myself," he said mockingly. "I was in a bad spot. Just got divorced, hadn't seen my son in a year or so, job market was bad, not much you can do with a literature degree if you aren't a professor. It just all snowballed. My depression was out of control." He got more serious. "So I would just get shit-faced, put on a bunch of porn, and crawl into a hole." He took another breath. "Everything just got worse. The porn on the peer-to-peer got more disturbing. But I didn't give a shit. I would go on weeklong benders. Blacked out most of the weekend. I saw all kinds of weird shit. I didn't care. Was really thinking of killing myself anyway."

He seemed oddly calm telling me this, but maybe the four years he'd spent at Elkton had given him enough time to process it, and I'm sure he'd talked it out plenty of times. "So when I got arrested and they let me stay on house arrest, first chance I got, I slit my wrists. I thought my dad was going to be gone for the day. Sonofabitch comes back mid-day to pick something up and sees my bloody mess in the bathroom and calls an ambulance. It really fucked him up. I just don't want him to deal with my mess anymore."

He seemed to accept his conundrum for the moment and moved on. "You know, a lot of guys here tried to off themselves when the shit hit the fan for them. When you meet people, try to catch a glimpse of their wrists. You will see."

Angry Buddhist was right. I counted at least five guys with scars on their wrists. All were discovered by a friend or family member shortly after the cuts were made. A few others had circular scars above their sternums, at the base of their necks: tracheostomy sites, I realized. After attempting suicide by drug overdose or a botched hanging, they were discovered by happenstance, revived by paramedics, and put on a ventilator for their stay in the intensive care unit.

MORBIDITY

This was not a person but was nonetheless a dominant character at Elkton. Evidence of self-induced harm was not the only common clinical finding I saw. Autism spectrum disorders were abundant, too. There were guys who were absolutely clueless about how to converse and read social cues, and would just talk over the other person, oblivious that they were pissing them off, right up until they were told to fuck off. A few others I would try to sit with at lunch or dinner would just stare at me after my attempt at initiating small talk, as if they badly wanted to say something. Instead just lowered their eyes back to their plate, put food in their mouths, chewing and swallowing and repeating that until the food was gone. And then they were gone.

There was senility and dementia among some of the grandpas who were there, though, everyone tried to help them through the day. There were war veterans with organic brain injury and frontal release syndromes and an overall slowness from being blown up by improvised explosive devices in Iraq or Afghanistan. I saw many craniotomy scars wrapped around the scalps of the many shaved prisoner heads, like the seams on a baseball, from motorcycle accidents, vaguely described head traumas, or brain surgeries. I also found myself observing numerous pathologic gaits—stroke, arthritis, injury, diabetic feet (missing toes), etc. It was a daily, nonstop bombardment of human suffering that my medical knowledge and curse of symptom recognition afforded me. Elkton FSL was the BOP's island of misfit toys, made possible by the Internet's ability to manufacture nonproduction/noncontact child pornography offenders and turn awkward forty- to fifty-year-old virgins into feared sex offenders. Given that 55 percent of male state prisoners and 45 percent of their federal counterparts have at least one documented mental illness (who knows how many have *undocumented* disorders), I am sure this bleak overall picture (in different details and faces) can be observed all over the country. Since the 1960s, when the system of public mental health hospitals began to be eroded, the streets and prisons have become warehouses for the "mad among us." There are now more than three times as many seriously mentally ill people in jails and prisons than in hospitals.

Over time, these realizations helped me to understand part of the disgust the Haters and other non-SOs had with the SOs there. Most of us just didn't belong there. Many, unfortunately—by mental defect or physical limitations—probably never belonged anywhere.

INSTITUTIONALIZATION

"I just don't get it, man," I began to tell Leonard, sitting on my bunk one afternoon after lunch, as he unwound from his morning pots-and-pans duty. "These Hater guys should be happy they don't have to worry about getting shanked, swindled, or their ass beat. Why do they complain when they finally get to a safe place?" I could see in Leonard's face that this was a topic near and dear to him, being an ex-CO and PO himself. But he knew I was not done talking and let me finish. "I overheard for the third or fourth time guys who came down from up top or higher securities say, *Well if this was a real prison, blah, blah, blah.* I mean, Jesus, no one here gives a shit about TV rooms. We just get up and walk out. And if we owe you money, lo and behold, you get paid back. They should be ecstatic to be here."

"Well, yes and no," he started. Leonard had been in Elkton for over a year, had been in high-security facilities, and up top, en route to Elkton FSL, and having an introspective and reflective soul, it was clear he had given this subject some thought. "You need to remember, some of these guys have been down in the system for years. Some for decades. They started at some of the highest levels, and with good behavior, worked their way down."

"OK."

"And in that time, they got used to a system—an expectation of what a prisoner is. There is a 'code,' a pecking order. When someone pisses on their seat, to mark their territory, there is almost an expectation of conflict, a push-back. When it doesn't happen, it throws them off."

"Hmm."

"And this place is unlike any prison they have ever seen before. They are the minority. Just about everywhere else, SOs make up 5 to 15 percent of the population. And most are touchers. The molesters—even *we* detest the molesters. Imagine how much *they* do. Now, they come here and 60 or 70 percent of the population are SOs. Do you think they make a distinction between us and the touchers?"

"Probably not."

"Of course not. Our society on the outside does not make that distinction." He paused. "God damn! Even some federal judges, who should know better, can't make that distinction. Can we expect these guys to?" I remained silent. "Hell no," he answered himself.

"But it's not just that. Sure, some of the knuckle-draggers assume we are actual chomos and detest us, but the ones who know better know what is up. I have seen some of them talking with you just fine," he said, pointing at me. I knew he was implying that the legal work he did for the Haters was analogous to the medical advice I gave them. "You are a doctor and play sports and look normal, so you don't fit that mold entirely."

Leonard was right, the free medical advice, etc., afforded me less hassle from the Haters. It was jarring at times, though, to go from advising a black inmate about his diabetic foot infection one minute to talking to a white guy with an "Aryan Brotherhood" tattoo on his shoulder the next about his mother's newly diagnosed lung cancer.

I had struck up a friendship, of sorts, with one of the Haters, a guy I called Tommy Gleevec. On the outside, he had a record but had walked the straight and narrow for over ten years—until he developed chronic myelogenous leukemia. All conventional chemotherapies failed. Then his doctor gave him some free samples of a drug called Gleevec, and he got a complete response: his affected lymph nodes shrank. But since Gleevec cost almost $9,000 for a ninety-pill supply, and his health insurance through the garage where he worked wouldn't cover it, he went back to making and selling crystal meth to cover the costs. He rationalized that he could pay for Gleevec through his drug sales, and if he got caught, the federal government would pay for it through BOP healthcare. He was right. He did get caught, and he received his Gleevec pill every morning, Monday through Friday, and was in complete remission.

"But really," Leonard went on, "the majority of the disgust comes from *who we are* and the shit that goes on here—not what we did to get here."

"What do you mean?"

"Look around. There are a lot of batshit crazy guys among us. Guys who don't bathe, guys who shit themselves or smear it in the stalls, shower sharks [gay guys who peek through stall doors or with mirrors in adjacent stalls, hoping for a hookup]—that's the kind of shit that disgusts them. And since this a special, low-security prison, if you lay a hand on someone just once, even shove someone, you are gone for good. So there is no way they can enforce the code here either."

"Really."

"Yes, there was a guy that used to be here named Bloody Bob. He always picked at the scabs all over his body, so his sores always stayed open. He bled everywhere. On his clothes, his bedding, in the showers. Man, you did not want Bloody Bob in the shower next to you. That red water would come over in your stall, right next to your bare toes. It was disgusting." Leonard paused to grimace at what had to be his actual memory. "If he pulled that shit up top or anywhere else, he would have gotten beaten down until he stopped. But down here, he is protected."

I soaked it all in and nodded. I had heard about Bloody Bob before. He'd told everyone he had a rare skin condition. But when he was told that he couldn't go to a halfway house because of his open sores, and would therefore have to remain at Elkton for the full six months remaining on his sentence, his "rare skin condition" miraculously healed in a week, and he was cleared to go.

Leonard continued, "Just picture Crack-Head Johnny [IQ ≈ 70], Hanson [schizotypal Dungeons and Dragons player], or Weird Mike [a morbidly obese endomorph with Coke-bottle glasses and a widely disconjugate gaze from a birth injury]—can you picture them surviving in a real prison?" Again I didn't answer his question. "They would get eaten alive."

"Yeah."

"And that is what bugs these hardened, institutionalized, non-SO guys. Elkton goes against everything they have come to expect."

In a half-joking way I asked, "Well, if it is so unbearable for them, can't they just ask to be moved back up the security levels?"

"They can't. The system only moves down."

Again half-joking, I asked while chuckling, "So—what? You gotta take a swing at someone to make that happen?"

"Yes. That is exactly what you need to do." He said in a very serious tone, as if delivering bad news.

"*What?*"

"Yeah," I could see in his face that he was about to deliver more disappointment. "Last spring, a guy here called Tall Dre just couldn't take it here anymore. He went to the COs and asked to go back up the hill. They said no. He asked his case manager and counselor, and they said no, too. So one day at lunch he walks up to a group of COs standing together, like they always do at chow hall, and tells them, *I am gonna knock that mutherfukker out and get the hell out of here* while pointing at his target out in the yard. And they warned him that if he hit someone, he would be sent back to the FCI. He walks right outside and sucker-punches a guy. Knocked him right out cold. Even a few teeth came out."

"Whoa."

"Yeah. The guy he picked was a well-known prison snitch. Tall Dre made sure he didn't make any enemies on his way back up top. By the time the COs came out—they watched the whole thing happen—he was already lying on the ground, on his stomach, with his hands behind his back. He went right to the SHU, lost all of his good time, and spent the rest of his sentence up top."

"Jesus. So the only way to go back up top is to cave someone's face in? Can't that be bypassed?"

"Nope. To move up in security, you need to do something bad."

We both chewed on that point for a bit. But I could see Leonard's mind churning. He struck me as someone who possessed the gift of learning something new just by hearing himself talk. "I guess that's the fourth reason people are here," he muttered, wrapping his head around his sudden epiphany.

"Fourth reason?" I asked. He collected himself. Then once he had it articulated in his mind, he spoke.

"I always thought there were three reasons people were in prison: Greed, mental health problems, and evil," he counted them off on his fingers. "Most think it is evil—like only bad people do bad things and go to prison," he said dismissively. "But even in a supermax, the sociopathy rate is only 25 percent. Most people are born good. No, greed and mental health are the big ones. Say some guy doesn't want to pay taxes, or is poor and steals something, or wants to get rich selling drugs. That's greed." He took a deep breath and moved on, "Mental health can be addiction, anger management issues, or bipolar, for examples. People can do bad things when those things flare up. Now if you are a poor addict and you start selling drugs to support your addiction—well that's a combination, isn't it?" I nodded. "But I guess the fourth one is institutionalization. It comes after the other three get your foot in the door. I knew a guy who was weeks away from getting out. He had no family, no job prospects, and was terrified of his heroin habit. So what's he do? He steals from cubes where he knows the security cameras are, and looks right into them, showing what he has taken, holding his loot right up there for all to see. He looks directly into a camera before smashing an office window. He did this over a day or two. He loses all his good time, gets another year added to his sentence. Problem solved. He doesn't have to return to the outside."

He then concluded, "You lock someone up long enough, and they don't know anything else. They won't want to leave, and won't mind coming back, either."

Chapter 6

"I am the walrus, Goo goo g' joob."

—THE BEATLES, "I AM THE WALRUS"

JON, THE JEWISH PRINCE, was always in my shit. Ever since his pressure-speech introduction to TV room politics, he had become a permanent fixture in my daily life at Elkton. In some ways, he was very helpful. Among other things, he wrote out the daily schedule for me and put me in touch with the "Elkton intelligentsia," which included the Northwestern University cancer researcher. But I soon learned to see through it, especially after his cellmates, Russo and Crazy Curtis, gave me a heads-up on Jon's MO.

Jon only associated with people he thought had intelligence or means. He took an exceptional interest in those he thought had both. Of course, being a young physician, I hadn't really had the opportunity to amass much wealth, and what little I did had pretty much melted away with the fourteen months of house arrest during which neither I nor my wife worked. But his hierarchy did not permit such logical conclusions to be drawn. If he did associate with those "beneath his station," it was to "help them." Of course, this altruistic assistance would be broadcast to everyone he knew, to show what a "good guy" he was.

Being right next door to a cell that housed a JD, an MD, and a master's was just too much for him. His nose, or rather, his ridiculous handlebar mustache, was in our business all the time. It was as if each tip of that whiskery monstrosity was attached to a silk thread connected to an invisible web he had cast over our cell—any muttering by Leonard, George, or myself sent an intellectual vibration along those lines that he would detect, follow, and pounce on. If we were working on a crossword puzzle (a Sunday-night bonding ritual we'd adopted when *The Week* magazine came in earlier in the week) or talking about history, politics, science, pop culture, or anything that required a modicum of knowledge, his sensors would pick up this frequency over the five-foot wall that separated us. Then he would swing over into our cell, insert himself into the discussion, and in short time, make it all about him. Everyone hated him. And there were moments when I did, too.

Every morning when I woke up and walked by his cube, en route to the bathroom, it was as if that was his cue to invite himself into our cube. I learned that, if he was sitting in his bottom bunk, with his back against the wall that separated my cube from his—the silk lines taut on his mustache-antenna apparatus—upon my return from the bathroom, I would see his ass sticking out from our cube entry into the walkway, as he leaned up against the top of my locker, which had become his self-assigned spot in our cube. This was beyond frustrating for me, as my locker was the only place I could stand or sit to write on a hard surface. It was my desk and office. On more than one occasion, he inserted his prodigiously furred upper lip between my face and the paper and asked me what I was writing.

It bothered him that I knew factoids and trivia, so much so that he once came up to my cubemates and me and delivered a little speech about it: "I finally realized something. You all know lots of things, but I know how to problem-solve. I am an innovator. Your claim to fame is rote memory—but I can see things that others can't, and I create new things. So I don't feel so bad anymore." He was so triumphant with this empty self-affirmation that I didn't have the heart to tell him I had a few patents pending prior to my arrest and had definitely found patterns in molecular markers in glioblastoma and rhabdomyosarcoma—when others had not. But he was so pumped up with his realization that I let him have his moment. The three of us just looked at each other, dumbfounded that he would interrupt us with an unsolicited announcement like that.

Regardless of the subject of the original conversation, once Jon entered, within a minute (seriously, you could set a timer) he would draw the focus onto one of his favorite topics: how much his income was, how cultured he was, that he had servants growing up, his world travels, and so on. When conversing with others, it was as if he paused his script when others spoke and then just resumed his monologue when the other finished talking. Interestingly, he was a strong proponent of eugenics and population control. He opined that we needed to reduce the population from seven billion to two, by getting rid of all the "dumb people." I would always look to see George's face when Jon went on this rant. George's father had been a surgeon in the Third Reich's Wehrmacht. The Nazis, of course, knew all about eugenics and the disposal of undesirables, some of Jon's relatives no doubt among them. But Jon failed to see the irony in his statements.

Jon had the most overt, raging case of narcissistic personality disorder I had ever seen. As a matter of fact, despite the evisceration I am giving him right now, he would probably get a hard-on from knowing that I dedicated a whole chapter to him.

He put the leaders of the cancer field at MD Anderson to shame, as far as ego was concerned. At least those people had actually done something remarkable. They *were* the leaders of their respective cancer fields—in the *world*. Jon, in contrast, was a disgusting old walrus who had burned through five wives and wound up a chomo at Elkton. But he carried himself as if he mattered. He didn't. None of us did. No one matters if he is a prisoner. Unless you are a prisoner for a righteous cause, like Nelson Mandela or William Wallace, you really don't matter. And that he couldn't accept this reality is what differentiated those, like me, who had narcissistic tendencies, from those who had the full-on disorder, like him. The worst punishment you can inflict upon a narcissist is to make him irrelevant. Jon would fight this designation tooth and nail.

Some of his more outlandish and disturbing claims (aside from his eugenics rants) are described below, with the number of times he personally told me that "fact" in brackets:

- He claimed he had millions of dollars in offshore accounts [three], yet often had little money in his commissary account and frequently borrowed money.
- He bragged about having had five wives [more than ten].
- He criticized his cellmates for pronouncing the frozen treat sherbet as "sherb*e*rt" [three], yet he later called vehicles that carry the dead "hursts."
- He said he was told by his high school guidance counselors that his teachers were intimidated by his intellect [eight].
- He insisted that flat-chested young teenagers [especially Asians] were his biggest turn-ons. "I am a hebephile, not a pedophile," he would boast [more than ten].
- He described the bodies of his daughters and granddaughters [three].
- He described how his fifth wife refused to share a spoon with him when eating ice cream yet licked his anus during sex [five].
- He claimed he had a can't-miss algorithm for earning $1,000 per hour at a roulette table [more than ten]. "It was not gambling," he reasoned. "It was a series of progressive bets." He said it was how he would get back into the wealth he became accustomed to after Elkton.
- How much money he paid in taxes in his lifetime [more than ten].

Still, I suppose I should be grateful. What better way for me to identify, correct, and work on my narcissism than to be adjacent to someone who had the full-blown disease and competed with me for the very oxygen that I was attempting to breathe? At one point I wondered if being placed next to Jon was a deliberate part of my prison sentence—to "learn" me, to show just how annoying my own traits could be.

Every interaction with him was an intellectual chess match, in which I had to make sure my acumen and logic were polished. Emotional, flippant comments would simply open me to factual attack. He was exhausting.

I was sitting alone towards the end of lunch one day when a Latino inmate, who wanted to understand the nature of the nasal septum defect that he'd acquired from snorting too much cocaine over the span of his life, came over and sat across from me at a table in the cafeteria. The constant irritation and vascular constriction of the drug causes the tissues to die off. He also wanted to know if I knew any good head and neck surgeons in Houston or Brownsville who could repair it. I advised him on what hospitals to check out once he was released. I'd explained to him that I had been out of the medical scene in the Houston area for quite a while, and staffing tends to change a lot, but that he couldn't go wrong with the places I suggested. Our discussion concluded with his words of appreciation.

"Thanks, homes! [fist bump] You are a good guy, Doc. Tell you what, give me your contact info before you go, and if you ever want to be a doctor in Meh-heeco, let me know," he said with that cool Mexican accent that makes white Midwesterners feel incredibly lame. "My family can hook that shit up, bro'." He made his voice softer in the loud cafeteria and looked over his shoulder before continuing. "One of the big cartels, bro'—not naming names, you know." Then his voice went back to his original volume. "Wherever you want to live, Maing, just lemme know." He then got up and gave me another fist bump.

It's hard to tell in prison if someone is bullshitting or not. He could have been a lackey who rolled on the organization and was at cushy Elkton, for protection—or he could indeed be a major player who had an easy, safe incarceration arranged through power and connections (like the one gangster guy with multiple murders who had his own TV room and was catered to by the COs). Either way, after that conversation I got a lot more hellos, what's ups, and nods from the Latino contingent at Elkton, and he would always single me out for a smile and his signature fist bump when I walked by him if he was in line or hanging out with his guys. I certainly did not follow up on his offer to become a physician on a Mexican drug cartel's payroll. Still, it was a good social investment during my time there, though. It cleared out a segment of people who could have had a potential beef with me.

When he got up from our encounter, however, I saw that Jon had ear-hustled me from the table behind me. *Damn! I didn't notice him there before*. He looked at me and shook his head. I couldn't talk to anyone or even check out a book from the library without his knowing and critiquing my decisions.

I could have bet the farm he would slink up to me within twenty-four hours of the event and tender his unsolicited advice. So the cynical side of me was satiated the next day. I was sitting on a bench outside with a book, trying to catch some sun, while across the courtyard, a group of black guys was playing dominos, and yelling and talking smack to each other. The stage was set for Jon's daily assertions, and he did not disappoint.

"You know, Chris, I'm sure you want to be the medical hero—running out of bounds to save the gay guy and dishing out advice to our friend from south of the border—but you need to watch yourself," he said, preening with his vast wisdom. "I know how the system works far better than you do," he said in the annoying condescending tone he must have sharpened throughout his life.

"What do you mean?" I said, playing dumb and enamored and buying time, already dog-earing the page I was on. At least he wasn't going to comment on the book I was reading and try to spoil it for me.

"There was this big cardiac surgeon [name drop], that was at the federal facility near D.C. where I was for a while. He was busted for insider trading."

"OK."

"He didn't think the medical staff at this place was competent, so he set up his own clinic in his cell. He was told to stop. He didn't. So they took away all of his good time and he spent the rest of his sentence in the SHU."

"Hmmm." I pretended to take the bait.

"I am just saying. You need to be careful—"

"Let me guess. This surgeon was a prick. A real asshole, right?" I asked curtly, closing my book. Jon stammered a bit. I'd learned how to deflate him. I guess I had enough narcissism in me to know what would sting him.

I had gathered great intel from listening to the spats he had with Russo, which wafted over the wall between our cubes. I'd learned what pushed Jon's buttons. One of the best prison moments I had was listening to those two going at it as I was waking up and pulling the earplugs out of my head one morning. For about a week, Jon had talked incessantly about one of his grandchildren being named a National Merit

Scholarship finalist and how he was going to help her with her application and essays—because her parents (one being Jon's daughter—the one with the great body, according to his lurid descriptions) were too simple and unsophisticated to guide her.

Finally, exasperated, Russo said, "That's right Jon. And when your granddaughter wins the Nobel Peace Prize, the first thing she is going to say is that I couldn't have done it without my sex-offender-crook of a grandfather, Jonathan Goldman, who single-handedly got me into Harvard from his prison cell." Jon was furious and called him a "stupid fucking truck driver." It was priceless and made even better by the silent thumbs-up from Leonard who was sitting in the bunk below me: I was not the only one to overhear that precious gem. My face flushed red and then broke out in a sweat from holding in my laughter. I still laugh out loud whenever I recall that moment.

In the yard, I pressed on about Jon's big-shot surgeon: "I am sure cleaning the sinks—like I do—would have been waaaay beneath him, and he would have told everyone about it, right?"

"Yes. He was an outright, arrogant asshole," he answered, defeated. His name-drop had lost its luster. I went for the kill shot.

"Right, so this openly defiant asshole, who told everyone how much better he was than everyone, was taken to task and had the rules enforced upon him?" He considered it.

I continued, "I am pretty sure the motivation for taking away his good time and putting him away in the SHU is a lot more complicated than me giving medical advice." He considered further. "Besides, I am not running a damn clinic just to thumb my nose at the authorities."

At that moment, the table of black guys playing dominos across the yard erupted into a cacophony of F-words and N-words and other shouts. Someone had just won big, but it came at a horrible time in my conversation with Jon. Shunted off his original course, he tried a new track. "Well, I am just saying, you need to decide if these lowlifes," he said, nodding his head toward the dominos table, "are worth you getting involved and in trouble." And having recovered his dignity by delivering his words of wisdom, he got up and slowly waddled away while the hollering from the table continued.

"I ain't getting' in any trouble over this!" I yelled over the din at Jon's disappearing ponytail. I couldn't let him have the last word. But it was over. I'd lost this round on a technicality. He never turned around. He just gave out a nebbishy *ehhh* while shrugging and kept walking away.

In that moment, I loathed him—like skin-crawling loathed. But also at that moment I came to the realization that I had sounded as obnoxious as Jon in the past. In moments of hurt or despair, or when feeling threatened, it was as if my hypothalamus took control of my thoughts and the mouth that spouted them. While I did not believe the horrific things I would say, they still came out, as if eliciting the worst emotional responses in those who had the misfortune of having to listen to me would elevate me above them or whatever it was that was threatening me.

Seeing how disgusted I was by what Jon had to say, I realized how disgusted others must have been with me—even if they knew what I was saying at the peak of one of my narcissistic diatribes was an exaggerated extension of the pain and anguish I was acutely feeling. I realized, through Jon, how damaging my personality had been. The blowhard, the exasperated douche bag, the drunk guy at the party who knew better than everyone else, the guy who mocked and ridiculed others who he felt had outworked and outsmarted—that was me. I was insufferable.

The thing is, only a few close to me saw this side of me. Nearly all of these blasts were shot toward Susan, at point-blank range. It was she who had to withstand these verbal and emotional onslaughts for over eighteen years straight, the way a rocky outcropping on a cold and windy coast withstands the constant fuming waves. But even the mightiest of rocks and mountains are vulnerable to erosion. I wore her out. Though most of my outbursts were not directed at her personally, the emotions they evoked had to be dispiriting beyond measure. In just a few interactions with Jon, I'd got just a glimpse of what it would have been like to tolerate his sort of crap for years on end. I could feel the anger and resentment rise within me with each word he uttered. But I could just walk away or tell him to go to hell. I was not locked into any kind of relationship with him. It was easy to see how he burned through five wives—just as I had completely fried one.

Yet in along with the disgust I felt toward him, I also felt a deep pity. I knew the origins of this behavior. His scars definitely ran deeper than mine. After hearing only bits and pieces of his family life, his emotionally distant philandering father, the drug use that ran rampant through him and his siblings, the fights, being told he was never wanted by his mother, I knew he had a huge hole right in the middle of him, one that pushed him past the point of merely trying to measure up. He needed to prove to the world there was a reason he existed at all.

Chapter 7

"All the time you spend tryin' to get back what's been took from you, there's more goin' out the door. After a while you just try and get a tournique on it."

—CORMAC MCCARTHY, *NO COUNTRY FOR OLD MEN*

JON LEFT ON FEBRUARY SECOND, and his departure marked a lessening in the severity of my incarceration. It also was the day I was notified that I would be completing my stint at Elkton on May 4, 2015, and going to a halfway house in Columbus. The extra day my judge added to my otherwise twelve-month sentence *did* qualify me for an earlier release due to the built-in "good time" policy after all. Thus, my sentence was set to be served for seven and a half months in prison, with the remaining ninety days spent in a halfway house.

That date that will always stand out as an important one in my adult life. February 1, 1996, a Friday, was the day of my interview at Northwestern Medical School. It was a day that the wind chill turned to minus 40°F (or it at least felt like that). On the tours of the campus and hospitals, anytime the group stepped outside the moisture from our breaths condensed and froze onto our nose hairs, converting them into little needles that would poke into our nasal tissues whenever we rubbed our noses to warm them up. I highly doubt they successfully recruited any of the candidates from California that day. At the conclusion of my panel interview, I announced that I planned to propose to my girlfriend the following day and asked them to wish me luck. I then spent the next eight hours driving through blizzard conditions on I-94. It should have taken only around four hours, but the warm, moist air of Lake Michigan, mixing with that painfully cold, dry air I'd endured in Chicago, had other ideas—lake-effect snow. And it was in full effect on that day.

I made that drive in my very first car, a gray 1982 Ford Fairmont, handed down from my grandfather's sister after she passed. She put very few miles on it, but it was old nonetheless. Driving in snow with this mode of transportation was a first for me. Up until then, my winter driving career had all occurred in compact cars with front-wheel drive and antilock brake systems. Several times I nearly skidded off the road into an embankment, or worse. Young and determined as I was, this occasioned more frustration than fear. The engagement ring was resting peacefully in the top drawer of my dorm room's dresser, waiting for me to place it on Susan's finger at the Brandy Wine in Jackson, Michigan, the following night. I was not about to let a car accident, stranding on the side of the road, or fatality derail my plans for February second.

Nineteen years later, on February 2, 2015, I woke up in my top bunk in a federal prison with the sole purpose of getting onto the TRULINCS email system and seeing if Susan responded to a message I'd sent her before it shut down the previous night. Around five thirty a.m., through my earplugs, I'd heard the rustling of Jon in the adjacent cube preparing for his departure, but I did not want to engage him. What I could hear of his final words of wisdom to his cellmates was enough. I went back to sleep, knowing that more things were going to change.

It had been 140 days since I self-surrendered to Elkton. In our numerous phone calls and emails, I'd never heard or read that Susan missed me or loved me at all. As time went on, each time I was to call her I was filled with more dread. Every time I called, the awkwardness of the previous call made the next one more difficult. Leonard and George would know when I had just gotten off the phone with her. They told me my entire countenance changed, that I would slam my locker a little louder or handle my belongings a little more roughly and that I would become curter in my interactions with them. Internally, I seethed with frustration, anger, and resentment, and I wondered how in the hell we were going to salvage anything, a hundred miles apart and with me on the sex offender registry when I came out, if we couldn't even talk *now*.

My email the night before had been very simple and to the point: "Do you miss me and still love me?"

Around the time of my plea hearing, on November 15, 2013, things had changed between us. Or rather we went back to our old ways. I think when my case first went public, the shock at what had befallen us triggered an urge in her to circle the wagons around me and the family, and she felt genuine concern that I had been suffering for so long. A lot of things finally made sense to her with how I behaved. But then a rapid series of events happened that shone a harsher light on things. An afternoon delight was interrupted by my pretrial services officer who unfortunately happened to make his monthly unannounced house visit at a time that should have been a private moment. She was interviewed by the neuropsychologist, Dr. Kimmel, who brought up many painful issues and observations about our relationship (some of which we were previously unaware of). We were hit by the fact that I could be hauled off to jail after I entered a guilty plea; consequently we got busy with power of attorney, living will, and trust paperwork (with the help of our estate-planner-lawyer neighbor). The capper was that, on the day of my hearing, Susan got to hear for the first time just how horrific and disgusting the files I'd viewed really were—and how angry and upset the court and society were going to be with me, for a long time. Her shock and numbness, which enabled her to initially stand by me, were replaced by an unforgiving reality check.

In their totality, these events showed her just how long this haul was going to be and how deep our problems had been for so many years. So we went back to our old isolation and separation in our home, the same way we'd handled pressures and problems before, when they originated from our interpersonal mismatch. Only this time, there were many more external and existential factors at work. For the next ten months, we were forced to stay in each other's oxygen because of the legal and financial restrictions placed upon us. We had to keep on a happy face for our children. And we had to do all this while not knowing what was going to happen, while I was getting vilified by the local news media and facing a legal system hell-bent on putting me away for at least four years.

After I made my instant coffee in my still-mustard-scented plastic cup, around nine thirty a.m. I jumped on one of the unit computers—as I always did. She'd written back. There was no simple yes or no answer to this. It was by far the longest piece of communication, in any form, she'd had for me since I left:

> This is something I have thought about a lot and I did not want to bring it up over 15-minute phone calls or emails that are monitored. I didn't know how to bring it up and I didn't want to be unfair to you. I did not want to throw this at you, when you are away and cut off and alone. But since you asked, I have to be honest with you and tell you that in many ways I have been relieved that you are finally gone. There are parts of me that had been missing for so long, I had no idea they were gone and now that they are back, I don't want to lose them again.
>
> I dreaded the thought of having to go through all that therapy together, to undo all the damage that has been done. To do that on top of you trying to reestablish yourself, personally and publicly, after this whole mess, just seems impossible. I think you would feel the same way.
>
> So, no. I do not miss you. I do care about you, though. I want to support you, but I just don't have enough left in the tank for "Us."
>
> I will be able to talk at around 2 p.m. Please call me back.

It was a relief to read this. I quickly wrote back that I understood and would call back around two as requested. It was the first time I actually wanted to call her. We were finally going to *talk*—even though the subject would be painful, it was going to be *some* kind of connection. I suspended all planned activities for that afternoon and hung around the phones, to ensure I could get one of the four phones when the two o'clock window opened.

There was always a tiny subsecond window of audible signal between the moment the person you called picked up the phone and when the robot voice said, "YOU ARE RECEIVING A CALL FROM— Chris Pelloski [in my recorded voice]—AN INMATE AT A U.S. FEDERAL PRISON. PRESS FIVE TO ACCEPT THIS CALL AND SEVEN TO DECLINE THIS CALL." Usually I would hear someone say hello or hear background sounds. Then it would go completely silent until the button was pressed on the other end and the call (and fifteen-minute time limit) commenced. This time, when I called Susan at 2:01 p.m. on February 2, 2015, I could already hear her crying. She was probably in the car and had got to the school early to pick up our children. Making extra time. So there was no background noise in her closed car. It was like she was crying alone in a sound studio.

"Ohhhhh—" she struggled, "hello?"

"Hey, hey, hey. It's OK. It's OK," I said, instantly trying to reassure her and help keep her composure—and mine. "We can talk about this." I heard a few more sobs, so I figured I would have to do most of the talking initially. "You *do* know that breakups are probably *the* number one subject of phone conversations in prison, right?"

"OK," followed by a nasally congested chuckle. I quickly continued.

"Yeah. And to be honest, this is the first time in a long time I have wanted to call you." The sobbing began to dissipate. "Every time I talk to you, I feel like you are being brow-beaten by a four-hundred-pound gorilla that's in the room with you." There was some more relieved, yet measured, laughter. "It's time to tell that gorilla to have a banana and take a walk while we talk!" Some nervous laughter escaped me, while my throat and nose began to burn a little. "I agree with what you wrote, Susie. And it's OK to say that while I'm here."

"OK. Yeah. I think we have given this every opportunity we can."

"I know. We have. And the prospect of hashing this out some more sounds like—like just more pain and torment." I said. "Since I got used to being here at Elkton, I realized the worst part of it was being on the phone with you and trying to have a conversation with you. Other than that, prison ain't that bad!" I said in a light way—trying to keep myself together.

There was another light, but very heavy laugh on the other end, "Yeeaahhhh—that is not a good sign."

"No."

"And it has been very good for me that you have been gone. I can't fully explain it."

"Yeeaahhhh," I parroted her, "that is not a good sign, either."

"No," she concurred. "I just didn't know how to say it, or bring it up. I didn't want you to feel like I was abandoning—" her sobbing returned.

"Susie—" the burning lump in my throat then felt like it was boring its way out through my neck, completely blowing my stoic insistence on levity, "You and your dad—" *Damn it!* I was crying in prison. You never cry in prison. That shows you are soft. I ducked my head into the phone well so that no one could see me. I could barely form audible words: nearly eighteen years of a marriage—one that was now clearly ending—was passing before my mind's eye. "Susie, you and your dad saved my life on that first night in Colorado." These were the hardest words I ever had to choke out. "You—" the lump in my throat was a hot coal, searing my vocal cords, "You stood by me—"

We might have spent the remainder of our conversation in mutual sobbing silence, but we were saved from that by, "This call is from a U.S. federal prison." The recorded reminder snapped me back to the here and now. That annoying message invariably triggered a joke between us of the *no shit* variety.

"You stood by me when it was *totally* unfashionable to do so," I said in my faux couture-designer voice, through tears, gallows humor temporarily conquering heartbreak. "And you made sure I could repair things with the kids, so I got to really know them as a father should. When it would have been so easy for you to just have—taken off. You have saved my life in so many ways already."

I could sense us both getting serious again. "So you, like, have done your duty for god and country when it comes to me." This time, the tension permanently eased.

"We have really been in rough shape, sweetie. I mean even before all this crap," she said, in a more conversational tone.

"I know."

"And I know all of that narcissism and masochism are part of what all happened to you—"

"Susie, you have dealt with a full-fledged PTSDer—who was taking amphetamines on top of it!—for almost two decades. You always pushed me to get better, but I shut you out."

"I tried—but I can't do the 'Chris Show' anymore."

"I know. When I think about it—prison gives you time to think, ya know—we have both been miserable with each other. There were only a few patches of time when we were both ever truly happy. It has been a hard road." It's the great moments that make it hard to let go. And they were fully present in my mind as we talked: Moving into our new apartment in Chicago, where our Boston terrier, Mehla, sprinted from Susan's arms into mine after running half of a block. Sleeping in the hospital room with our newborn twin babies for the first time and hearing their coos and gurgling—making those babies may have been the only two things we did right. Roasting marshmallows over a firepit in the backyard of our dream home with our children.

But those moments had been fleeting ones amid the constant drone of unhappiness and resentment. Fighting and worrying about money, slamming doors, falling asleep alone and furious. Basically 90 percent of the filler time. "I think we have fought against everything from the beginning. Your mom dying, me not being right, school—all of it. We have had the deck stacked against us."

"I know."

"And it's not your job to monitor my stability, for you to be walking on eggshells all the time."

"I know. And I know you are better now, but you still have a long way to go. I've just got nothing left."

"Yeah."

"I need to be your friend again. We have always been great friends. Had we not been such good friends, we probably would have 'peaced out' a long time ago. It's why we stayed together so long."

"Yeah. I agree." It was if we needed to convince each other, and ourselves, of the obvious. "Susie, we just spent fourteen months together and have been apart for 140 days and neither of us feels any sense of loss. I think that means we are done. Why wait any longer? We have to end this unrelenting sense of obligation and expectation and just be parents and friends."

"I think so too." Relief had overtaken our voices. "If we tried to make this work—"

"It would be more years of misery and the kids putting up with pissed off parents."

"Yes. Exactly."

It was our first true accord since deciding to remain in our home and stay together during my house arrest. The rest of the conversation was logistics. She would talk with a family law attorney and figure out what all needed to happen and what I needed to do once I got out—which if all went to plan, was thirteen weeks away.

"Good god, I'm glad we talked," I said.

"Me too. It was getting unbearable."

Beep-beep-beep—time was running out on the phone call, only about fifteen seconds left.

"I know," I said.

"OK. OK. I know we are about to run out of time." And then for the first and last time ever I heard, "I love you." Whatever resolve I had to hold back tears was now entirely gone—the faucets had been cranked to full in an instant, as Susan continued, "and I have got your back. But not as your wife. And you need to get your mind back into oncology!"

"I love you too," I mustered in a harsh whisper. "And thank you."

The line silently shut off, the hiss of the connection turning into a pure, black, empty quiet like it always did.

Once again, something very brief but hugely important, one that determines a life's path, had just happened. And I had nothing but time to process what in the hell had just transpired. It was a conversation that should have happened long ago. Failed attempts had occurred so many times: Sitting across from each other in the hallway of our Chicago apartment at two a.m., when I was in medical school and Susan in law school. Several times in Houston, before our children were born. One time after moving to Columbus. But we were always afraid to pull the trigger. There was always an excuse: Maybe this is how it feels when you are first married? What would our parents say—they'd be crushed. Maybe it will be better once I get that federal research grant, then I won't be so stressed out. The statistics say it is better for the kids if the parents can gut it out together.

And so on.

We had run out of excuses. We'd used them all up. The fact that our children were thriving in my absence essentially debunked that last excuse. Further, the fourteen months I'd been able to spend with them made it clear to them that I was their dad and that we all loved each other. Ironically, had it not been for my house arrest, I probably would have spent less time with them than that over my entire career-crazed life, and they would have grown to hate and resent me. And then I would have been dead by the time I was forty-five, at my own hands—directly, or indirectly through work. Instead, they got to know me as someone other than "Yelly Daddy." Now was the logical time for Susan and me to part. Prison had showed us that we could be separated and everyone would still live, breathe, and, surprisingly, thrive. We could be happier, and the sun would still rise—even with my incarceration as part of the conditions.

Still, it was numbing. For the first time since coming to Elkton, I didn't do anything to keep my mind occupied. I just sat, doing nothing but thinking and staring off into nothingness.

My mom, when I called her, was relieved to hear the news. Not only were the logic and rationale for a divorce obvious, but she'd known it was coming since our medical and law school days in Chicago. She said she hadn't the heart to tell me, and she was surprised we had made it so long.

I remembered working in the intensive care unit during my internship, in October of 2001. There was a shriveled old woman whose liver failure was the worst I had ever seen. She was so jaundiced the whites of her eyes looked like orange peels. But the family wanted all heroic measures taken to keep her alive. And every fifteen minutes or so she would go into cardiac arrest. So, every fifteen minutes or so, we would go into the room and pound on her chest, further cracking her chalky ribs pushing her floating, detached sternum into a new starting position with each resuscitation. These futile code blues served no purpose, other than to give the interns practice at CPR and the family a false sense of hope. The life they were clinging to was just an illusion and a blip on the EKG machine by that point. Eventually, out of respect for the already-dead woman, the MICU staff put an end to the nonsense. Sometimes an outside source can help guide proper decision making. It was still very sad when she died, though, for all involved.

Like that family who had held onto an empty promise for too long, but eventually agreed to pull the plug in the face of reason, I felt a suffocating sense of loss with our decision to divorce. It was the same feeling I'd felt when my grandfather passed, after years of horrible dementia, even though in his lucid moments he had wanted it to end. A loss is still a loss.

You cannot say the word *divorce* without a sense of failure—and ours was colossal. We were a doctor and a lawyer. Beautiful kids. Beautiful home. We had everything. But we had nothing. We were just friends who tried to make romance and passion happen by rubbing two platonic sticks together and hoping for the spark that never happened. And it took eighteen years of immeasurable frustration and resentment—fomented by my unresolved mental health issues and my unrelenting pursuit of professional immortality—a publicly humiliating downfall, near bankruptcy, and a prison sentence to prove that it just didn't work.

Chapter 8

"The most difficult subjects can be explained to the most slow-witted man if he has not formed any idea of them already; but the simplest thing cannot be made clear to the most intelligent man if he is firmly persuaded that he knows already, without a shadow of doubt, what is laid before him."

—LEO TOLSTOY, *THE KINGDOM OF GOD IS WITHIN YOU*

ANGRY BUDDHIST HAD survived his suicide attempt, like a lot of other guys who were at Elkton who bore the scars. But not everyone who endured the humiliation of the charge and the public spectacle that followed made it to prison. When I was on house arrest, a friend of mine directed my attention to the story of Ryan Loskarn, the chief of staff for Tennessee Senator Lamar Alexander. He had a reputation for getting the job done and working well with both sides of the political aisle—something which seems to be a uniquely valuable and extremely rare skill these days. When I read his suicide letter, which his mother published online, I wept. It could just have easily been my letter:

> On December 11, 2013, I was arrested for possession of child pornography. Writing those few words took

a long time; seeing them in print is agony. But I owe many, many people an explanation—if that's even possible—and that's why I've written this letter.

The news coverage of my spectacular fall makes it impossible for me to crawl in a hole and disappear. I've hurt every single human being I've ever known and the details of my shame are preserved on the Internet for all time. There is no escape.

My family has been wounded beyond description. My former boss and colleagues had their trust broken and their names dragged through the mud for no reason other than association. Friends' question whether they ever really knew me.

Everyone wants to know why.

I've asked God. I've asked myself. I've talked with clergy and counselors and psychiatrists. I spent five days on suicide watch in the psychiatric ward at the D.C. jail, fixated on the "why" and "how" questions: why did I do this and how can I kill myself? I've shared the most private details of my life with others in the effort to find an answer. There seem to be many answers and none at all.

The first time I saw child pornography was during a search for music on a peer-to-peer network. I wasn't seeking it but I didn't turn away when I saw it. Until that moment, the only place I'd seen these sorts of images was in my mind.

I found myself drawn to videos that matched my own childhood abuse. It's painful and humiliating to admit to myself, let alone the whole world, but I pictured myself as a child in the image or video. The more an image mirrored some element of my memories and took me back, the more I felt a connection.

This is my deepest, darkest secret.

As a child I didn't understand what had happened at the time of the abuse. I did know that I must not tell anyone, ever. Later the memories took on new and more troubling meaning when I became a teenager. They started to appear more often and made me feel increasingly apart from everyone else. In my mind I instigated and enjoyed the abuse—even as a five and nine years old—no matter the age difference. Discussing what had happened would have meant shame and blame.

I always worried someone might look at me and know, so I paid close attention to others for any sign they might have figured it out. No one ever did. By my late teens I reached a sort of mental equilibrium on the matter. I couldn't stop the images from appearing altogether, but I generally controlled when they appeared.

As an adult I thought I was a tougher man because of the experience; that I was mentally stronger and less emotional than most. I told myself that I was superior to other people because I had dealt with this thing on my own.

Those I worked with on the Hill would likely describe me as a controlled, independent, and rational person who could analyze a situation with little or no emotion. That's how I viewed myself. In retrospect, the qualities that helped me succeed on Capitol Hill were probably developed partly as a result of the abuse and how it shaped me.

In the aftermath of my arrest and all that followed, the mental equilibrium I had created to deal with my past is gone. Today the memories fly at me whenever they choose. They're the first thing I see when I wake and the last thing I think about before falling asleep. I am not in control of anything anymore, not even my own memories. It's terrifying.

In my life, I had only ever mentioned the abuse to three friends, and then fleetingly so. I never spoke to a mental health professional about this or any other matter until I was in the D.C. jail. I talked with a counselor there about my crime and the horrible hurt I had caused so many people. I didn't talk to him about my past. I didn't think it mattered because I intended to kill myself as soon as possible.

The session ended and I left to be taken to a cell. Before I'd gone far, the counselor called me back. He said there was something he couldn't put his finger on and he wanted to talk some more. And then he just stopped and looked at me, not saying a word. He was the first person in my life who I think had figured it out. And he was the first person I ever spoke to in any detail about those memories.

That conversation was the first of many that have already taken place, and many more to come, as I begin the process of trying to sort this out and fix myself.

I understand that some people—maybe most—will view this as a contrived story designed to find some defense for defenseless behavior. That it's an excuse. In some ways I feel disgusting sharing this truth with you because in my heart I still struggle to see my five-year-old self as a victim. But I'm sharing this with you because it is the truth, not an excuse. And I believe it played a role in my story.

To my family, friends and Capitol Hill colleagues: I've had individual conversations with each of you in my mind. I've pictured your face as I admitted to my failure and heard the shock in your voice. I lay awake at night reviewing these conversations over and over again. They are among the most excruciatingly painful aspects of this terrible, terrible nightmare.

To those who choose to sever all ties with me, I don't blame you. No one wants to think or talk about this subject matter. All I can say is: I understand and I'm sorry.

To those of you who have offered words of com-

> passion to me and my family: your kindness has been remarkable. Compassion is harder to accept than condemnation when you feel as disgusting and horrible as I do, but it means a great deal. I'm more grateful to you than you can possibly imagine.
>
> And last, to the children in the images: I should have known better. I perpetuated your abuse and that will be a burden on my soul for the rest of my life.

Does this sound like the rantings of a remorseless monster?

On January 23, 2014, Ryan hanged himself in his parents' home while on house arrest. He was thirty-five years old.

Immediately after reading this letter, I reached out to Ryan's mother. She responded, and we keep in frequent contact to this day. She was the first person to write a review of my first book on Amazon. We both understood what Ryan went through. This letter, and his taking his own life, underscores for many that this is a mental health issue—not a public safety issue, as is typically believed. But myths persist.

I often compared my experience with Ryan's. In the first five days, Ryan was put on suicide watch in a county jail, isolated from the ones who loved him unconditionally, who had they been there would have supported him and told him that the media circus was all bullshit and they knew who he really was, that they knew he had struggled and that the fear and shame could be behind him one day. He never got that chance, and stewing over his humiliation and focusing on his loss was all he could do. What is further soul-crushing and bitterly ironic is the fact that Ryan's plan to take his own life was hatched while he was on suicide watch.

In contrast, I was able to spend the first five days after my home was raided with my wife and children in Colorado's beautiful mountains. I began healing almost instantly. I had the opportunity to regroup and see what was truly important. It gave me the strength to handle what was going to come to me next. Had I been thrown in jail or put on diesel therapy from the get-go, as many are, and had nothing to do but think about all I had just lost in the blink of an eye—after working so hard for it my whole life—I would have done the same damned thing as Ryan. The contrast between Ryan's situation and mine provides further evidence that there is a better way to handle this problem—and a reminder that (with a very sharp pang of guilt toward my condemned brethren) the ball bounced the right way for me at almost every possible turn. It made me realize just how fortunate I had been. But my eyes were opened to how bad it can get.

On February 12, 2015, my first book, *Trauma, Shame, and the Power of Love*, was published online by Qui, who was busy enough starting a radiation oncology practice of her own about forty-five miles from Elkton. In the months prior, she and I worked tirelessly, through the slow mail system of Elkton, the TRULINCS email system, and during her visits, which she managed to make every other weekend (which entailed closely following my visitation schedule)—including holidays. I initially wrote the book during my house arrest as a by-product of my journaling and abuse/PTSD cognitive behavioral therapy—and so that I could give my children something to read one day to help them understand what their dad had done to get his "consequences" and have to go to "camp."

I'd asked Qui to take a look at the manuscript while I was on house arrest. After she stayed up an entire night to read it, I was hit with texts the following morning, telling me of her nearly continuous tears and a few much-welcomed moments of laughter as she read. Her conclusion was that my story must be told to help others and to counter the misrepresentation that the news media created about me. It was she who garnered support among my colleagues who financed the necessary editing and book design efforts. She put me in touch with the editors, too. I was grateful to hear she thought the book was worth pursuing, in part because I wanted to get it out before my medical board hearing, which would come on the heels of my release. Thus, our Herculean efforts to get the project into print at a breakneck pace.

The result was that my book came out while I was still incarcerated. For a while, I had told people I trusted that I'd written a book. This statement was frequently met with something along the lines of, *Yeah, you and about a hundred other guys here.* But when the first copy arrived during mail call, that skepticism quickly evaporated. Word spread like wildfire throughout the FSL. In a few weeks, there were four or five copies floating around. After my inner circle read it (pointing out a few typos), the book spread until it reached all units of the FSL. For the last two months of my stay, on an almost daily basis, someone would appear red-eyed and unannounced at my cube. After a while I knew the routine. Seeing them standing at the entrance, I would say, "You read my book and want to take a walk around the track, don't you?" The response was a silent nod. This was followed by four to ten walking laps around the track, which served as the backdrop for intense, often tear-filled discussions.

My book struck a chord. And after someone had just read about my personal life and its gory details, they felt compelled, or at least comfortable, sharing their stories with me. This may have been the most therapeutic aspect of my time in prison.

As I gathered the stories, I noticed some trends in how their cases went down. There were four major factors that determined what happened to an individual.

WHEN THE DEFENDANT WAS SENTENCED

The cutoff date was December 2012, when the Sentencing Commission's Report on Federal Child Pornography Offenses was released. Before this, about 50 percent of federal judges thought the sentencing guidelines lengths were a bit draconian, but their hands were somewhat tied. After the report was released, it gave judges some teeth, a document to point to, such that the number who disagreed rose beyond 70 percent and sentencing lengths plummeted. Prior to this, many judges who gave short sentences feared an appeal would overrule or remand decisions they'd made in good conscience, but this threat diminished once the report was released. The Southern District of Ohio, where my case was held, had formalized its disagreement with the sentencing guidelines. I, and several other of the more recent arrivals to Elkton, were given sentences of twelve to twenty-four months—something unheard of previously. And while I was the recipient of some elbowing and the "short-timer" moniker, most of it was good natured. Several people commented that it was about time the punishment matched the crime and that they hoped the newer cases like mine ushered in a new era. In some ways, I felt like a solider returning from the front with some good news for once.

THE DEFENDANT'S PREVIOUS STATUS

A lot of people assumed that I got a light sentence because I was a doctor and had means. This was a big misconception. It really comes down to the judge, and having held a position of trust could just as easily count against you as in your favor. On the one hand, a judge could say about a doctor, lawyer, teacher, *Well this person did a lot of good, let's cut him some slack and get him back out there in the world.* Or a judge could say, *This guy should have known better. He abused the trust placed in him, so let's hammer a nail through his scrotum, shall we?*

Money didn't always help either, but neither did not having it. I met a retired Air Force colonel—someone who'd been heavily involved in the "wars on terror" in Afghanistan and elsewhere, who spent over $150,000 on his defense. He got eight years and a $250,000 fine. However, many poor guys got stuck with subpar public defenders who could barely keep up with their caseloads and received extremely harsh sentences as a result. These weren't Air Force officers or doctor/lawyer types. While I heard stories of great defense attorneys—public and private—the only ones I heard complaints about were public defenders. So being limited to this option carried risk. In short, the defendant's previous standing in the community had an impact, but the nature of that impact was very unpredictable in the multivariate analysis.

THE DEFENDANT'S AGE

This one was bimodal in distribution, with the very young and very old representing one group and everyone else comprising the other. The effect on senior citizen offenders was obvious: no one likes it when people die in prison. And, really, who is some crippled old geezer going to hurt? So keeping sentences shorter for older guys is understandable. That was the story with Mr. Bistline, the elderly man who was sentenced before me by my same judge. He had already spent three years on house arrest and completed sex offender treatment. My judge did not want to send him away for five years, so his case kept getting kicked around—to placate both the law (with the numerous appeals) and society—in the hope the delays might let him die in peace at home. He ended up serving twelve months somewhere. About 30 of the 150 men in my unit were older than sixty-five. They tended to have shorter sentences.

It is with mixed emotions that I describe the "shorter sentences" received by the younger guys in the unit. Judges tend to give younger defendants a chance to still maybe have a life—because nothing says you are going places more than being a felon and a registered sex offender. While most of these young men's sentences fell below three years, which was relatively short, *how* they were prosecuted was often reprehensible. Several of the kids there (I use the word *kids* deliberately) were in high school when they first got involved with child pornography, trading pictures and telling their buddies to check out this crazy stuff. Then, after they turned seventeen, they were arrested and tried as adults. In other words, due to an arbitrary measure of the number of times they'd seen the earth go around the sun—plus a few extra revolutions on its axis for good measure—these kids went overnight from being boys to fully attaining the rights, responsibilities, and (supposedly) decision-making capabilities that the legal definition of adulthood confers. Of the stories I heard at Elkton, it was these that were the most appalling. Several inmates told me similar stories while I was there, and I heard second hand about a few others who left before I got there. This is somewhat terrifying, knowing that many teens in high school send explicit pictures of themselves and their friends to each other—which technically is production and distribution of child pornography, since the subjects of the media are under eighteen years of age, even if the subjects are themselves. And yes, cases are emerging where teens are considered to have victimized themselves and are punished for it as if they were abusing adults, while state laws (including Ohio) are being drafted to further criminalize this common activity among teens.

The most egregious story was that of a twenty-two-year-old man who was the head orderly of my unit. He was my boss. When I needed Lysol spray, rags, or extra Scotch-Brite pads for cleaning the bathroom sinks on the weekend, he was the guy I reported to. He was also the guy who'd let me know if I did a good or bad job—and he did. He was such an intelligent kid, with patience that takes most people a lifetime to develop. He had a somber and contemplative young face behind his glasses, and possessed equal parts physical awkwardness and confidence. I will never forget how calmly he told me of his undoing while walking the yard one day after I'd insensitively offered, "You seem like a smart kid, what are you doing here?"

His response will stick with me for a long time. "You know, me and some guys back in high school found this website where girls that were like our age, or freshman maybe, were showing off their tits or playing with themselves or whatever. They probably were posing and doing stupid stuff on their smart phones. I was like, *Hey! Nice!* I was still a virgin, you know. I hadn't seen a girl my own age naked—*ever*. I mean, look at me. Who was gonna fuck this, even back then, right?" he chuckled, pointing at himself. "So we did this for a while. And two days after my seventeen-year birthday, I get arrested. It was a state case at first. They were like, *OK man, you don't do this shit again, right? You get probation. And we are gonna watch you. Oh, yeah, and we want you to go to college, too—that is part of your probation—go to college and shit.* So I am going to college and doing really well, man. I got like a 3.6 GPA that first semester."

Then came the pause that so many stories had.

"Next thing I know, it becomes a federal case. I have no idea how, other than maybe some local federal prosecutor caught wind of it. I get pulled out of college, I have a trial, and I got four years of federal prison. So I have one year left here—and I have no fucking idea what I am going to do now."

It was another disgusting irony, given that the laws that ruined this child's life were written to protect children.

Chapter Eight

WHAT THE DEFENDANT LOOKED LIKE

Justice is *not* blind. Facial symmetry and proximity to what society deems attractive matters in court just like everywhere else. Almost every person I met who got less than three years was among the more attractive guys—or at least they looked "normal." People have told me I look OK, and I believed them. And I also believed that helped me in my sentencing. George, my cube mate, looked like a TV news anchor. Perfect hair, great skin, amazing smile, well-spoken. He kind of looked like Doug Flutie. He was only five years younger than my father, yet he only looked five years older than me. (He also added a master's in microbiology to the law degree and medical degree that comprised our cube. We ended up being called the University Cube and were visited by many inmates seeking medical and legal advice. Jon, the Jewish Prince, was quick to call us, the Doctor, the Lawyer, and the Candlestick Maker—but George, the consummate salesman, took that slight in stride.) He'd had over a million files of porn on his computers. I am not sure what percent was child pornography, but 1 percent of a million files is ten thousand files, just for reference. Handsome George got two years.

It seemed that the guys who got more than six years just didn't look "right." Often they resembled stereotypical child molesters from TV and newspapers: misshapen heads, rodent- or amphibian-like countenances, bad mullets, wispy facial hair, Coke-bottle thick glasses, an affinity for Members Only jackets, etc. Despite being nice, totally harmless guys and clearly noncontact-type SOs, they had something Gollum-like about them. It was easy to imagine judges—not having much knowledge of the offender and in light of the extra weight that anything related to child pornography carries— adding a few extra years to these guys' sentences, just to be safe.

The upshot was that, if you were in your thirties to fifties, had a low-paying job, were sentenced before the winter of 2012–13, and appeared unsettling to strangers—well, you were toast.

After my book came out, I received an email from my attorney, Wadsworth, who told me that a local veteran news anchor wanted to interview me to discuss the book and my thoughts about anti–child pornography advocacy and law reform. Of course, the warden instantly denied that request, but it did get me thinking about what I would say. After talking with so many inmates and getting to know them, and then being posed this question, I came to some more realizations.

I almost never heard from the men anything like, *You know, when I was viewing children being sexually abused and exploited, it was during the best time of my life and I was so pissed when I was made to stop.* (The few exceptions were Tweak and maybe two others who gave me the creeps—three guys out of over a hundred.) Never did I hear, *It should be legal.* Never did I hear, *I thought about it, and what better way to hurt children and add to a pervasive global problem than to view the worst moments of their lives—so that's what I did!*

What I did hear a lot of was, *I was so relieved when I was caught. It could finally stop*. And I heard, *I can't believe I did that. I am beyond ashamed*. And, *It was the worst time of my life*, followed by any number of qualifiers:

- *My [mother/father/wife/brother/sister/best friend/etc.] just died...*
- *I just lost my [job/marriage/house/life savings/etc.]...*
- *My [mental illness—PTSD and dissociative disorders were especially common] was totally out of control...*
- *I was doing a ton of [alcohol/drug of choice]...*

Concluding with, *when I was doing this shit.* Frequently, there was the added statement, *I knew it was wrong on some level or another—but I felt too sorry for myself to care.*

I was amazed at how strongly these themes resonated with me. One the most profound moments of my life was the morning after the raid on my home, after I told my wife that I had been abused and that I had viewed child pornography, and I learned that she and her father were going to stand by me. I was walking on the University of Colorado's campus during a beautiful Rocky Mountains sunrise. I felt like Dorothy swept from the dingy gray world of Kansas and set down in the Technicolor Land of Oz after the tornado. I was not alone in this feeling. The relief of being caught was almost universal among us.

The other common theme was that of early childhood sexualization. About half of the SOs I met were, like me, sexually abused as children. Some abuse was mild or moderate, like the teenage babysitter who fondled a guy's genitals when he was eight. Some were horrendous, like the uncle who routinely sodomized one of the guys when he was eleven, or the grandmother who frequently made her five- or six-year-old grandson shove his whole hand and wrist into her vagina, and then rewarded him with ice cream.

Among those who hadn't been sexually abused, often a traumatic experience at a young age had coincided with an exposure to sex and sexuality. The most striking example of this was a guy who had watched his father beat his mother nearly to death (complete with a skull fracture and a long hospitalization) and was then sent away to an extended family member's house for a few weeks while the dust settled. There, his fourteen-year-old cousin showed him an X-rated movie that involved high-school teachers having sex with their students. (Of course, this was *legal* porn, since all participants were at least a day older than the minimum required age, even though they looked years younger.) He was nine years old at the time.

The equation for creating a nonproduction/noncontact offender might look like this:

childhood sexualization + childhood trauma*

\+

mental illness/addiction

\+

adult life stressors

\+

Internet

=

NP/NC child pornography offenses

*This would be a single event in the case of childhood sexual abuse.

The guys I'm talking about were not pedophiles. There was no evil or malice in the actions they'd taken. They were not hoping to be part of an underground cabal for the sole purpose of exploiting children. Rather, what they'd done was a maladaptive coping mechanism that the ease of access and massive abundance of online child pornography created for them. Anytime a noxious agent is made readily available to the public, problems are going to arise—see what the overprescription of opioids has done to us. And it is not a harbinger of future contact offenses. There is plenty of scientific data that repeatedly demonstrate this observation.

A peer-to-peer network download and its search engine capability put thousands of files at their fingertips. And the combination of sex, early childhood trauma/despair felt compellingly familiar to them. For the vast majority of the men I met with the NP/NC charges, though the harm they caused was indeed real, it was unintended. Just as the drunk driver, whose judgment is impaired (and whose use of alcohol is a manifestation of an addiction disease), does not intend to run his car into a minivan, killing a family of five.

Of course, this view is a far cry from the monster moniker conferred by the news media/law enforcement/prosecutor/legislator complex, members of which have a tendency to exaggerate their heroism and pander to the public demand for surrogate victory in crimes against children. As Amanda Knox eloquently said in the recent documentary about her murder trials (and eventual acquittal), "People love monsters. And when they get the chance, they want to see them. It's people projecting their fears. They want the reassurance that they know who the bad people are, and it's not them." From what I could see, these guys, myself included, are not monsters either.

Being immersed in this situation, I had to wonder if there was a better way to deal with the problem than crushing partially broken people, labeling them as the worst of all human beings, and then warehousing them, compounding old traumas, and creating new ones—while spending billions of tax dollars to do so without putting a dent in the online child pornography stockpile and its related activity. It also seems that for those investigating, evaluating, and prosecuting these crimes, it quickly becomes apparent that a significant number of the offenders who are caught are not what the general public assumes. There needs to be some kind of off-ramp from the current default process for offenders who are, once thoroughly vetted, proven to be nonviolent.

Currently, NP/NC child pornography cases comprise 85 percent of federal sex offender cases. They become federal because of the nature of the Internet—it crosses state lines. And since the federal government has, for all intents and purposes, unlimited resources (despite being $21 trillion in debt), the sentencing length is not bound by the normal fiscal limitations of most state budgets. That is one reason why some state molestation and rape cases result in shorter sentences than federal NP/NC sentences.

A more effective and less costly approach would be to create a diversion program, like those that exist for nonviolent drug offenders, perhaps at the state level, to free up the courts and police resources to pursue more dangerous elements in the world of sexual crimes, like human traffickers and rapists. Diversion programs mandate education and counseling for offenders (with the goal of understanding the reason behind and preventing future offending behavior), restitution for the victims and fines to fund future law enforcement efforts, and avoidance of situations or restrictions specific to the crime (in this case, for a computer-based crime, computer monitoring). These programs are typically run by police departments, the court, the district attorney's office, or an independent entity. They can generate revenue for combating the more egregious sex offenses. Completion of the program would result in the charge being dropped or reduced (avoiding full prosecution and incarceration), which helps keep people's lives intact while addressing their issues. Failure to comply would result in the full or a heightened charge being applied, bringing with it the full measure of shame, personal loss, public humiliation, and prison time. This would give first-time offenders a chance to redeem and repair themselves, as opposed to just throwing them away for sixteen years, like Jelly Roll. Going by the majority of the men I met, NP/NC offenders just need a nudge in the right direction—not a sledgehammer blow to shatter them. Given the very low recidivism rate of these offenders (around 2 to 4 percent) the success rate could be expected to be very good.

Diversion programs have been proven to be effective for low-level drug offenders. It is true that when the offender buys pills, heroin, or crystal meth, they participate and fund a market and illegal trade that often entails murder, corruption, and the destruction of families and communities. But addiction, not a thirst for violence, is what drives those activities. And individually their overall impact and the magnitude of harm they generate is miniscule. The drug abusers in these programs are a far cry from the cartel leaders and other crime bosses that law enforcement should be targeting.

The same can be said for NP/NC child pornography offenders. They are low-level, nonviolent offenders. While their maladaptive coping mechanism leads to the retraumatization of the victims and may encourage others to engage in the activity, they are often too mired in their own mental health issues and suffering to be aware of the harm they are creating. And, as with low-level drug offenders, the harm generated is largely abstract. Even Supreme Court Justice Samuel Alito (a George W. Bush nominee) struggled to quantify the harm of viewing child pornography files. As he wondered aloud during oral argument in the 2008 case *Paroline v. United States*, "Determining the harm created by viewership is difficult to measure. Once images of sexual abuse have been viewed 1,000 times, is it even theoretically possible to assess the damage caused by the 1,001st viewing?"

I was struck by a case I read about while I was at Elkton, where a guy with child pornography possession charges actually took his case to a federal jury trial. This is rare, since computer forensic evidence is indisputable. Nearly all cases are plea-bargained in exchange for shorter sentences. Federal prosecutors often use the threat of a massive sentence to deter defendants from taking their case before a jury, essentially leaving whatever plea bargain is offered as the only option. *If you plead guilty, we will give you two years; if you go to trial and are found guilty, you get thirty*, is how it goes. Most federal defendants take the first option.

Of course, the guy in this case was easily found guilty. But for grin's sake, the judge (James Gwin, who presided over the 2015 case, in Cleveland—the Northern Ohio District) polled the jury about what they thought should be the appropriate prison sentence, even though their decision would not be enforced. The sentencing in federal court, as in most courts, is entirely up to the judge. The jury in this case recommended fourteen months and were aghast to hear he was facing a mandatory minimum of five years, while the prosecutors wanted twenty and federal sentencing guidelines recommended twenty-seven. The judge issued five years—and caught a lot of flak for it.

This unusual case provides a rare opportunity to illustrate multiple problems. For one, it shows that when all the facts are thoroughly presented to members of the public (not the selective, sensationalist spin that comes from news media), there can be some quantification in harm. In this example, the defendant's peers, composed of typical members of the community who made up the jury, felt that 1,500 illicit files were worth fourteen months in prison. The second point is summed up best by Judge Gwin himself, when he stated that the jury poll, "does reflect how off the mark the federal sentencing guidelines are."Where is the will of the people when they say fourteen months and the legal statutes (purporting to reflect the will of those same people) say twenty-seven years? Since 97 percent of federal cases are disposed via plea bargain, direct exposure to the unfiltered evidence (including the psychological profiles, motives of defendants, and other mitigating factors) is rarely presented to the lay public, which further widens the information gap surrounding these crimes.

My intent here is not meant to minimize the victimization of those children in those media files. But if a system is to deliver life-altering, crippling sentences for a crime that, when brought to light, induces some to commit suicide, the harm generated should (A) match the severity of the punishment, (B) be easily quantifiable and substantial, and (C) not be open to such theoretical musings.

Law enforcement and prosecutors are incentivized by good PR and convictions to go after the low-hanging fruit that NP/NC child pornography offenders represent. (It doesn't take a Sherlock Holmes to track an IP address, nor does it take a Jack McCoy to prosecute a case with irrefutable digital/computer-based evidence.) As a result, to bring these cases to court, these agencies have compromised in ways that are morally and ethically flawed. In a 2017 article in *Reason* magazine, Jacob Sullum charged that the FBI has become one of the largest distributors of online child pornography. When the FBI commandeered The Playpen (a dark web source of child pornography) in 2015, it operated the site for two weeks. During that time, about 100,000 people visited the site, accessing at least 48,000 photos, 200 videos, and 13,000 links. The operation led to 200 arrests, or just 0.2 percent of those who committed the crime.

This example is sobering for three reasons: (A) It demonstrates just how prevalent this disturbing activity is. A small Internet task force in Wisconsin, similar to the one that investigated me, once reported that over 18,000 people in its area (a few counties) engaged in this activity and had accumulated enough evidence on their computers for prosecution. (B) It undermines the rationale of deterrence and allows if not encourages continued harmful behavior, given that 99.8 percent who participated were not arrested (though, granted, many of the website visitors may have been outside of the U.S., and thus the FBI's jurisdiction). (C) Perhaps the most troubling reason is that the continued victimization of the abused was facilitated by law enforcement, regardless of the intent. And consider, if each of the 100,000 visitors viewed or downloaded ten files (which is very easy to do with today's technology), that would be *one million* more victimizations.

In the name of "catching monsters," the FBI in many cases is committing more serious crimes than the people it arrests. Federal prosecutors routinely bring cases that were made possible only by the Bureau's repeated victimization of children—thousands of times.

In a 2002 *New York University Law Review* article, Howard Anglin argued that victims of child pornography actually have legal and moral grounds to sue FBI agents who mail images of them to the people they are targeting for arrests. "If, as courts have held, the children depicted in child pornography are victimized anew each time [an image] changes hands, this practice inflicts further injuries on the children portrayed in the images," Anglin argued. "The practice of distributing child pornography in undercover operations exposes federal agents to potential civil liability and undermines the integrity of the criminal justice system."

Moreover, each time the FBI distributes a single image, it essentially commits a federal crime that, under different circumstances, would be punishable by a mandatory minimum sentence of five years and a maximum sentence of twenty years. The argument that this convenient bending of morality is acceptable because it is for the greater good holds no weight when considering that over 80 percent of those who are caught and imprisoned are nonviolent, nondangerous NP/NC offenders who are otherwise productive members of society. If putting away guys like Deaf-Con 5, Jelly Roll, Leonard, the kids just out of high school, and the grandpas in their walkers are the end result of this practice, that only makes a further mockery of the suffering those children have already endured. The children are victimized three times in these cases: first by the primary abusers and producers of the media, second by the people who viewed it, and third by the law enforcement agents who permitted its viewing for the sake of arrests, when they had the chance to remove it instead.

Efforts should be focused on eradicating this media wherever found, reducing the supply whenever possible—not leaving it out there, or actively putting it out there, and using it to catch people. The supply far outweighs the demand using this approach. Another common refrain I heard from my fellow Elkton inmates was, *I didn't start out looking for this stuff. It found me.*

Reducing the supply is a daunting task (whenever one site is taken down, others are put right up, creating a game of technological Wack-a-Mole), but it would at least shift the focus from passively waiting to see who looks or downloads and pouncing on them to making an actual attempt to put a dent in the actual problem. With a new direction and shifting the emphasis away from low-level offenders, more time and resources could be put toward developing more sophisticated cyber-strategies to eliminate files and paralyze distributing websites.

Based on my observations, personal experience, and research into this subject that few consider, I can say with extreme confidence that something really needs to give here. The disconnect between the reality of the offenders and the public's assumptions, between the stated goals of the current policies and the actual outcomes, simply could not be greater. A rational discussion on combatting this problem needs to happen—one that is based on the ample available data (which are often ignored in favor of sensationalist myths) and an honest and rigorous cost analysis. Fear, demonization, projection, and the discomfort our society feels about anything sexual need to be set aside. Because, by and large, what I saw at Elkton was a massive waste for everyone. This includes the inmates and their families, the prison officials, taxpayers, and, most importantly, the true victims of child pornography.

Chapter 9

"Then–as he was talking–a set of tail-lights going past lit up McMurphy's face, and the windshield reflected an expression that was allowed only because he figured it'd be too dark for anybody in the car to see, dreadfully tired and strained and frantic, like there wasn't enough time left for something he had to do."

—KEN KESEY, *ONE FLEW OVER THE CUCKOO'S NEST*

"MAN, I COULD go for an American Spirit as soon as I get out of here." I had told Leonard and George a few days before I was due to leave. "But, I would feel so weird, you know—" they looked puzzled. "Asking my mom to get me cigarettes. A cancer doctor?" I struggled. "I think she would be so disappointed in me."

"Dude," Leonard said, "your mom is picking you up from a federal prison." Trying to be delicate, while simultaneously busting my balls a bit, he continued, "I don't think you can disappoint her any more than you already have."

There was a pause. And then our cube erupted in laughter.

"Good point," I conceded.

I still didn't ask my mom to bring cigarettes, just some left over Reese's Peanut Butter Eggs, squirreled away for me since Easter a few weeks before, and some no-bake cookies.

"So what are you going to do when you get out?" George asked me, after the laughter subsided.

"Well, I am going to the halfway house in Columbus for ninety days, as you know. I have no idea what I am going to do for a job while I'm there. Hell, I don't even have a car. My wife sold it!" We laughed a bit. "I just wish I could have been released to Cincinnati, but that halfway house don't take any sex offenders."

"Why Cincinnati?" George asked. "That area is where I am heading in a week." George's sentence was coming up on completion, too.

"I have a research job lined up at a paint company in Kentucky, about ten miles south of Cincy."

"Paint? Really? What kind of paint?" I thought this was an odd question to ask, but then again, George was a chemical salesman.

"It's weird paint. It's not like the stuff you paint the walls of your home with. It has a ton of zinc in it and keeps metal from rusting. The automotive industry is their main purchaser." I could see George's smile forming. "And a weird class of chemicals—pyro-strontinates"

"*Pyro-strontinates!?*" he broke into a laugh. "Are you going to work at Hammond? Hammond Industries!"

"Yeah," I said, surprised. "How in the hell do you know about Hammond?"

"Are you serious? I sold strontinates to them. They were my largest account! How do you know about Hammond?"

"My dad helped to build that company. He has been there for almost forty years. When my case broke out, the founder and chairman said I could always have a job there—you know—to use my science background and all and help me out," I explained. I thought about the coincidence and chuckled again. "Man, small fucking world, eh?"

"Yeah. So you know DJ—he is the lab manager—and Tad, the general manager?"

"Man, I have known those guys since I was a kid."

"Great guys. Great guys. I always liked visiting that place. And DJ was great. He would always test out new products in the paint and get back to me on how it performed. He was such a great customer and researcher." George paused, allowing this new discovery to settle in. "Wow! What are the odds? You can tell them I said hello."

"I will. Too funny." All three of us shook our heads in disbelief for a while.

"What about your medical license and being a doctor again?" Leonard asked.

"I don't know. The medical board wanted to wait until I got out to have my hearings with me in person, and they will see. I was surprised they waited for me. So we'll see what happens. I don't know how long I will be at Hammond."

"Jeez. More shit, eh?"

"Yeah."

George chimed back in then. "Well, try to end up in Clermont County. You don't want to mess with Hamilton, where Cincy is. It's a busy, crowded inner-city type sheriff's office." George was referring to the upcoming hassle of being on the sex offender registry. "Clermont is more laid back. Suburban and rural. Try to get a place in Batavia, Milford, or Amelia. I'm moving in with some friends in Milford. Whatever you do, don't live in Cincy."

"OK, man. I will keep that in mind."

The event of my departure, on May 4, 2015, was somewhat unceremonious. There was no big send-off for me the night before; there would be none for a guy who stayed at Elkton for only seven-and-a-half months. I just hoped I wasn't so much of an ass that there'd be a party *after* I was on the other side of the fence. I'd seen that happen a few times. Even months after Jon the Narcissistic Walrus left, a few dark recollections about him surfaced from time to time, and we all fervently hoped he wasn't coming back (for our own sakes). Although the bonds I developed with the men there were, in both depth and number, accelerated by my book coming out and making the rounds of the units, plus the odd heart-to-heart walk-and-talk on the track, a "short timer" simply does not garner enough regard to get guys to dip into their commissary for the week to throw a good-bye party.

But those who knew me gave me their well wishes: "Get back into cancer, man." "Write about me in your next book." "Let people know what's really up." "Don't lose hope—you will be fine."

Vanilla was among them—or he did the best he could. He recounted his entire Elkton softball career to me, season by season, as I laid in my top bunk and he stood in the walkway, elbow up against the brick wall that prevented me from rolling off and landing four feet below on the hard concrete floor. (One old guy from H unit had rolled out while I was in Elkton and got himself a subdural hematoma and a craniotomy to fix it.) Vanilla had five years and five softball seasons behind him, and now it was spring training again. But the status of his shoulder and knee were in doubt, so he was deciding between the spring season versus the real summer league, and whether he would play at the A or B level hung in the balance. His dissertation lasted almost fifteen minutes, while I politely listened and gave him advice, baller to baller. As it happened, he was the guy who'd led me to my bunk on the first day. So it was fitting that he held the floor on my last night there and took the longest to say good-bye. "Well, take it easy on the outside," he abruptly concluded, just as I thought he was going to explain his plate-coverage philosophy and his approach to being two strikes down. Then he disappeared into the darkness.

"What the fuck was that all about?" Leonard asked when he knew Vanilla was out of earshot. He was laughing, giggling, and even in the dark I knew his face and ears were red. I tried to keep my chortles quiet, since I did not have the soundproofing the bottom bunk provided. We hadn't laughed that hard since Angry Buddhist put the smack down on our post-meditation state of serenity.

Leonard and I laughed about it again as we walked to the receiving and discharge door, at five forty-five the next morning. It was the first time I ever walked toward that door with its posted "R&D" sign and recalling Vanilla's soliloquy took some of the edge off. "That institutionalized motherfucker," Leonard said with a chuckle.

"Well, I can leave now, knowing V's softball rehab program." *Rehab* was a poor word choice. Vanilla had turned down the residential drug abuse program (RDAP), which would have shaved a year off his sentence, because it was up the hill. The entire social network and laundry hustle he had built at the FSL would have been leveled; he would have been a chomo with no life up there. Remaining on the Island of Misfit Prisoners for another year was the better option. I couldn't fault him for that. Besides, what is one more year on top of eight if your personal safety is essentially guaranteed?

As we approached the door, we became quiet. Leonard still had about a year and a half to serve on the three-year sentence he received for having deleted links to fifty-one photos of mostly teenage girls—roughly the same age of the girls who abused him when he was eleven years old. He was the only person I met whose sentencing enhancement numbers were *lower* than mine—yet he got three years to my seven and a half months of actual prison time. His mother died five days after I arrived at Elkton. His father died five days before I left. He missed both funerals. So I knew it was hard for him to be happy for me that I was being released, but he still genuinely was. And he showed me the graciousness he always showed.

"I am so glad we were cellies, man," he told me with a smile. "I had some dickheads before, but you were clearly not one of them." He added, "You are going to be scared shitless. You have no idea what is coming. It is going to suck for a while, but it is going to be OK, man. You are going to defy the odds. You always do.

"And don't *awfulize*—you'll drive yourself crazy," he said, giving me his last-minute pointers as we stood in the atrium. I carried my laundry bag, full of everything I owned at that moment. I turned in all of my prison-issued gear to the laundry room, where the CO jokingly told me not to come back. I am sure that was his canned line for all the guys who were leaving—but there was a sincerity to it too.

"Hey, man. I can't tell you how lucky I am, to have been with you and George—" I was too numb to articulate. What could I tell him he didn't already know? He and George had kept me sane for what amounts to a coffee break in the time scale of federal prison sentences. Anything I could say would sound contrived. A lot more was said with our glances at each other. Men are not good at goodbyes. Even sensitive PTSDers like ourselves.

The pregnant pause hung on the buzz of the pallor-inducing fluorescent lights fixed in the yellow-stained drop ceiling. I heard rustling behind the bolted door, with its thick bulletproof glass. Leonard needed to go or get yelled at for being out of bounds. The R&D anteroom was for those leaving only. "You take care, Doc," he said, and with that, stepped through the door and quickly disappeared into the darkness of the morning yard. The glass door quietly swung shut, becoming a flat slab of obsidian in contrast to the artificial brightness of the room. As I tried to distinguish his silhouette out there, I heard a voice from behind me.

"Inmate Pelloski?"

"Yeah. That's me."

"Come this way." The guard walked me to a half-lit room. It was silent. He went through some of my paperwork and then got annoyed. "God damn it, they always forget this shit!" He picked up a phone. "Have a seat." He hit a few numbers. "Yes. I have Pelloski here in R&D. Yes. You guys forgot that again. Yes, he's not getting picked up until noon. He'll need to get that—" I stopped listening.

My mom was picking me up. It was either that or go to the Youngstown bus station. My counselor had prepped me on how to avoid being knifed at the Youngstown Greyhound station. But my mom said hell no to that. She was staying the weekend at Susan and the kids' new place, just a few blocks away from our old home (Susan sold it in February), and then heading out to get me on that Monday. I only thought about seeing her outside of the fence. All of my phone and email had been shut off Friday morning, so I would have no way of finding out if something came up and she couldn't make it. Nor did I know what would happen to me if that was the case. Inmates are not allowed to make calls on another inmate's behalf, either.

The drive up the hill was very different from the drive down 230 days before: no shackles, no ankle-breaking anti-escape shoes. I was wearing my sweatshirt, the shiny aqua shorts that I wore nearly daily, and the black running shoes with the white Nike stripe that I had run with on the track, dropping me to my 210-pound release weight. After all the paperwork and clearing of manifests, it was about nine a.m. Had I needed to take a bus, I would have left then, to allow for the seven-hour trip from Lisbon to Columbus. But since I was getting picked up at noon, I had three hours to wait in a holding cell. Having grown accustomed to waking up at nine thirty, I propped my laundry bag on the concrete slab and went to sleep to pass the time.

A buzzer indicated the unlocking of my cell. A face appeared in the door. "Pelloski," it said, "you are outta here." I was led through the maze of gray-painted cinderblock hallways to the exit. When we entered the vestibule I could see my mom's green Ford Escape—an apt model for the occasion—down the slope of the parking lot. I had seen that car parked so many times in our driveway when she visited us in Columbus. I promised myself I would hold it together, but as soon as I saw her silhouette in the driver's seat, my throat and eyes began to burn. I am sure I looked part sailor, getting off his ship to embark for shore leave with his sack of clothes slung over his shoulder, and part misfit, in my oversized and unmatched clothing, reminiscent of Warren Beatty's character in *Bulworth.* But I am sure I looked all parts pathetic, with red eyes beginning to well with tears. I was certainly a far cry from the staff physician she'd seen when I gave her an unofficial facility tour of MD Anderson several years before, his chest swelling with pride as he made his mom proud.

I don't know how long I held onto her and sobbed in her ear. I had no idea why I was crying so much. It's not like I had been away for years or decades. I was so mad at myself for those tears, but I couldn't stop. She just returned my embrace, saying, "This part is over, this part is over," and running her hand through my hair as though I were still a five-year-old who'd just gotten a booster shot.

Eventually, we had to pull it together and get on the road. I only had three hours to get to the halfway house, or the federal marshals would come looking for me. The conversation on the drive was somewhat scattered and pressured at times, punctuated with long silences. There was a lot to cover in the short amount of time we had.

"How are the kids?" I asked. I hadn't seen them in 135 days. Susan brought them just once while I was in Elkton, in December.

"They are doing great. I have pictures from my visit on the phone already set up for you to see."

I instantly grabbed her iPhone and saw my daughter in her glasses, looking up from a book she was reading and smiling. She looked happy. Instantly, I began crying again. I was seeing her in her new life, a life I was not really going to be part of anymore and hadn't been since I left. The next was a picture of my son sitting on his hams on the dark wooden floor of what I deduced was his new room, beside the Lego AT-AT that he built by himself in under two days (something that in another life he and I would have done together). I scrolled through a few more pictures and saw things I recognized from my previous life in a new setting and arrangement. The plate and fork we received as a gift for our wedding, the end table from the old living room, the lamp from my daughter's room, the coffeemaker. All, like my wife and children, in a new place now.

"They do look happy," I choked out the words. Then I came across a picture of Susan, sitting on the couch. She looked tired but had mustered a smile for the camera. "Is the new place OK for them?"

"Uh, yeah. It's just fine," Mom said. I was surprised by her terseness. I stopped crying and started to realize why my mom held it together. She'd come to my pickup with a different emotion from mine. A few minutes passed in silence. "I was taken aback by how nice the place was, actually. All new furniture. Not Ikea or milk crates, but good, top-of-the-line stuff. The whole place was fully furnished." There was more silence as I started coming out of my fog of sadness. She continued to look forward, eyes on the road, gripping the steering wheel at the recommended ten and two o'clock hand positions. I recognized the tightened jaw of my mom's anger from nearly twenty years of pissing her off as a kid. "The real kicker, for me, was the new BMW in the garage—I just wasn't expecting to see all that." We drove on. "Did she ever send you any money? Be honest."

"No. But Ma, she had a lot to deal with. She stood by me when all this went down—"

"I know. But to see you like this. Jesus." Her voice trailed off. "I guess she stopped standing by you." I could see the hurt in her eyes and hear it in her voice. "It's a slap in the face after all the money your father and I sent to her, when you were away. I want us to retire someday, you know." My parents had sent us money every month since my house arrest started, to help us stay afloat. And they continued after I went away. She and my dad had bailed my brother out, too, when he hit his legal woes. They had "adult child support fatigue" from the last eight years. Expecting some frugality and discretion on the receiving end was not out of line. I felt horrible for her, and responsible.

She sensed this defeat in me and changed the subject, knowing I had a lot on my plate at the moment. "All of my friends read your book. My entire Bible study group read your book," she said, in a more upbeat fashion. "They said it was excellent and that you are one heck of a writer."

A relieved smile came to my face. "Well, that's good to hear."

"I told them, 'Of course, Chris has always been a good writer!'" she laughed. "Kelly Farnsworth said it is a book that *everyone* should read. Of course, she was abused, too. And I learned about a few more friends that got abused," her voice lowered, "because they read your book." I nodded slowly. That seemed to be a common response, to divulge painful personal history after reading my book. "You know I can't read it. I will one day, but not now. It's too soon. I'm too close."

"I know, Ma. I know." I decided to segue into another subject on my mind. "I hope the medical board reads it and knows what all actually happened. Hoyer decided to submit the whole book as an exhibit for my hearing. I just hope they read it. If they just go by the headlines, I am screwed," I said with a nervous laugh.

"Yeah, what *is* going on with that right now? Do you have a chance?"

"I don't know. Hoyer has been surprised by how the whole case is being handled. They have kept agreeing to push the dates back for the hearings. It's like they really want to give it time and consideration and that they want me to be present. They pushed back the hearing like three times over the last year and a half—without any protest. I gotta think if they just wanted to cut me off, they would have back in July 2013 when this all began." My mom nodded. "Hoyer said usually for this kind of stuff, sexual crimes or misconduct, they just revoke the license, with no questions asked. But they have handled me differently."

"Well, I hope you get your license back. You are too good of a doctor and you have done your time, for Christ's sake. It's time to move on."

"I hope so, Ma."

A sick, sinking feeling hit me when I saw the Columbus skyline for the first time coming down I-71. It continued the whole way in. I felt like a ghost coming back to the places where he had once lived and walked. We drove by parks and venues where we had taken the kids, baseball fields where I used to pitch games in the men's league for which I was an All-Star in the two previous years. But to me, then, they seemed part of a physical world that I could not touch, as if in a parallel dimension that was passing me by, on the other side of the wormhole that was my mom's Ford Escape.

I was a man without a country. My old home was sold, and I was not welcome in Susan's new place—she'd erupted in anger and fear at the mere suggestion that I might put it on my release papers for the halfway house. She had secured the place through a leap of faith on the part of the landlord, who knew all about my case. Plus, I was going to be on the sex offender registry, and her new condo was across the street from a middle school. It was, perhaps, a subconscious strategic move. There was no way I could put my name and that address together on any documentation.

It was difficult enough knowing that for the next ninety days I would not be seeing my children, but the remainder of my supporting cast had drastically dwindled while I was away as well. My closest friend since fifth grade had stopped talking to me a few months before I was to be released. There was once a plan that he would pick me up from prison, something that he joked was on his bucket list (#11—Pick up a friend from prison or jail). It turned out he couldn't have anyway, as only immediate family can perform the transport from prison to halfway house. It is permissible if someone is leaving custody for good, but not if the new location is under the jurisdiction of the Federal Bureau of Prisons. But his sudden disappearance was troubling nonetheless. Nearly my entire lab group—people who'd made nearly weekly pilgrimages to visit me when I was on house arrest—had disbanded and moved out of the Columbus area. My main animal technician went to Cleveland; my post-doc went to Philadelphia; one of my students went back to New York to help his parents with their real estate business, and the other students went on to medical schools, far away. And Qui, who had been my rock when I was at Elkton, who lived nearby and saw me frequently, was also about to become a long-distance friend upon my return to central Ohio.

Up until that point, I had been in a bubble. During house arrest, I was in my fancy wood-floored white-sided Colonial home, with my wife and children, bonding and healing with them while being visited by friends, family, and neighbors, all of them in my corner and telling me how ridiculous and wasteful all this was. I was getting the therapy I had always needed and was writing a book. Then I went to a prison, where over 60 percent of the inmates were in my lot. Every day I was surrounded by over a hundred guys who had been through the same things I had. Every day at Elkton we talked about therapy, healing, coming to grips with our offense. I'd spent a lot of time discussing the need to reform our justice system, prisons, and sex offender laws with guys who had PhDs, JDs, and master's degrees or were self-educated, self-made prolific readers. Deep thinkers who had a lot to lose and had lost it all for their emotional lapses.

But now, for the first time in my journey, I was entirely stripped down, bare to the bones. I was not going to have my family, home, support network, or even access to my own money (Susan shut me out of our coffers) to buffer my return. I was returning, naked and weaponless, to a city that once had my face plastered all over its TV airwaves, that had vilified me as a monster who brought shame to their beloved flagship, *The* Ohio State University. I was going to a place where the chomos were going to be vastly outnumbered, as in most correctional settings, and most likely I was going to be recognized, on top of it.

After I watched my mom drive off—she was abruptly asked to leave by the halfway house staff—it seemed my personal punishment had truly begun.

PART II

Home

Chapter 10

"Either they don't know, don't show, or don't care about what's going on in the hood."

—JOHN SINGLETON, *BOYZ N THE HOOD*

ALVIS HOUSE, with its big blue roof, looked like a repurposed IHOP. The halfway house stood out from the predominantly industrial buildings and county jail a block north. The young man conducting my intake was equal parts pleasant and by-the-book. My mom had brought me two plastic storage bins of toiletry supplies and old clothes, including the blue jeans I wore every day on house arrest, even in the summer, to hide my ankle monitor from the kids. The hems were frayed in back from being stepped on after I lost twenty pounds and the waist hung lower. Spots of white paint from when I touched up the porch and repainted the basement TV room were still there, a pleasant, familiar sight—a connection to my previous life.

"Four white T-shirts, two brown towels, toothpaste, two blue jeans, a mobile phone," he rattled off as I pulled each item out of the bins. "Oh, you won't be able to have this one."

"What do you mean? I have never had Internet access on this phone. My mom called and verified that it was OK to bring it here, as long as it did not have Internet access."

"Well," he sighed, "it has a camera lens in it. It has camera capability."

"OK?"

"A few weeks ago, some of the guys took pictures of themselves and flashed gang signs and all, and they posted them on Facebook, and they gave the name of the house, too. Took pictures of the premises here. The probation offices and administrators were not too thrilled about it. So they banned all phones with cameras in them."

"But without Internet access, how could the pictures get out?" I asked. "It sounds like they had phones with Internet—which would be against policy, too, right?"

"Well, the new policy is that it will not have cameras in them—in addition to no Internet access."

I panicked, "But all of my contacts are on this phone. Everyone I would possibly want to reach out to are in there."

"I am sorry, you can't use it."

He did let me turn the phone on and get all of the contact numbers I had stored in it. Under his supervision, of course. I thanked him profusely.

"So you were a doctor?"

"Yeah."

"What is the medical board saying?"

"Not much. They have held things off so I can make a personal appearance. That is unusual for them. I gotta figure if they were just going to cut me loose, they would have a long time ago."

"Hmm," he said, going through his checklist. "Not to dash your hopes, but I wouldn't count on good news. Every doctor I have seen here has lost his license." The way he said it, it was clear he wasn't just trying to be a dick; he felt some regret giving me this news. "The last one we had here was from New York. The board said," he glanced up and then slowly returned to his list, "that once the public trust has been violated, one loses the privilege of treating that said public."

"Yeah, I know."

"Sad, really. We don't have enough doctors." He added, "but you will find something if it doesn't work out. I have to believe with all that schooling you did, you know how to do a lot of things." He became more contemplative. He had permanent stubble for a beard, black as midnight, and a straight part on the left side of his straight jet-black hair. He was a white guy, but his hair was all Asian. "It's incredible what you guys have to deal with."

"Yeah," I answered, assuming he was referring to the rigors and sacrifice of becoming a doctor.

"I grew up in Indianapolis, near a prison release center. And when my dad drove me by a bus stop, I would see these guys looking shell-shocked and standing out like a sore thumb." I then realized that in my arrogance I had missed the abrupt change in subject. It was not the plight of a young doctor's sacrificed twenties he was talking about. "They were former prisoners. Newly released. Just standing there with their knapsacks and not knowing what in the hell to do next. They just got out. The system said it is time to go, and they just let them out. That bus stop was the first stop on a new life, with no plan. No guidance. What we do to our criminals and prisoners is criminal itself," he said. "My dad explained to me what they were up against—that's why I do what I do for a living." He said this with pride and sadness. "The guys may think I am a hard-ass. You might get annoyed with me. There are rules. But I really do want you guys to move on from this human catastrophe. I got a degree in social work, but I chose to do this. To make some kind of difference."

I had a soft spot in my heart for social workers. It was a social worker who diagnosed me and fixed me, when the MDs (psychiatrists included) and legal folks danced around the crux of the issue and took positions that had to do with everything else but the problems I actually had. This guy was one of those social workers who saw through the bullshit and probably slept well at night knowing he did his part. More so than I ever did when I was performing expensive procedures on patients with advanced stages of cancer, knowing full well the procedures wouldn't save their lives, because the hospital demanded that I keep up my billings in order to maintain the department's financial solvency. This redistribution of wealth enabled us to continue doing research. That rationalization worked for me, at least, at the time.

I envied him. He made a conscious choice and was living with it. He was very young to have taken such a mature stand. I'd used my white coat to make people feel they were making the right choice on their own, that the miracles of modern medicine would prolong their life—when I should have just told them to keep that money and spend it instead on a blowout last trip to Maui or put it away for their grandchildren's college. This guy probably made close to minimum wage and had more balls than I ever had. I was humbled in his presence. He did not assert his authority over me. He didn't need to.

"The food here, now, is absolutely terrible." He changed the subject, yet again, as if to shed the heaviness.

"Really? I heard from some of the guys who left Elkton a few months ago that the food was incredible. Bacon, home-cooked meals, pot roasts—"

"Yeah. Management decided to save some money," he said disappointedly. "We let go of the cooking team that had been here for over five years to make way for a low-cost contracting company. The god-damned leeches. It is outsourced. Contracted. We don't have to pay them benefits the way we did with the old staff. The food now is disgusting. This place is the last stop before the food gets thrown out. Or maybe they pull it from the garbage and heat it up here. I have already filed multiple complaints. Absolutely disgusting."

"Shit."

"Yeah. Your food is probably going to be worse than what you had in prison. But," a rebellious look came over his face, "a lot of the guys stop by McDonald's or KFC or whatever on the way back here after work. That is technically a violation, since they aren't approved," he said, looking over his shoulder. "But as far as we are concerned, if it's drive-through, it's on your way home. And anything to go against this *bullshit* is OK by us. Anything is better than this garbage they are feeding you."

"OK. Good to know." But without a job and car at that moment, I was going to be stuck with that food for a while. And it truly was atrocious. It literally was that food's last chance to get eaten before it was turned into garbage or fertilizer—or even past those points. It made Elkton's food look like Morton's Steakhouse. I stayed thin, despite not being able to exercise much anymore.

"Christopher Pelloski, please come to the front desk," I heard over the PA system. I had been at the halfway house for only a few days and hadn't been assigned any work duties or was due for any appointments. I had spent most of these days in the computer lab, reconnecting with people from the Yahoo email account I had not touched in nearly two years, when I wasn't applying to and getting rejected by convenience stores and gas stations for clerk positions. It turns out that Angry Buddhist was at the same halfway house, so we'd reconnected by reflecting on the Elkton experience over an American Spirit or two. I'd also met some of the other guys at the house, and we shared our job-search woes—over a smoke as well. Smoking was verboten at Elkton and if you got busted, you went to the SHU and were then banished to the FCI, never to return. So I never got to play poker for smokes or have one after a long day in the prison yard like in the movies. But hey, at least I got to smoke in a setting equally as depressing as prison at some point during my custody. It just wouldn't have been a complete experience without that.

The circulation desk was manned that day by the woman who made it a point to let you know how she would much rather have her intestines ripped from her still-conscious body than to spend an extra breath in communicating with you. Her eyebrows were raised so high on her forehead with disdain that I thought they would lift right off into the air above her. At first I assumed it was because I was a white, and that my "white privilege" annoyed her blackness. But she was an even bigger A-hole to the black guys there. I learned from them that so many of the inmates (we were not "clients," as the halfway house staff purported) had complained that she was knocked down a few pegs in rank—which made her only more bitter and dismissive. She nodded toward the small, windowed meeting room across the hall without looking up from what she was doing, keeping motion and eye contact to a minimum. "Your probation officer is over there. She wants to meet with you."

A serious, attractive, middle-aged African American woman stood in the conference room. She wore her dark Federal vest with the embroidered seal on it and was looking at her mobile phone. But she knew I was there.

She looked up and signaled me into the room. "Mr. Pelloski, I am Gloria Evans. I will be your probation officer. My office is in the Southern Ohio District at the Kinneary Federal Building in Columbus." She shook my hand with a warm smile. "I know Hank very well, and he said you did well under his supervision." We both sat, on opposite sides of a small coffee table.

"Yeah. Hank was a good guy toward me." He was my pretrial services officer.

"Here are some papers that you need to sign. There is also a questionnaire that I would like you to complete and give back to me the next time I see you." She handed them over to me with a pen. "Don't overthink these answers—just answer them honestly."

"OK."

"What are your plans for your three months here?"

"I really don't know. I have a job lined up around Cincinnati, working in a lab. Pretty good pay, too." I handed her the offer letter I had from Hammond Industries. "They started the paperwork for the halfway house when it was assumed I was returning to my family in Columbus. I asked them to change it to Cincinnati, but they said the Cincy house doesn't take sex offenders. Then my wife moved to a place I can't live, and we decided to divorce kind of recently. So I am stuck here."

"This looks like a very good job. And it is research. But you won't be able to start that until you are out of here. This job is over a hundred miles away and crosses into another state. Do you even have a car?"

"No. My wife sold it."

"Well, when the time comes, you can transfer to the Cincinnati office, it is still within the Southern District, and this is a worthwhile employment opportunity. So I am sure it will get approved. But for the time being you are going to have to find employment. Have you started to look?"

"Yes."

"Good." Then her tone softened a bit. "How is the relationship between you and your wife right now?"

"We have our own issues to deal with. But the one thing," my throat tightened and burned and I could barely choke the next few words out, "the one thing we agree on," tears rolled down my cheeks, "is to do everything we can to get our kids through this. This has been our goal from the very beginning."

"I think you two will get through this. If you can keep that goal in mind, yes, you will get through this. I have seen it when people lose sight of the children. And that never ends well." She waited for the next question. "Are you going to see them while you are here?"

"I don't know." My throat still burned, but I could breathe again. "Just me being here, back in Columbus, is like, completely nerve-wracking for my wife. It's like kicking up that big dust cloud again."

"Well, you let me know when and if you will see them here. I will have to vet your wife's new home and talk to her."

"Yeah. Not right now, though. She doesn't want to deal with any of this at the moment. I put her through a lot already." We both hung on that statement for a while, until I asked, "Can I legally see them, now? Am I allowed?"

"The conditions of your probation will not deny you any of your parental rights. However, the conditions between you and your wife, decided in a family court, will determine when and how you will see them. Regarding being around other children, well, I have an obligation toward the safety of the community—"

Safety? The word stung, and pulled me out of my sadness.

"You are not allowed to be around other children, however, without supervision of adults who are related to the children, whom I have contacted." *Safety?* I thought. *I had three different federal judges declare me safe and not a threat to the community at all of my hearings. Why am I now considered dangerous—when I wasn't before, when I was temporally and psychologically much closer to my offense? I took a lie detector. I...* But I said nothing.

"Which reminds me, have you gone down to the Franklin County Sheriff's office to register as a sex offender? You need to do that within three days of arriving within the county."

I panicked. "I have been here five days and I haven't been allowed to leave yet, I –"

"It's OK. They give some leeway to new releases into the halfway house setting. Just make sure you get permission to leave and go as soon as possible. For something like this, leave is typically granted. If there is a problem, just tell me."

I relaxed. "OK."

"You will also need to start your counseling and therapy. You have served your punishment for your offending behavior, but now is the time for the hard work to start and put in the time to get better."

"Start? I underwent a lot of counseling for PTSD, even before I went to Elkton. That was the root cause of my offense. As a matter of fact, I kept contact with my social worker and she has agreed to keep working with me."

"Well, she is not a mental health professional who is contracted with the federal government for the specific purpose of sex offender treatment." These words hit me even harder. *Just getting started? I spent over a year in intensive PTSD therapy during house arrest. That was the cause. Is all of this to be ignored now? All thirty-seven one-on-one sessions that were voluntary and cost me almost $4,000 of my vanishing life savings? Am I going to have my diagnosis rewritten to fit the public policy agenda like those poor guys at Elkton? Am I...* My mind raced, I was so taken aback. But I fought to stay outwardly calm and quiet. "You will need to undergo treatment with an approved vendor. "

"But I have gotten a lot of therapy. I—" *Don't argue. This is your first meeting. You can't come across as a contentious ass.* "I mean, I addressed the causes of my offense. I even wrote a book about the whole experience."

"You wrote a book?"

"Yeah. It was published back in February. It's available on Amazon. I actually have a copy if you would like?"

"No. That's OK. I will order it. I want to read it." *Good. Maybe you will see that I have gone through all of the mental exercises and conclude I don't need to do this and let me go back to the therapist who saved my life.* "I can provide you with a list of referrals. But if you are going to move to Cincinnati in several months, we can hold off on that for now." There was another long pause. I'm sure my face betrayed that my mind was running all over the place. Crying about my kids, learning that my previous therapy was going to be largely ignored—and perhaps overwritten. I felt like defeat must have been emanating from my face, despite my efforts to conceal it.

"Well, you have a lot to absorb and think about. So I will let you go for now. You will get through this—I have no doubt," she reassured me as she rose from her chair. Then she returned to her more businesslike tone. "Please have that questionnaire ready for me the next time I come by in a few weeks. But for the long run—well the next few months—you need to find work for the meantime and figure out how and where you will relocate to Cincinnati. You really are starting over. And that can be overwhelming for anyone."

The inmates at Alvis House were more representative of the general U.S. prison population than I'd encountered at Elkton FSL. Most half-way houses don't take sex offenders. They are considered violent criminals and the address requirements (like not being within a thousand feet of a school or park or where children may congregate) complicated things further. The guy who bunked under me had done twenty years for murder. Like most of the house's population, he was black (the twenty-five or so African Americans tended to dominate the scene). He had a phone with a camera *and* Internet, but it never got confiscated, despite him showing it at the checkpoint when he returned from his daily construction job. I assumed the rules must have been applied case by case. I wondered if I could get away with walking in with a Glock and a list of people to kill, since my offense was looking at something on the Internet, rather than murder. But I didn't try it.

One of my two other roommates (there was four to a room) was another black guy who was out from drug charges. He worked at Columbus Crew's soccer stadium, cleaning it after events. The fourth guy, who occupied the top bunk across from mine, was none other than Angry Buddhist. He had a gig with Home Depot as a manager. Once again, I was blessed: two black guys (who don't care what got you here), another SO, and no redneck Haters to share living space with. The prison gods had favored me yet again. Another SO who'd come out of Elkton a few months before had to switch rooms because his meth-head roommate described all the ways he would kill his "pedophile/chomo ass" every night as he tried to fall asleep.

The other reason I was somewhat grateful for the predominantly black drug-thug population at Alvis was that I would not be instantly outed upon my arrival. I'd been all over the news in Columbus, but these guys had been down for a long time, and they probably didn't follow the *Channel 6 OnYour Side* news anyway. Maybe I could have some anonymity while I stayed here.

It was not to be. On one of my first nights, a very loud and proud Middle Eastern guy came up to me as I sat in the computer room, looking for work. He stood out like a sore thumb there. He always had a briefcase, sported a Rolex, and dressed in designer/tailored clothing that left his densely hairy chest (adorned with prominent gold chains) and bushy forearms exposed. Strong waves of his cologne greeted you long before he did and lingered long after he left the room. In these and other ways, he seemed to play into—if not boisterously revel in—the western stereotype of a man on the make from that part of the world. He even drove a recent model Mercedes Benz, which stood out in the parking lot full of jalopies purchased from Craigslist that featured rust and/or primer in a sort of urban camouflage not intended by the manufacturer. That included the 2004 Dodge Neon with 135,000 miles on it donated by my parents and brother. When the car was idling, the steering column shook violently (it needed a new idle air control valve), prompting the halfway house staff member tasked with inspecting the car for approval to quip snarkily, "I thought doctors had nice cars."

Though we hadn't met, I knew the Middle Eastern guy was earning his master's in business from Ohio State and working with some kind of financial entity. It was never clear to the rest of us how he landed there, but it seemed clear he was there for tax evasion, embezzlement, or some other financial crime. He certainly was not hurting for cash.

He waited for the room to empty out before he came to talk to me. "My friend, I know who you are," he opened in his thick accent. I felt a familiar instant panicky rush throughout my body: heart pounding, numb hands, the usual crap.

"Oh yeah?" I replied nervously, pretending to focus on the monitor before me, trying not to appear rattled.

"I knew the face. I remembered the name—but, I did not put it together until I was at OSU the other day. In the library."

"Yeah?" I finally looked at him. His eyes were very serious. His olive skin was oily from the day's efforts, which only made the exchange more intense.

"I read up on all of the work you did, man. Great fucking work. Important work."

"Thank you." I was relieved.

"Look, my friend. I don't give a fuck about what you did—or what they said you did." He then leaned in toward me, to keep his voice down, even though no one else was in the room. "You need to get back to what you were doing. The amazing work. Saving lives. Don't let this bullshit hold you back. Those motherfuckers all want to be heroes. But don't let them win." His tone became more defiant. "You have a gift, my friend. Do not let them take it away from you."

"I think they already did. It's all out of my hands these days, anyway."

"Fuck all that noise. You will find a way back. You really do need to get back."

We both sat on that for a bit. Then I resumed the hunting and pecking on the keyboard, finishing up an email. The clicks of the keys sounded like thunder in the otherwise silent room.

"So you had Dickins as the lead of your defense team?" he asked.

"Yeah."

"Wise fucking choice, my friend. Top notch. I went with Smolinsky—but it was between Dickins and Smolinsky, though. Either of them are the best," he proclaimed. He then began to smile, changing gears. "Imagine that, I went with the Jew! But, I am an Arab!" he exclaimed with irony and bravado. "But when your ass is on the line, you go for the Jew who will be a bulldog and run those numbers line by line, eh?" He let out a big belly laugh as he pointed at me in proclamation.

I laughed a bit, too, the tension all subsided by then. "I considered Smolinsky. But I think he was out or not taking new clients when I caught my case."

"Eh, you did fine, my friend," he assured me. "Dickins is smooth. A gentleman. Maybe that was the better way for you. Who was your judge?"

"Martin. It was Washington at first, but he recused himself. Thank god. He would have buried me. He had a reputation for giving tough sentences on cases like mine."

"I had Washington. He was reasonable toward me. I took a lot of money, you know, my friend," he said with a big grin and laugh.

"I see," I answered awkwardly.

"I am Aziz," he said, extending his hairy hand, which I shook. "Don't worry about this shit, my friend. Do all the shit they tell you to do, and just go along with it. You have a gift. You have many gifts. Get back on your feet and move away from this awful place."

I pointed to the computer. "I am trying, but I can't even get a job at a gas station from here."

He grimaced in dismissive disgust towards the monitor, "Psh-ah! Fuck that shit. Anyone with half a brain will take you on in whatever the hell you want to do for your life and theirs. Save that bullshit for the rubbish. These motherfuckers here don't stand a chance," he said, waving his hands around, to signify all who domiciled in the halfway house. "You will see, my friend. You will see." And with that he was off, briefcase in hand, leaving me with something to think about, and the scent of Drakkar Noir in my nostrils.

"The computer room closes at nine thirty, and it's nine forty-five. It is time to shut it down." The woman covering the front desk for the night shift had poked her head in the door.

"Oh, sorry!" I said sheepishly, "I didn't know." I hurriedly logged off of my email—something that others who had been down for years did not do, exposing their accounts to others. I was very careful to close everything out.

Aziz was right. As I sat in my reentry classes, I saw just how behind the eight ball these guys were. Some had been down for ten or twenty years and had never worked at a legitimate job before. Instructions as basic as "Don't swear during your interview" were among the primary topics of the presentations, along with what to wear, how to hide tattoos, etc. It was like teaching someone how to walk. What was sad was how naturally intelligent these men were. They ran complex organizations. They could readily calculate percentages of profit based on per-ounce prices of their product in their heads. They networked. They were charismatic and articulate. They could lead. To run a caper beyond state lines (thus making it a federal case) required a lot of balls and brains. And these guys certainly had both. In different circumstances they could have led hugely successful, legal enterprises. In my work, I always prided myself on building a team based on talent, not the letters and degrees after the names. I always made it a point to give the talent—not the title—equal sway and a seat at the table when it came time to running a lab. In many instances, the MDs and PhDs I came across could not decide themselves out of a paper bag. Their degrees were obtained largely as a function of the circumstances into which they were born.

In my lab, I had undergrads and other none-degreed people running the show and helping me innovate. Harnessing their talents, I gave them the freedom to troubleshoot and explore options, and they gained confidence along the way. I learned that approach from my father who, without a formal chemistry degree, transformed an industry and helped build the company in which I was to have my soft landing from incarceration.

Many of the men I sat with would have as easily fit that bill, had they had the same advantages of birth I did. You can argue they made bad choices and took the easy way out—but with the money incentive and the limited choices they had, I found it difficult to judge them. And then, once they went down that path, there really was no way out. It's not like there is a scholarship program for drug-dealing high school dropouts. These guys had no education, experience, or credentials—and on top of it, they had a felony on their record. Who was going to hire them on a cold call?

The kind of cash they were working with—tens of thousands of dollars per week—was mind-boggling. Seeing the uphill battle they faced, struggling to secure a job that paid $8.15 per hour when *that* other opportunity waited, along with a red carpet welcome as a reward for not snitching—how could the recidivism rate for drug offenders *not* be around 65 percent?

My skin color, privilege, and skill set comprised an embarrassment of riches, despite my being at the bottom of the convict totem pole: a sex offender. To be sitting there knowing that, in that group, was tough at times. It is not that I just felt guilty for the advantages I'd had in life, I was shamed by how recklessly I'd thrown it all away. And they knew it. It was like they were pissed at me for the same thing—not resentful for what I'd had but because I lost it. From their perspective, they had to do what they did. Me, I *chose* to make a mess of my life and shred my meal ticket. At one point one of them said, "God damn, Doc! How could you fuck that up?" I could only acknowledge that it was a great question.

And while they struggled to get a foothold, my background bailed me out again. Within a month of my arrival, a friend of mine, a medical physicist with his own fledgling consulting company, asked me to come work with him. I was to help write reports and run code for his software, which commissioned and assured the quality of medical radiation equipment (X-ray machines, CT scanners, MRI machines, radiotherapy linear accelerators) using a web-based platform. I was also there to advise on clinical operations and provide a radiation oncologist's perspective. I only made $10 per hour, but I would have *paid* a lot more than $10 an hour just to get out of that soul-sucking halfway house and out in the real world for fresh air (and the occasional Baconator Combo from the nearby Wendy's). It also eliminated the arduous task of searching for employment from a halfway house after serving time for a sex offense. My background and connections had already moved me to the front of the line, just as Aziz said it would.

Each drive to and from work was a blessing. Listening to sports radio again on the way home (my favorite show, *Jay Mohr Sports*), having a smoke washed down by a Mountain Dew—it was incredible. I almost cried when I was given my own computer and a desk and was able to pull up my old Pandora and iTunes accounts and listen, through my prison-issued headphones, to the same music I did when I wrote my grants or checked treatment plans.

It was as if small pieces of me were coming back that I'd missed. Things I thought I'd forgotten, but hadn't. It took me awhile to regain my sea legs, though. After that first full eight-hour workday in nearly two years, a far cry from the around-the-clock schedule I used to work, I was completely exhausted. I guess I was learning to walk again, too.

On a random day in June, on returning from work, I parked in the small lot in my usual space adjacent to the facility. Aziz often got there the same time I did, and he would hang out in his Benz right up until his check-in time, as if to maximize every minute outside that he could. On my way inside, I gave him my usual wave and received his usual nod in response. Just as I turned the corner to enter the building, I saw a thin young man in a Kevlar vest and navy blue pants running toward me, holding an automatic pistol in his right hand, pointing it toward the ground while silently waving me off the sidewalk with his left hand. The message was plain: *Get the hell out of my way.* I leaped onto the grass. He made no sound as he ran by me, moving like a leopard through a thicket to pounce upon its prey. As I turned to look over my shoulder, I saw two large black SUVs with tinted windows pull up from opposite ends of the lot. One roared behind me, the other came up the driveway I had pulled into a few moments before.

The SUVs converged on Aziz's car, blocking it into the parking space. When the doors swung open, several large crew-cut men in more Kevlar vests jumped out. One held a shotgun and the two others had assault rifles—all aimed at the guy I had just waved to. I couldn't see how many men there were in total from where I was standing, since my view of the proceedings was partly blocked by the building's corner.

"Slowly get out of your vehicle with your hands above your head! You are surrounded. Get out of the vehicle, *now*!" the thin young man shouted, pointing his pistol at the Benz. There was a lot of fire power trained on that car. I supposed the federal government really wanted the money it felt it was owed. It would have been unfortunate had there been a loud noise or sudden, misinterpreted movement that triggered the emptying of countless rounds into that opulent sedan—and, inside it, Aziz. But that was a risk the feds were willing to take.

After a few seconds, which felt like hours, the men simultaneously lowered their weapons and darted out of my sight. Then more silence, no sound of a scuffle. It was sunny out, with a slight breeze. Birds and grasshoppers made their usual noises. Gnats made their usual cloud around the bushes in the front of the building. Nature went about its business, ignoring the human drama unfolding around the corner. Those gentle sounds seemed louder while I stood there, stupefied. Eventually, I heard a few car doors shut. Two of the men came back into sight, circled around the SUVs, got in, and shut the doors, and disappeared. Nearly complete black-tinted windows obscured any view of their interior. Then, as quick as they'd arrived, they drove off. No thin young guy with a pistol or Aziz, just an obsidian black Mercedes with gold hubcaps one space over from my beat-up silver Neon. His car would stay there, abandoned, for a few weeks before eventually being impounded.

I slowly walked through the doors to the reception desk. The two women working the desk looked at me and my slumped shoulders with pity.

"Did you guys know that was going down?" I asked them.

Katrina, an attractive young African American woman with an infectious smile, looked at me, uncharacteristically sad and disappointed. "Yes," she sighed, "they usually give us a call about ten minutes before they raid."

"Ugh, Aziz." I shook my head and started to empty my pockets, remove my belt, and take off my shoes for the metal detector sweep and pat down. "He was working on his degree—" I said as her hands did their usual assessment.

"We really can't say what happened, but I don't think he was where he said he was all the time. He got in trouble again. We liked him here—he was always making us laugh."

It was my turn to sigh. Then I put the breathalyzer straw into my mouth and blew clean. A beer would have been very nice at that moment.

"I'm really sorry you had to see that, Mr. Pelloski," she said sweetly and earnestly as she handed me back my shoes.

"I really need to get the fuck outta here." I said, defeated and exasperated. I usually didn't swear around the staff. But this was a lot to take in and I didn't care much in that moment.

She evidently appreciated my frankness because she smiled back at me as she handed me my shoes. "It will all be over soon, Mr. P. Very soon."

Susan was right to not bring the kids there to see me. It stung me deeply to know they were so close (only about six miles away) and were not going to visit, but my selfish needs took a backseat. Something like Aziz's ambush could have happened at any time, and that would have completely thrown a wrench into our "Daddy went to camp" story. In the eighty-seven days I was at Alvis House, the place was raided four times: twice during visiting hours and once during dinner time, when we all had to stand in the hall and watch drug-sniffing dogs comb through the entire cafeteria. I'd wondered if the horrific food we were provided would be effective at masking the scent of illegal narcotics.

It wasn't.

Chapter 11

"Be kind and compassionate to one another, forgiving each other, just as in Christ God forgave you."

—EPHESIANS 4:32

IN EARLY JULY, I started to panic. I needed to find a place to live, near Cincinnati, so that I could start working just over the border in Kentucky and remain within the Southern Ohio District. I had tried a few apartment-management companies, but after a few credit checks (and the subsequent dings to my score) and the blanket policies against felons and/or sex offenders, I needed a different approach.

Craigslist was the way to find private individuals who would be more flexible with their rental policies. So, I composed a response to hundreds of listings in the Cincinnati area. I didn't have time to beat around the bush only to get rejected later when it came out that I had a criminal record. I had to own it and just get myself out there, or else end up in a shelter or live in my car, as other sex offenders had to do in the area. Full disclosure was my only option if I were to be efficient. And I made sure to emphasize the whole doctor thing and the starting salary and the book I wrote. Anything I could to put some silver lining into a random sex offender asking for housing from a halfway house—any advantage I could possibly have over the typical ex-con, especially someone with my terrifying offense. I had to follow Aziz's edict of moving to the front of the line if I had any hopes of pulling this off in those last few weeks. I didn't have time anymore to deal with the blowbacks and mentally process the influx of rejections. I copied the Craigslist-issued email addresses from the advertisements and used them to compile a mailing list. Then I wrote the following message and sent it to twenty-five addresses at a time. Any more than that, and Gmail would have automatically assumed the email was spam and not sent it.

> Hello,
>
> I am looking to relocate to the Cincinnati area and seeking a 1–2 bedroom apartment or similar room to rent. I saw your advertisement on Craigslist.
>
> I received my medical degree from Northwestern University Medical School in Chicago in 2001 and trained at one of the top cancer centers in the world, MD Anderson in Houston. I had been a cancer doctor and researcher for quite some time and look to eventually return to the field. I have the support of many of my colleagues, friends and family.
>
> I have a good-paying research job awaiting me near Cincinnati. So financial responsibility will not be an issue with me.
>
> Before I go any further, I must ask, will you accept someone with a criminal record? I have one. I know this is an emotionally loaded question, but please let me provide some background information about myself. What was portrayed in the news is nowhere close to the complete story.
>
> Regarding my offense, I have undergone lie detection and have been extensively investigated. The federal judges presiding over my case have said, on the record, that I never was nor ever will be a danger to *anyone*. As a matter of fact, the only thing I have ever directly done to another human being was try to save their life if they had cancer. All of these factors explain why my

> sentence was extremely short. My offense was viewing things that are free and publicly available online that resonated with things that happened to me when I was a child. There was no predatory intent. This has been proven and is well documented.
>
> I have also completed therapy for the abuse I endured as a child and am looking to restart my life. I hope the fact that I committed this offense does not dissuade you from giving me the opportunity to live at your place.
>
> As part of my redemption, I have written a book about this whole experience, so that others may learn from this tragedy. It can be found at: http://amzn.com/1500755532
>
> Please consider this additional information.
>
> Thank you,
>
> *Christopher E. Pelloski, MD*

Out of about three hundred requests, I received around fifteen declines due to "policy" (there were some commercial/nonindividual renters in the group, it appeared). A grand total of three responses said they would consider me: 1 percent. The rest never responded. At least there were no messages calling me a chomo with wishes that I get hung from a tree and set on fire with gasoline. It's the small victories, right? But the bigger victory here was that I had three leads, which was three more than zero. One that stood out came from the owner of a rental I had eyed during my search. The unit was a completely furnished, basement apartment near Milford described as a "Bachelor Suite," and was all-inclusive (utilities, cable, Internet, etc.) for only $600 per month. The reply was encouraging:

> I appreciate your frankness and honesty about your situation and would consider renting to you. I am a Christian woman and believe in forgiveness and giving people a second chance.

> That being said, I will need to meet with you first. That would go for anyone who I will rent to, not just because of your background. Please call me to set up a meeting time.

I jumped from my desk in the medical physics office, astounded after reading this. A miracle after reading so many sex offender housing horror stories. I paced around that empty office—the guy I shared with was onsite at some mammography center. All the moisture seemed to have deserted my mouth and found its way to my palms. I called the number with trembling hands.

"Hello?" an older woman answered, somewhat tersely. I could hear a sink running in the background and an occasional dog bark. I was definitely catching her at a bad time. Damn it!

"Hi, uh—" I could barely speak.

"Yes?"

"Uh, this is Chris—uh, Chris Pelloski." *Jesus.*

"Who?" She seemed to be getting annoyed.

"I uh, am interested in renting. I am the guy with, uh, the record." *Idiot, why are you leading with that?*

"Oh, oh! Yes." She warmed a bit. "Wow, you called back pretty quickly, I think I just sent you the email a few minutes ago."

"Yes." I gave a nervous laugh. "Yes, um, I uh, really need to find a place to live before July 30th." It was quiet, except for the running water, one more dog bark, and a *shut up!* In the background. "So, I, uh, called right away."

"OK. Well, can you come by the place and see it?"

"Sure, just let me know when a good time is for you."

"OK. How about Tuesday the 14th? Like around one p.m.?" It was Thursday. Five days away.

"Sure. No problem," I lied through my teeth. I had no idea if I could get clearance, but I had to keep my foot in the door.

"OK. I will mark that down in my book and see you then. Sorry, I have a lot going on at the moment."

"That's all right. Thank you for giving me a chance. I really—"

"OK, see you then. Goodbye." And the phone went silent.

Halfway house approval was granted for the visit (at the eleventh hour and at the great expense of my nerves) and the address was nowhere near a school or park. So the location for the residence itself was approved by the probation office as well. All I had to do was nail the interview. But that was no easy task given my station in life.

It was July 15, 2015, sixteen days before my release. I was driving down I-71, en route to Cincinnati. The last time I drove this stretch of road was in April of 2013. I was going as a visiting professor to Cincinnati Children's Hospital to give a lecture on the radiation research program that my lab was developing: testing new chemotherapies to make radiation work better by irradiating anesthetized mice that had tumors implanted in their flanks. I was also going there to meet and establish collaborations with the researchers at that institution. It was part of the arduous but necessary legwork that went into building an academic empire, making allies, and signing treaties with other kingdoms. Now I was going down that road, hoping that a woman I'd never met before would take a chance on a crook that she'd never met before.

I did everything I could to make a good impression. I brought my twenty-page CV; a copy of my credit score; my hiring contract from Hammond, which disclosed my income; and a copy of my book, lest she have any questions about what happened.

I wore a new black polo shirt (from Walmart), one that showed off my prison biceps and broad shoulders. Fortunately, it was a good hair day, and my contact lenses had arrived in time. It was the first time I'd worn them in a long time, so my corneas were a little annoyed, but it was a sacrifice they had to make. Pedophiles always seem to wear glasses on TV, so anything I could do to make me look less chomo-ish had to be done to assist with this miraculous foot in the door.

The house was beautiful, set in a quiet, middle/upper-middle class neighborhood. The front yard teemed with colorful flowers and included a koi pond. An old black Ford F-150, like the one my maternal grandfather had in the 1980s, sat with dirt piled in its bed and various shoots, leaves, and roots sticking out.

I slowly approached the front door, took a deep breath, and knocked. Dogs instantly began to bark. I heard the latch disengage, and then the door opened. Eleanor was bigger than life and had a booming voice: "All right! All right! Knock it off!!" she scolded her dogs, and then moved them away from the door. Molly, the bigger dog —pit bull mixed with beagle, with the deeper bark—Scruffy, the poodle with his incessant yipping, and Eleanor together blasted apart the serene silence I'd experienced walking up to the door. "Come in, come in!" she implored me, "Just don't let these pains-in-the-asses escape! Ha ha ha ha!"

It was like stepping into a whole new world. She had eclectic artwork and bulky furniture from all over the world: Africa, Russia, China, and Western Europe. The house had a warm chaos to it, and the scent of a pot roast on a slow flame filled the air.

I could not place her, agewise. She was tall and burly and looked very strong. Her hair was a deep red. I could not tell if it was dyed or natural. Her mannerisms and speech made me think of a red-headed Large Marge (from *Pee-wee's Big Adventure*). Only she was no ghost. Her eyes and rosy cheeks imbued life into whatever room she entered.

She mentioned she had just been in between checking on her roast and working on her flowers in the back yard. "Have a seat, have a seat," She said, motioning to the dining room table just off the foyer.

I sat at the table and she took the chair across from me, where a contract and rules and regulations were already waiting. "Here, read these. They really aren't strict rules, but more like guidelines. And it really isn't anything too crazy, just common courtesy stuff. You'd be surprised how rude people can be these days." I began to read it. "So remind me who you are. I have a few people looking into the place and can never keep track of everything." Then she added, almost without a breath, "I am pretty busy for an old lady. Ha ha ha! I am president of the Cincinnati Women's Business Board; I volunteer at the Aronoff; I do stand-up comedy and am in an acting troupe that does those dinner/ murder mystery shows you hear about; I am on the board of the Order of the Eastern Star—should be president next fall. Oh, and I have a hair salon in my house. I used to be one of the top stylists for Paul Mitchell Studios—so I have clients coming in and out all the time. I got to tour the world, you know. I noticed you looking at my artwork. Pretty nice, eh?" Before I could answer she sailed on. "And I have an agent to get me acting gigs—mostly commercials or extras in movies. I used to be a model you know. You probably couldn't picture that now, could you?" she said grabbing her belly. "Sorry to ramble, who are you again?"

I was a bit nervous. This woman was part of decent society. I felt like I had no business sitting in her home. I cleared my throat, "I'm Chris—" It pained me to say my full name out loud to someone I didn't know. "Chris Pelloski." She looked at me, still unsure. "I am that doctor with, um, you know, a checkered past."

"Oooohhh! Yes. We talked on the phone last week. Right?"

"Yeah."

"I see." Eleanor said, studying me as I read her rental policies. "Well, you don't look scary." I had been petting Molly, the pit bull mix, who had set her snout in my lap so I could scratch behind her ears. "And Molly seems to like you. That is a good sign. I use her to screen applicants," and she gave a hearty laugh to ease the awkwardness.

"Yeah. About that—" I reached into my bag and pulled out my book, "Here is that book I told you about. There was a lot more to it than the news reported and I think you should read it before—"

"The news is all a bunch of bullshit anymore," she offered, shaking her head wistfully. "I am sure there was more to the story. There always is. But thank you, I will read your book." She took it from me. I sensed that despite her very terse and gruff exterior, she had an extreme vulnerability to her. I had seen that phenotype before, in my grandparents.

I continued while the iron was hot. "And here is my credit score. Not bad. Right? And here is my CV, resume. See, I actually did do some good things for humanity, at least." A little nervous laughter here from me, while I pulled one last thing from my folder. "And, maybe the most important, my contract that tells you I will actually get paid and will afford my rent," I said with a smile. She laughed.

"So, what all happened to you?"

"Well, I looked at stuff that is illegal. You know." I knew the question was coming, but no matter how many times you think you have prepared for it, your heart rate shoots up and rings in your ears while your throat clenches. All the eloquence of your many rehearsals, talking to yourself while driving or while looking in the mirror, the writing out of your thoughts formulated as twenty-point dissertations on mental health and the inadequacies of our social support systems—all of that goes out the window, and you just have to fess up to doing something deplorable to someone who doesn't know you. It's about as uncomfortable a thing anyone can do.

I continued painfully, "Some pretty disturbing stuff. I'm—I am not very proud of that, of course—"

"I see. And did you pay for this, or something?"

"No. It was all free and publicly available. You know about Napster—with the free music?"

"Yes."

"Well, there are other Napsters out there, with all kinds of stuff on them."

"Wait, so just looking is illegal? I didn't know that. I thought you had to be part of some club or pay or something—for it to be illegal."

"Um—it is, uh, very illegal, actually. I assure you. I can personally attest that." Again, nervous laughter.

"So what brought you to that?"

"It's a complicated question. But I can tell you that some bad things happened to me when I was a kid. And I could kind of relate to it. I, uh, got diagnosed with PTSD out of all this. This was a kind of symptom of it. I never in a million years would have guessed PTSD. And, it's not like I was *into* kids or anything like that. And I took a lie detector to prove that. And if I was or did something like, you know, hands on," I did a creepy-guy hand gesture, miming lecherous groping of an invisible victim, "I would have been put away for a *long* time, and I would not be here now or allowed to move about like this."

I caught myself talking a bit too quickly and intensely for a stranger to absorb and slowed down. "But that information never gets made known—to anyone. It doesn't scare people enough to mention that or point it out in the news."

Eleanor sat for a moment and pondered that revelation.

"My brother had PTSD." She became more forlorn. "Yep. He went off to Vietnam, and he had *a lot* of problems when he got back: drugs, alcohol. He did weird things that don't even make sense to him now.

He spent some time in prison, too," she said with empathy, rolling her hand toward me. "So I know what a lot of you guys are up against when you get out. It's not how it's supposed to be. He wasn't a bad person; he just made some bad choices, is all." Her face had lost its lightness. "I had some very bad things happen to me, when I was a kid, too." She caught herself letting her guard down and quickly pulled herself back to the interviewer role. "So I am curious to read what's in your book."

We both kind of sat on that for a bit. Molly continued to be my new best friend as I went on petting her behind the ears and looking down at her, her eyes slitted with happiness under my hands. If I'd had a steak to give her, I would have. She was helping my cause more than any other living being could have in that moment—I was passing her rigorous screening test. Another life debt owed to a growing list of warm-blooded creatures who helped me along the way.

"Well, let me take you on the tour and see if you even like the place," she said with typical Midwestern pragmatism. The basement apartment was perfect. It was private, separate from the rest of the house, fully furnished with its own kitchen and bathroom. The backyard was gigantic, with a hammock that Eleanor said I was welcome to use to relax. I tried to not let my hopes get too high.

It helped that Ms. Evans had told me that if this didn't work out I could live in an extended-stay hotel. That took a little of the pressure off, but still, I wanted to be *here.* Not in the city, but out somewhere quiet, like George recommended, to begin my recovery. With someone who could keep an eye on me, like an aunt who cared. Someone who understood my situation in life. Dogs and a yard would also help make things feel more normal, too. This felt almost like too good of a setup. I had grown to distrust things that looked too good to be true. For me to land somewhere this safe and sound was definitely that.

Two days later I got an email from Eleanor:

> I am more than halfway through your book. You are an incredible writer and I can't believe what all you have gone through. There are a lot of things in there that helped me make sense of what happened to me, when I

> was little. Thank you for your bravery in writing this and for sharing it with me. I will finish the book, but I don't need any more questions answered. The place is yours. Just send me a deposit of $600 to secure it. Let's get you back on your feet. You need to get back into cancer medicine. What has happened to you is ridiculous.

Eleanor had made a point of mentioning she was a Christian in our first communication. As a man of science, I never gave religion much thought. But when you get punched in the face and lose everything, your perspective on human experience gets broadened a bit. In addition to reconnecting with my love of history and learning some psychology and psychiatry—again—I opened up myself up to religion in a way I never did before. It started with a neighbor across the street in Columbus, who'd invited me to his church while I was on house arrest and insisted that he bring his family (including his children) to my house for Easter. After the meal, he talked to me about suffering, atonement, redemption, and the path of Jesus. I'd noticed that the acquaintances who really reached out and supported me fell into one of two camps: the "libertarians," who thought that just looking at a crime was a vast chasm away from committing a crime (and were very concerned with civil liberties being encroached upon by Big Brother), and devout Christians.

Of course, when I mentioned the Easter dinner to Hank, my pretrial services officer, he had to call each and every neighbor who was going to show up with their children to verify that they were aware of my charges (as if the news vans and helicopters might have escaped their attention), that I was an imminent danger to their children, that I should not be left alone with children lest I eat them with fava beans and a nice chianti, and not let the children, or me, out of their sight.

I had not been to church since I was about six or seven, when I went with my grandparents. That was right about the time my last few rounds of sexual abuse happened. I was still at an age when discerning myth from fact was a bit of a struggle, what with Santa Claus, the Easter

Bunny, and the Tooth Fairy still making regular appearances. Jesus fell into that mix, too. In hindsight, since that was when my life began its tailspin, religion—faith—never really had a fair shake with me. I was burned by cynicism and betrayal much too young to give something like faith a chance.

When I began going to church, listening to the sermons, and reading the Bible, I was struck by what an incredible man Jesus Christ was. What courage, to preach love while being loathed, to fight hypocrisy with moral points that only bring to light more hypocrisy from the opposing side if they chose to argue further. The genius of this approach is in its subtlety. Rather than a confrontational stance, which forces people to throw up defensive walls, it allows the opposition to change its own mind. Which is a far more effective strategy to create permanent change in thinking. To demand that only those who have not sinned cast the first stone. What power. What confidence. What vision. And to do all that in such plain language, for all to understand.

Jesus didn't raise an army against oppression. He embraced the powerless, the misfits, the cast-asides, the sinners, the whores, the perverts, the diseased, the dregs, the unwanted. He embraced humanity with all of its faults. He led by example, not by force or fear. He led by love. He forgave those who hammered nails through his wrists and ankles—that takes an incredible, special Someone. He preached against hate and vengeance. He said it was not the province of man to ultimately judge and punish. That was God's realm. His Father's.

Whether you believe in the Virgin Birth and the Resurrection is irrelevant. There is no denying that Jesus was an incredible man and figure in history. Even other religions have acknowledged his wisdom, leadership, vision, and the sense of humanity and morality that few ever achieve.

At first, I drew comfort from the idea that Jesus would accept and forgive a sinner like me. Being a social leper, a sex offender, it gave me hope. But then I came to a more troubling conclusion.

The United States is one of the most religious and most Christian of all Western countries. A 2011 Gallup Poll found that 92 percent of Americans believe in God, and over 70 percent are Christians. The first syllable of *Christian* is Christ, so I interpret that word to mean someone who bases their life and philosophy on the teachings of Christ and example he provided. The same Jesus Christ who embraced the powerless, the misfits, the cast-asides, the sinners, the whores, the perverts, the diseased, the dregs, the unwanted. Yet people with felonies struggle to get housing, employment, or other societal benefits because of having committed a crime—or sin, if we are speaking religiously here. Why is that? And why is it that despite having only 5 percent of the world's total population, the U.S. has 25 percent of the world's prisoner population at any given time? Do Americans sin more often than the rest of the world?

I then learned about Finland, a country like many other European countries, where Christianity is not such a big deal anymore. Only 33 percent of that population believes in God, and they tend to go to church only on Christmas and Easter. Over a quarter have no religious affiliation at all. In other words, Christianity is not a fixture of its culture. Interestingly, the average prison term in Finland is about eight months. *Across the board.* The system looks to see where someone went wrong. Was it mental health, was it access to education, was it something else? They identify the problem and rectify it. Companies and housing agencies compete to get newly released prisoners to work for them and live in their places because they know these people will work extra hard and take extra efforts to ensure they get the most out of their second chance at life. Finns forgive, in a very Christian manner, even though— as a country, and often not as individuals—they are not Christian. They understand that people make mistakes. Whether it is a lapse of the individual or of the system, it gets fixed. The recidivism rate is just 4 percent.

Compare that to the U.S. system. The average incarceration term is nearly five years. The average recidivism rate is 77 percent at the state level and 45 percent at the federal level. This is because once you commit a felony, it becomes much more difficult to get a job, to find a place to live, or to get an education. It puts you deeper into a financial hole. If you got a shitty education, had few options, resorted to crime to make money, and got busted, being branded a criminal in the United States is the cherry on top. With a felony on your record, you go from marginally employable to virtually unemployable. So what do people do? They go back to the only "job" they know, where few questions are asked.

Eleanor rented to me—against all odds, after uncountable rejections and no-replies from hundreds of inquiries. *Sorry, no felons* and/or *no sex offenders*. She withstood backlash from her housing association when I first moved in. A sex offender in their neighborhood? No way. *Screw you*, she said eloquently. *It is my house and I will do as I please.* The other person she rented to, Larry, had a drug felony. He'd got hooked on opioids and then heroin (because it was cheaper) in the aftermath of a shoulder injury sustained while serving in the United States Marine Corps. He couldn't find housing either. Between the two of us, we were making more than $140,000 per year, yet Eleanor provided us our only housing option that wasn't located in a drug-infested war zone or under an overpass. She once joked, "What the hell am I running—a three-quarters-way house?" But it shouldn't come down to Eleanor for Larry and me. If we were truly a Christian nation, Eleanor would be the rule, not the exception. She was living her beliefs—a true Christian, as she stated in her first reply to me. Forgiving and giving someone a real second chance. Larry and I were lucky. Many are not.

After learning more about Christianity, the one definitive thing I can say is that J.C. would be most displeased to see the lack of progressivism in the U.S. version of Christianity. Why is it that the predominantly atheist/agnostic Finland is, in its actions, more Christian than the extremely Christian United States? Where is the forgiveness? Where is the chance for redemption? These are two *huge* hallmarks of Christianity, yet they are disgustingly lacking in our society—which according to most Christians was founded by Christians.

To me, as a relative outsider and newbie to religion, one who is just starting to understand, nothing says that you lack faith in your God more than the notion that your righteousness allows you to permanently condemn (or kill) others who do not conform to your vision. We are all mere mortals, powerless. And those who condemn sinners for the remainder of their earthly lives are a blasphemy personified. If what others do is that reprehensible, then the Creator will sort that out in the afterlife. That is not our domain.

If you deny those who have sinned the opportunity to atone, to make things better in their life and to convey what they have learned from their errors and repairs, then you are no better than the Great Deceiver. You are doing the Devil's work. Not His work. You are a fraud if you subscribe to condemnation. You are the very hypocrisy that Jesus spoke against. He would challenge you to throw that first stone, and in His presence, you would have no choice but to rightly walk away after being called out by your Savior.

Given the deplorable outlook for the lives felons must face after prison, after they have paid their debt and served their mortal punishment through loss of freedom for often-exorbitant periods of time for nonviolent, non-dangerous offenses, and given that 92 percent of Americans believe in God and more than 70 percent are Christians, and given that the U.S. was founded by Christians, it is hard not to conclude that American "Christianity" is a colossal failure. If He walked among us again in the States, Jesus would be furious and disappointed at this, and he would probably do more than just flip a few tables at the market on a Sunday.

Chapter 12

"No one expects the Spanish Inquisition!"

—*MONTY PYTHON'S FLYING CIRCUS*

"PELLOSKI—I KNOW THAT NAME," the woman at the security desk told me with a smile, as I gave my identification and signed into the visitor log. I was in the multi-gymnasium-size marble-and-granite lobby of the Rhodes State Office Tower, where conversations and the clacking of heels and dress shoes reverberated into a continuous sonic gibberish. "I am not sure why I know that name," the pleasant woman continued. She was a middle-aged African American woman in a sharp uniform with a walkie-talkie clipped to her shoulder strap. Two armed guards stood in the background by the elevator bay. It was August 4th, 2015, and I was only six days out from the halfway house. Part of me expected to be searched and made to blow into a breathalyzer before being granted access to the upper floors (as I'd had to at the halfway house), despite having had a few nights to regroup in the dark, quiet peace of my basement apartment and in the hammock in Eleanor's sunny backyard while reading Sun Tzu's *The Art of War*. I found it very unsettling that my name was recognized so readily.

"I am not sure why you would know my name," I fibbed. I glanced over at my attorney, Nancy Hoyer, who gave me an empathetic smile and nod, sensing my uneasiness. Soon we were in the elevator.

"My god, even the guards are aware of my name."

"You *are* in Columbus, after all," she said with a dry grin. "It will be fine."

"Ugh! This suit!" I said, pulling the front of my buttoned jacket away from my chest. The gap was huge. "It's like I borrowed my dad's for prom. I even had it taken in, but I'm swimming in it." I tend to complain about little things when huge things loom on the horizon.

"Yeah, I noticed that. You look like you melted away. Did they feed you at Elkton?"

"Yeah, but, you know, no stress and plenty of time to work out. This suit was bought when I was about 240. I'm 213 now." We both chuckled. "I'm sure I will sweat my way to 205 today."

"Just relax, you'll do fine today." I wasn't going to relax. While I was in Elkton, I wrote elaborate statements and speeches on why I should stay in radiation oncology and cancer research. I had all the utilitarian arguments canned in my mind. I was an innovator. And an educator and communicator. I'd learned my lesson. I'd turned myself around. I have much more life to live. The public investment that was made in me—what about the loss? The whole nine yards.

But starting early on at the halfway house, I just didn't have it in my heart to fight anymore. Maybe I would try to be a doctor overseas, but trying to be one in the United States was going to be an uphill battle. Convincing people who had already made their minds up or who were under pressure from the uninformed public—having to always explain myself where ever I went—it would all get old very quickly. I wanted to just stop dragging things out and just let the state take my damned medical license. But friends and family urged me to fight for it, so I agreed to try—mostly for them. I just didn't have enough left to fight for myself.

When we arrived on the State of Ohio Medical Board's third floor, a group from Channel 6 News was already there with a camera prepped to roll. (*Channel 6 On Your Side?* My ass. More like *In My Side*.) Good god, those guys were always there. Of all the local news networks, they were the ones that followed me the most. They stayed the longest when the entire Columbus local news armada laid siege to my house. They were at every one of my hearings—plea, cancelled sentencing, and final/real sentencing—when the other news stations decided to move on to the latest city councilmen banging his intern while taking bribes from local businesses or other train wreck *du jour*. It was their crime beat reporter who tried to interview me when I was at Elkton, but the Warden put the kibosh on that. So it wasn't surprising that they were the only news crew on hand for my hearing.

Once it became clear that I never touched anyone, other news stations just didn't care. But not Channel 6. Maybe they thought I would put a gun in my mouth and shower the crowd with fragments of skull and gray matter—or that I would be gunned down by some Puritanical lunatic—when I left the building. It certainly would have made for compelling TV. Pulitzer Prize material. And they would be the first and only to feed that voyeurism and scoop up the resulting ratings surge.

Hoyer told me to wait in the meeting room and told me where to sit while she discussed things with the hearing examiner and the *two* Ohio assistant attorney generals (AAGs). Apparently, they called in backup for what usually requires just one AAG: attempting to revoke a doctor's license to practice. When I opened the double doors to the hearing chamber, my blood instantly became ice water while my face felt hot.

Sitting at one end of the large table with his back toward me—in the witness's seat, as I would learn—was Detective Starr, the police officer who'd investigated my case. He looked over his shoulder and I gave him a nervous nod, which he returned in kind. Walking over to the defendant's side of the table I could not look at him. I'd talked with him by phone on that very first day, when my home was raided and tossed, but I'd only seen him once, when he presented his findings at my plea hearing. I knew he would be testifying at this hearing; I just didn't expect him to be there already. The air felt like a bath of mercury, weighing on my head and shoulders and squeezing my chest with its immense density. Of all the awkward silences, this one bordered on otherworldly. I have no idea how long it lasted, but it felt like hours. It was kind of like meeting your Maker, or at least the one who'd set in motion a life-shattering chain of events. Finally he spoke, as I averted my gaze toward some paperwork sitting on the table before me that might as well have been written in Mandarin in that moment.

"Chris, I just want to let you know that I am not here to make your life worse—or any more worse than it already is." I heard a completely unexpected warmth in his voice.

I slowly raised my eyes from the table, probably looking like I was seeing a ghost, or a unicorn. Some mythical, implausible thing.

"They asked me to be here," he continued, "to confirm or clarify what is in my report." He paused and then added, "I didn't ask to be here." I just stared at him. I am sure it was awkward for him, too. "I want you to know that. I am not here to make your life *any* more worse than it already is. There is nothing I will say here that I haven't already said or written up before." I couldn't speak, so he changed tack.

"How have you been doing? How have you been holding up from all of this?" he asked me.

I finally snapped out of my trance. "You know," I began to gain some coherence, "this is probably the worst and the best thing that has ever happened to me." His smile became more inquisitive. "I mean, I am, by far, the healthiest I have ever been. I feel, oddly, at peace—with myself." He seemed to understand. "It's just all this stuff," I said, gesturing to indicate the space around us—not just the room but the whole legal apparatus attached to my offense. "Now I have to go through all this stuff."

"So what is going to happen? Are you going to be able to treat patients again? Can you at least do cancer research?" he asked with genuine concern.

"I don't know. This charge is—well, *you know.*" I motioned toward him, with a sheepish smile. "It is so emotionally charged, and scary for people." I paused for a bit. "I'm not expecting any good news from this." We both let that statement hang in the air for a while.

"You know, I read your book," he said.

"Really?" I did not want to ask him what he thought about it. I was afraid he would attack it and say I was making excuses or lying.

"I liked it." He stated, taking me fully by surprise: I had kind of railed against the system toward the end of the book. "It gave me a different perspective—from the other side. I thought you did a good job exploring all the issues." And then, as if to let me know he agreed with some of the themes I discussed in the book, he added, "Yeah. We have been pretty busy catching and putting away some very bad guys: producers, enticers, and human traffickers." I nodded, secretly wishing I could have gotten a warning and then the counseling that I received while they went after *those* guys.

I think he could read my thoughts in my face at that moment, because he switched tack again.

"I didn't know you were a pitcher," he exclaimed. "Sounds like you have a pretty good arm, too," he said, pointing toward me. "I'm a catcher. I play in an old-guy's league, too. Of course, being old, I need to use those knee savers, but I can still hold my own," he chuckled. "Believe me, I would have much rather talked with you about pitch selection and handling hitters."

"I know. Me too."

Then, as we both sensed this window of private discourse was coming to a close, Detective Starr circled back to the task at hand. "Look, Chris, they are going to ask me questions, and I am going to answer them honestly. This is nothing personal against you. It will be strictly professional."

"I understand," I said quietly. "I appreciate your words." Unexpectedly, I felt a sense of closure between law enforcement and myself. I still had a long row to hoe legally, but with this exchange, it was as if both sides had said *no hard feelings*. It was a very therapeutic moment for me.

Before Starr could reply, the double doors opened and the attorneys and hearing examiner entered, along with the Channel 6 cameraman with his gigantic video camera.

The hearing examiner was a stern-looking older man, maybe in his sixties, in a well-tailored gray suit that matched his hair. He'd probably been a physically imposing man in his younger years—vestiges of his youthful self remained—but time had made him smaller. He addressed me directly as the others assumed their positions at the table, bringing out their files and paperwork. "Dr. Pelloski, this is a public hearing and Channel 6 has requested to have their cameras rolling during the proceedings. You have the right to object to this, but in lieu of the camera, a reporter can be here to record and document what is said here. Do you object to the camera operating during this hearing?"

"No," I said, "the camera can record this." And so the tribunal began.

Detective Starr was first examined by the Ohio AAGs. After verifying his credentials and the facts of the case, which took quite a while, they started chiseling away at my story. "Can someone *really* open a file, expecting one thing, and get something else on a peer-to-peer network, as Dr. Pelloski alleges he did? He alleges that he was looking for adult porn from the seventies and he came across child pornography *by accident.*" This from one of the AAGs, demonstrating his doubts about the veracity of my claim. He was a pale, heavy-set, sweaty guy, reminiscent of the anthropomorphic Mr. Toad, but accessorized with a goatee. Aaron G. Carpenter, Esquire, was his proud name. His reddish brown hair suffered from male pattern baldness, clinging just to the sides of his head, but he'd tried to compensate by growing a goatee that looked out of character. His suit looked shrink-wrapped on him, and very uncomfortable, while his collar dug into the razor-burned wattle that began at his chin and substituted for a neck. The other AAG, a younger blonde woman, barely spoke. In time, I tuned out her presence.

"Well, in these peer-to-peer networks," Detective Starr said, "anything can be named anything. You may think you have downloaded Disney's *Bambi*, but when you click it on, it turns out you have *Debbie Does Dallas*." Mr. Carpenter bristled at that.

"But it was clear that Dr. Pelloski knew what he was looking for when you were following him through your task force operation."

"Yes, but as he admitted, he first came across child pornography while living in Texas. And in the national databases, the IP address he had in Texas checked out. So we cannot attest to the circumstances of his first-time viewing. But that being said, we can tell if someone comes across that by accident. Once, maybe twice. But is becomes clear that a file-share user knows that they are looking for this material when it happens more frequently than that."

"When he erased the peer-to-peer software from his computer—do you think he was trying to evade being caught? Dr. Pelloski alleges that he did this to make it harder for him to return to the share file system."

"I can't comment on his motive for removing the program after he viewed what he viewed. But regardless of that action, once your IP address shows up in the system, we have it logged and filed, whether the software is downloaded and constantly running or used intermittently the way he did. There are far more sophisticated ways to evade detection, but he did not do these things."

There were a few other clarifications, but these were the big ones.

My attorney's cross-examination was very brief—like one-question brief: "So based on everything that Dr. Pelloski has said to the investigating authorities and what he has admitted to, are there any impossibilities, inconsistencies, or anything incongruous to his side of the story? Anything that is just patently false, based on the evidence you have collected?"

"No."

I was next. Hoyer led me with her questioning through my life's story, my professional ascent and personal life. For the umpteenth time, I had to go over all of the details of my abuse and memories and flashbacks, with the Channel 6 News camera rolling and the eye of the blank lens staring at me, unblinking. I had already been humiliated so much that this was starting to feel normal to me.

When it was Carpenter's turn to cross-examine me, he tried to minimize what was done to me (contact offenses by three different adults, penetration of my mouth and anus, and groping of my genitals), and maximize my offense to make it seem that I'd committed an act that bordered on cannibalism for the purpose of predation and inflicting maximal pain on innocent children. Eventually he worked up to his gut shot: "Was what happened to you really *that* traumatic?" he asked.

It was the only time I lost my cool during the whole ten-hour, two-day hearing. "Are you saying I was not raped or molested?!" I shouted involuntarily, while Hoyer grabbed my arm to calm me down. I understood the gamesmanship of cross-examination, but this was disgusting. Out of every moment of my surreal journey—my home being raided, prison, the labels, the shackles, the losing of everything—this was the vilest, lowest thing that was done to me, a close second only to that old guy sticking his dick in my mouth. And in that moment, I felt the most contempt I have ever had toward another human being.

The most unusual line of questioning, though, concerned my book. One of the reasons I'd wanted it published so quickly (while I was still in prison) was so that it could be given to the medical board, so that they could know everything that happened. So they could understand and look beyond the superficial, sensationalistic news coverage. But from that book—in which I detail the things that happened to me when I was a very small child, where I detail my therapeutic process and talk about my grandmother's experience in Nazi concentration camps from the ages of ten to fifteen, where she was repeatedly raped and assaulted, leading to unquestionable pelvic inflammatory disease and multiple miscarriages later in life—Carpenter found only material for disturbing sucker punches. The first one caught me entirely off guard.

"So, Dr. Pelloski, let's talk about your book," Carpenter said smugly. "In it, you boast of your prowess as a lover, did you not?"

"Uh?" I fumbled, squinted my eyes, and tilted my head in confusion, "Um—" I went through my mind, trying to verify. Yes. I wrote a passage where I described how, because I dissociated during intercourse (because I had been sexually abused and wounded in that arena of life), it took me a lot longer to climax than the typical college-aged male, thus *appearing* to be a more competent lover. It was intended as an ironic, a tongue-in-cheek, somewhat bitter quip, to take some of the heaviness out of having just revealed that sex was a problem for me. It could, in fact, be seen as a metaphor for my life. Because of my psychopathology from abuse, PTSD, etc., I had compensated by overachieving, which led me to become one of the top radiation oncologists in the United States at my level of seniority. But it was driven by the unhealthiest of reasons. The point I was trying to make in that passage was that even the act of intercourse for me was fool's gold. And later, I'd gone on to say what a chore having sex with me became for my partners, or at least the ones I was with for a while, because I was so detached. Because there was no intimacy. Because it didn't register in my mind that it had happened. That is not really boasting.

So I was thrown by this question, because either the State of Ohio was recruiting from the Derek Zoolander Law School for Kids Who Can't Read Good (as he completely missed the entire point of that section of the book)—or he was cherry-picking an insignificant line from several pages of painful text to paint a picture of me that served his ends. "Yes, I did write that, but—"

I was quickly cut off by the next question. "And in your book, you mention how good of a baseball player you were, in your mid-thirties career—a pitcher and how hard you could throw?" *So,* I thought, *this is what it's going to be like? This is what we are going to ask? This is a child pornography case with a career on the line and we are talking about men's beer league amateur baseball that I wrote about in a book?* Carpenter struck me as having been the kid who always got picked last on the sandlot and was making up for that humiliation now through his current position of power. Seeing that there would be no discussion of the real substance of the book, I dug in and became more deliberate in my responses.

"There was a period of time in my life where I was happy. My kids were born, I was no longer a resident, and I was playing baseball again. I had a hobby and outlet. And I worked at it. And I wanted to show the reader that there were more sides to me than medicine and someone who was a doctor and committed a crime, I—"

He cut me off again, "And you wrote extensively about when you met with an intellectual property attorney because your name was removed from a manuscript that you had written, on your research."

"Yes. I did."

"Well," he said with staged exasperation, "Here you are, spending thousands of dollars on your legal fees, losing your career, looking at prison, in the middle of a federal child pornography case, and you take the time and spend more money to look into this?"

I took another deep breath. "I was urged to look into it by my colleagues and my wife. My name had been taken off my own work. That is technically academic fraud, and, if I ever decided to go back into medicine or research, not having been acknowledged for my work would have been detrimental to any career I might attempt to salvage. So I looked into it—at their urging." Carpenter seemed like he might have been expecting response more along the lines of a narcissistic *how dare they?* "So I did my due diligence but decided not to pursue it any further. And it wasn't just *one* manuscript; I had my name taken off of *several* papers," I continued, evenly. I would not give him the satisfaction of getting another rise out of me.

He then turned to the last, in his view, major point of the book, and attacked it. "You wrote a lot of pages on the discussion you had with your friends about your case. In chapter sixteen, there's a lot of diatribe about how unfairly you were treated. I wonder why you took such great pains to write that out. Did you and others really have that conversation—or were you just trying to attack the criminal justice system and be the victim?"

"The conversation did happen." I said calmly. "And I had to shorten it significantly, or it would have gone on for many more pages and dragged down the flow of the book." He didn't respond. "And my friend, the defense attorney, he had offered a viewpoint that I hadn't heard before up until that time. It was *that* conversation which propelled me to do some research on my offense." Miraculously, he let me continue. "And so, that discussion served as a segue to the second half of chapter sixteen, where I discussed the case law and statistics that my attorney friend was referring to."

Prior to the hearing, Hoyer had submitted my book as an evidentiary exhibit. What was interesting, in addition to some odd and minor points of the book the AAGs had attacked to paint the picture of me as a braggart, was that they objected to including chapter eight as part of the exhibit. In that chapter, I'd described my experience with the voice-stress analysis, where I was asked if I had ever passively or actively sexually abused children or got off on any prurient thoughts about them. The AAGs labeled the chapter hearsay and said that because lie detectors are not allowed as evidence in criminal cases, that material should not be allowed in my medical board case, even though the same rules of evidence do not apply across all jurisdictions.

I find it very interesting that polygraphs and lie detector results are readily dismissed when they don't support the narrative one side is trying to espouse. If these examinations are scientifically pieces of shit, why was I being made to take them in the first place? Certainly, there must be some research to support their routine use in criminal investigations. CIA and FBI agents have to take them to enter and remain in those agencies. Is the argument here that these government entities have it all wrong? I am sure if I failed this test and more things were revealed, both the federal prosecutor and the AAGs would have *led* with that finding, not tried to bury it.

Upon learning of this objection, Hoyer and I procured a copy of the audio recording of my voice-stress analysis interrogation so that it could be submitted in lieu of chapter eight if it was to be excised from the book. In the end, though, the book in its entirety remained as evidence. Still, I had doubts the book was going to be read.

Carpenter then made a point of listing the details of the content of three of the fifty-seven files I had viewed. The ones he chose were very different from those the federal prosecutor chose to highlight. In my federal case, the media in which very young children (ages five to six) were abused and tortured were reported. Given that younger age of victims and sadistic elements are used for sentencing enhancements, this was the strategy for maximizing prison terms. I learned from some of the men I met at Elkton that this happened to them, too. What they were looking for were teens (ages fourteen to seventeen). But embedded among those files were even more disturbing files with images of younger victims and sadistic acts, and those were what drove their sentences. For me, however, it was these more disturbing ones that resonated most with me, probably because I was of a similar age when I was abused, as they most effectively put me into a dissociative, near-catatonic state afterward.

The AAG in the hearing did the opposite and decided to highlight files in which the victims were teens. Perhaps he was trying to show that what I viewed did not match my childhood experiences and that I had a wide variety of deviant tastes. Interestingly, neither the federal prosecutor nor this AAG decided to highlight the media I viewed that *did* match my childhood experiences: women fondling and molesting little boys, or men forcing fellatio upon and anally penetrating boys as young as five or six. I saw these horrific things, too. But inclusion of this information did not fit the lawyerly gamesmanship in either case. Both attorneys also purposefully omitted from their presentations the randomness of what files actually showed up in the peer-to-peer's search engines, to further frame my intent in the way that would best suit their different legal aims.

My attorney objected to this, saying, "All of these details are in the police reports," but she was overruled. Carpenter's argument that "the State of Ohio Medical Board hearings need to have this on the record, in our transcripts," won out.

It was then that his demeanor significantly changed. His speech became more pressured, his body language more animated. He read from his report all the gory details in a sanctimonious tone. As he built up his dismay and disgust, I noticed beads of sweat form on his forehead. Eventually, he arrived at the last one:

> The title of the third video is "Laura 14Yo (Anal Frontview Upclose - Pthc New 2007).mpg." The description states, "The length of the movie is four minutes, two seconds. Description: Color video of a prepubescent, approximately twelve-year-old female, lying on her back while an adult rubs something on the area of the girl's anus. The girl complains that it is cold. She is later anally penetrated by the condom covered penis of the adult male. The female is chewing gum and continues to put gum in her mouth during the sex act. The adult male has a British accent and keeps telling the girl to keep her legs down. There is a TV on in the background that has people speaking with a British accent. The girl grimaces and groans towards the end of the sex act."

He was *really* into the descriptions. I wondered if I should have taken cover from the hail of fire and brimstone that would have soon been emanating from his portion of the table surface, which seemed to grow (along with the volume of his voice) and transform into a pulpit. As he read, I was struck by his psychomotor agitation. I wondered if some compensation or projection was occurring.

I recalled the story of a man in my hometown who led a crusade against the adult movie theater on Woodward Avenue: Studio North. My friends and I, being curious and developing boys, could not wait until we were eighteen and could just walk into that dark and mysterious place and see what being an adult was all about. This man fronted groups of picketers carrying signs first in front of the theater, and then later on Woodward's median strip, when the police forced them off the privately -owned property. He frequently wrote letters and editorials to the local newspaper decrying the evils of smut and the derelicts who consume it. Eventually, Studio North shut down, much to the disappointment of us boys.

It was discovered later, of course, that this guy had been molesting and raping little boys left and right. It turned out the guy who thought others could not handle material of a sexual nature could not handle his own sexual nature. You need to watch out for moral crusaders. Whenever someone is eager to cast that first stone, or has a reaction to an issue that is disproportionate, you have to wonder what they are hiding, and why they are so eager to direct others' attention away from themselves. So I had to wonder, *What in the hell was Mr. Carpenter hiding?*

"Dr. Pelloski, did you view these movies?"

"Yes. If that is what is in the report, then that is what came up in the queue."

"Did you view them in their entirety?"

"I rarely ever watched a full movie. Most of them didn't resonate with me. I would watch for a bit, turn it off, and wait and see what else came up. I could only see what came up in the queue. It was random. I wasn't there very long, and had no control over what came through." I felt like this was the thirtieth time explaining what I did.

"But you do admit to seeing these videos?"

"Dr. Pelloski has already admitted to seeing everything he saw," Hoyer began to object. But, I answered over her.

"Yes. I saw them. I wish I hadn't. But I saw them. And I went to prison for it. That's what all this is about."

"Dr. Pelloski, do you think you should have gone to prison for what you did?"

"Yes," I said softly. "Yes, I do."

"You said in your statement that your actions harmed children. Did they?"

"Yes."

Again, he was trying to bait me into saying I was treated unfairly—waiting for some Colonel Jessup-like rant about why the rules didn't apply to me. He went back to his original questioning. "Well, here is where I get confused—what does a fourteen-year-old girl getting sodomized by a grown man have to do with what you purport to say happened to you as a little boy. Why would you even look at something with that title, knowing what happened to you and what you were looking for?"

"I don't know." He'd made the point I knew he was working toward, and I really didn't have an answer. "It doesn't make sense. I am still struggling with that myself."

After over three hours of nonstop questioning and answering, my examination was over and we broke for lunch. My armpits were soaked through my T-shirt, dress shirt, and suit jacket—despite the generous application of the clinical-strength antiperspirant I'd been happy to reunite with after I left Elkton and its suboptimal deodorant-only options. All I could do was drink small sips from the bottled water to keep my mouth moist. The thought of food made my empty stomach nauseous.

It turned out that Dr. Kimmel, the forensic psychologist who evaluated me around the time I pleaded guilty in November of 2013, who testified after me that day, had a much more sophisticated answer to that last question. Ever the academic in his bright neon green glasses that clashed with his older man's visage, he sat at the end of the table, a rock of reason and data, ready for the onslaught of waves of hysteria and misperceptions that were about to crash against him. He was well versed in this exercise. Hoyer knew this question was a sticking point, so she posed it to him during her examination. His response was far better than I could have articulated.

"There is no rhyme or reason to what gets viewed and what strikes a chord with the viewer. It may not make sense to a healthy mind. But the unhealthy mind of the viewer does not make sense. It doesn't have to be the exact match to what the viewer experienced previously. The victimized children could be boys or girls of any age. The abuser could be a man or woman. Sometimes it's just the setting of the images that triggers the response. Sometimes it's the very act of going through the steps of getting to where one can see children being abused that is sufficient to induce the reaction."

What Dr. Kimmel described is a lesser known but well-established behavior of someone with PTSD: the compulsion to repeat, reenact, or reexperience trauma. Freud called it Repetition Compulsion. It's a form of masochism that gives the sufferer a sense of control over the event, determination of purpose of the event, or is a manifestation of an attachment to something familiar during moments of stress. A more common example of this is soldiers who return from combat in Iraq or Afghanistan and play online war games like Call of Duty or Medal of Honor all the time. An article that discusses this phenomenon, written by PTSD expert Bessel van der Kolk, was submitted by Hoyer as an exhibit of evidence for my case. It was obvious Carpenter hadn't read it. When he asked me why the content I viewed didn't match my experience, I was too fried to make this connection, and even if I had provided an answer eloquently describing it, he would have dismissed it as some kind of contrived excuse for my actions.

Kimmel continued. "Chris indicated to me in interviews that he uninstalled the peer-to-peer program to make it more difficult for him to get back there. Many times, he did not go through with it, since it took a long time to connect, suggesting the barriers he put up were often effective—but not always, of course."

"You don't think he did this to evade detection."

"He is a smart man. I am sure he knew that once you are detected, you are detected. It was just a matter of time, given his standing in the community. I believe he was trying to limit his viewing activity—and it worked, sometimes."

My attorney also asked Dr. Kimmel about the distinction between contact offenders and those with my charge, about the thought that viewing leads to committing contact offenses—or wanting to, at least.

"That's a huge misunderstanding," he responded. "They're two totally different animals. Individuals who offend other human beings are one group of people. And actually, a very small group of people, if you look at numbers. A lot is written in the press, but it's a very small group of people. A very, very much larger group of people look at inappropriate pornography not with any intention of touching or injuring or offending another human being, but for self-gratification, which is typically the story—or there are some of these outlying or unusual cases, where there is a different motive."

"And you think his case is an outlier?"

"Yes, many of those convicted of this offense will admit, more often than not, that they then fantasize sexually, that they fantasize intimacies and become aroused and masturbate. The difference here is that I have no information, including discovery and including the voice-stress-analysis test, that that was Chris's purpose in looking at child pornography. And that's what makes his presentation so unusual."

"Why do you think his presentation was so different?"

"Chris's presentation is that of a researcher, that of an academic. And he's also, in my opinion, rather stubborn, rather self-centered, and rather unwilling at that point in time to seek help and ask *Why am I having recurrent images? Why am I having memories? Why am I frightened?* He didn't seek out help. Frankly, I think that was a huge mistake, but it's history. But given who he is, he thought he could explore and figure out the problem himself. I commend him, obviously, for having done that, but it's not the easy way to go. Maybe he does nothing easy. But it's not the easy way to go."

"You think he didn't seek help because he was too stubborn?"

"I think Chris shows many narcissistic tendencies, and what that means in plain English is he thinks he can solve his own problems. He thinks that he, at this point in time, was able to look at his own issues and figure them out and try to work with them and resolve them. I think there is clearly a shame factor here, where he didn't want to advertise his weaknesses. He's very unlike an individual who would come for counseling or therapy, because that's a very revealing life experience. I see a number of physicians and attorneys and other professionals who aren't seeing me by choice because this is not their character."

He continued, "This, again, is sort of an exaggeration of that example where Chris appeared to be, to me at least, somebody who knew he had issues and yet he was a top performer. He was able to do everything else while underneath all of this—there was this huge ball and chain, if you will. There was this huge area of concern that he couldn't understand and didn't know what to do with. But yet, as a researcher, he thought he could learn to deal with it himself. Very unusual."

When asked about the chances I would ever do this again, he replied, "Noncontact offenders such as Dr. Pelloski have a very low rate of recidivism, between 3 and 4 percent. I would place Dr. Pelloski's risk at less than 4 percent. The low risk can be attributed to such offenders not realizing the risk of being caught and the severity of the potential consequences." He added, "They're scared into not doing this again."

When it was Carpenter's turn to cross-examine, he basically tried to discredit the thirty-plus years of education and experience Kimmel had in his field (a master's in clinical psychology from Xavier University and a doctorate in psychology/criminology from OSU), where a third of his practice was devoted to making risk assessments of sex offenders for state and federal courts, prosecutors, and defense attorneys. The AAG tried to cast doubt on everything Kimmel said—which sadly for him was backed up by research and actual statistics, not supposition. Carpenter also intimated that everything I had said had been some kind of elaborate hoax, to hide my real danger to society.

On redirect, Hoyer asked, "You mentioned Dr. Pelloski is a very smart man. Could he be making this all up? Is he *that* smart?"

"He is an intelligent man. But you can't fake emotional scars, and his run deep. Some very bad things happened to him. There is no question. And his very infrequent use over many years, with the low file numbers—we are talking fifty-seven or sixty files that were deleted here, when I have seen defendants with tens of thousands, even hundreds of thousands of files, who actually collected them—this all speaks to his unusual presentation. He did not fake this."

"Have you read his book?"

"I have."

"What was your impression of the book? You are in it, after all."

"I thought it was a very candid and spot-on assessment of himself and the events that happened—in his childhood and adult life. I think it was good for him to write."

Toward the end of the hearing, during the morning of the next day, several of my colleagues and former residents gave statements of support over the phone. Oddly, this affected me most, bringing me to tears knowing that I had let them all down, and that they took great professional risk to support me. Or maybe I was just too mentally exhausted to handle hearing good things about myself for the first time during the proceedings. The AAGs tried to undermine their statements by asking if they would have still supported me had I been aroused by children's abuse—completely ignoring the evidence and Kimmel's testimony—and implying that the support was conditioned on a motive that they worked vigorously to discredit.

One of my former residents, when asked if the program director who took over my position was able to do the same good job that I had, responded, "When Dr. Pelloski took over the residency program, it was in horrible shape and facing probation. But the changes he made were so sweeping and lasting that anyone could have taken over the position and just run what he implemented with continued success."

Again, at every turn, it was a battle of narratives: the one that everyone assumed to be true, and mine. Finally, it was over, after two grueling days. Now I just had to wait. In the meantime, I was going to start my new job in five days. I had another big transition coming up.

Chapter 13

"Be careful to leave your sons well instructed rather than rich, for the hopes of the instructed are better than the wealth of the ignorant."

—EPICTETUS

AS PART OF the intimidating MD Anderson panel interview for its radiation oncology residency (which took place at a long table flanked by at least ten staff members, with the candidate at its head), the candidate is to give a five-minute story or presentation on something not related to medicine. The idea is to give the residency review committee a glimpse of what the person is like as a human being, rather than one of the medical drones we were programmed to be by the fourth year of medical school. Some people played an instrument. One talked about their mother rising from the dead after having a massive brain tumor. One related a tale about swabbing tree toads for fungal spores across the U.S. as part of her senior thesis. I talked about the summer I spent at the company where my dad worked before I got married and went to medical school, Hammond.

My father played Division-I college football on a scholarship in the early seventies. A lot of shady stuff went on then. He spent the summer between his senior year in high school and his freshman year (where he was a beer bitch for Conrad Dobler, later dubbed "pro football's dirtiest player" by *Sports Illustrated*), at a football camp. He left Ferndale, Michigan a somewhat-awkward 190-pound halfback who ran a 4.8-second forty-yard dash. He returned weighing almost 220 (with all of his body fat melted away) and even more fleet of foot, with a 4.6-second forty-yard time. In addition to the rigorous daily workouts and training, he'd been given special "milkshakes" (perhaps spiked by some ingestible androgen or testosterone precursor) to drink. Regardless of the overwhelming anabolic overtones, my father insisted it was incredible that I did not have an older sibling, as my mom could not keep her hands off him that summer of 1970, a few years before I was born.

Despite, or perhaps because of, being the first in his family to go to college, he'd developed a disdain for pure book smarts. Instead, he prided himself on his innate intellectual ability, where all was put on the line. He was a C student at best—thanks in no small part to a continuing, undiagnosed post-concussive state (he had taken tests he could not remember and had never-ending headaches after football practice)—and never formally received his college degree. Football and midterm hunting and fishing trips interfered with that goal, and being handed the reins of the research program at Hammond Industries rendered it unnecessary. There, he single-handedly changed an entire field of science and created a unique niche for the company envied by competitors around the world. He ate PhDs and engineers for breakfast when it came to the chemistry and chemical engineering that went into the anti-corrosion coatings he himself had pioneered. Which, of course, only strengthened his disdain for academia. Some of the greatest minds in science and industry never earned a college degree but went on to change the world—Edison, Tesla, Gates, Zuckerberg —so my father is in good company. And his ideas not only put Hammond on the map but several competitors, as well. He was so innovative that a few people he took under his wing, mentored and entrusted with critical information and ideas, then left to start their own companies. So I am not exaggerating when I say that my father's ideas launched a whole industry.

Still, despite his skepticism, my father impressed upon me the importance of getting all A's if I was to become a doctor like I said I would. It was weird to hear, simultaneously, that I had to get all A's *and* that grades don't mean shit in the real world, when dollars and people's lives are at stake. But my father was just being my dad here, not trying to make sense. So, I abided by both sides of his mouth.

As a result, that summer after getting my bachelor's, when I worked in my father's lab, the summer of 1996, was when I crossed the threshold between academia and the real world. And it was the first time I could gain intellectual respect and approval for what I could bring to the table—respect and approval that my near-4.0 collegiate grade-point average had failed to earn me.

There was an issue with one of Hammond's coatings, and I was charged with helping one of the paint formulators solve it—a man I had known since I was about six years old. A chemical reaction was happening that made the paint "seed out"—precipitate—such that solids like bits of sand fell out of the paint emulsion, gumming up the machinery in the facilities that applied the paint. A customer was pissed because their big, expensive machines were getting clogged with particulate, bringing their operations to a standstill. Millions of dollars were on the line.

Just out of college, I attacked the problem with pages of potential chemical reactions, after analyzing the chemical structure of all the paint's ingredients. For my pains, I was ridiculed by a Hammond veteran: *I haven't seen that shit since college—none of that hocus-pocus works, schoolboy,* and so forth. Nonetheless, I plugged away, eventually using Le Chatelier's principle to figure out what chemical to add to the idle vats of paint to reverse the reaction—to dissolve the "seeds" and get the customers' machines up and running again.

I will never forget the anticipation, complete with sweat on my brow on a hot July 1996 day, waiting after several five-gallon buckets of the complex alcohol that I'd suggested adding were dumped into the massive pool of stagnant coating. Finally, the mixing components of the machine became unstuck and the mixture within the cauldron became true again. The sound of the machine fell from a high-pitched lurching to a quiet, low-pitched hum. The little crystals I had predicted would dissolve actually underwent dissolution. It was a huge coup. Hammond solved the problem for its customer, and for our efforts, it gained the customer's eternal loyalty. But for me personally, I had showed my father that I could come through when the shit was slinging off the spinning fan and everything was on the line. It showed I had the spark in me that my dad was unsure of—despite the high-GPA book smarts I was cursed with. It was huge for me.

So that was the story I told, sweaty palmed, at my MD Anderson interview. I had been there for two months as a visiting medical student, living in squalid conditions, sharing an apartment with a cockroach that crawled across my chest one night and the frequent late-night lip smacking of my native-born-Chinese roommate, whose village custom was to chew as loudly as you could with your mouth full to convey appreciation of a dish well made. I didn't expect the story to make any difference. I assumed the panel would despise me, since this was how my mind worked at the time. So, I was surprised to learn much later, after I'd done my residency and was on the faculty at MD Anderson, that my talk was one of the ones that had stood out. Many people told me they found my five-minute story refreshing, as it showed me asserting myself from a position of inferiority (as opposed to assuming I had the world on a string, which was the norm for the typical overachievers who had the CV to be granted an interview) and bonding with and earning the respect of a demanding father.

As I built my short-lived career as a physician scientist, I kept my father's perspective with me: to not get wrapped up in the credentials, but to assess the person. My lead animal technician was an art major. The guy who helped build our world-class mouse irradiation devices was the department's fabrication tech. The physicist who helped make the device physically viable and technically reproducible had been marginalized for years within OSU's radiation oncology department. But, thanks to my father, I could look beyond these paper-based "deficits" and see the true value and talent in people. And this enabled me to accomplish a lot in a limited time.

A great deal happened between the summer of 1996 and August 2015. After I left my internship at Hammond I got married, went to medical school, became a doctor, became a hotshot, and then lost it all. News vans, helicopters, court hearings, prison, halfway house, sex offender registry, divorce, no money left, and right on the heels of an invasive and painful medical board hearing.

Hammond was the answer to my current situation. We had made this plan and set things up even before I went to Elkton. Without hesitation, the owner of the company, who had been through thick and thin with my father for almost forty years, extended an invitation to me to join the company. He was disgusted with how my case had been handled, by both the news media and the policy makers, and it didn't hurt that he was a cancer survivor. I would go to the company's Kentucky facility, just over the state line from Cincinnati. I could stay in the Southern District of Ohio, be able to drive up to Columbus and see my kids on weekends, and start rebuilding my life.

Hammond had meant so much to my family over the years. My grandfather, my dad's dad, was the first Pelloski to work at Hammond. He started as a janitor when the company was just one facility in Troy, Michigan, in the mid-seventies. Both of his parents died by the time he was ten, and his oldest brother, Pete, assumed the mantle of head of household. Then, when Pete was called up to serve in World War II, my grandfather took his spot instead, allowing his brother to keep the family running smoothly in Harbor Beach. Grandpa got hit by a German mortar shell just after D-Day, but you could say smoking saved his life: His metal cigarette case protected his heart from a piece of shrapnel. He earned a Purple Heart, met my beautiful Austrian grandmother, and begat my dad, another Pete.

When Hammond management caught wind that my then-janitor grandfather had done some early work with computers in the army, they put him in charge of shipping parts, to better track their inventory using the primitive digital systems available at the time. He was dedicated. He would always weigh out coated bolts to ship, then drop a few back into the company pile (within the margin of error), to help the greater good. His gruff staff sergeant demeanor was both revered and feared at the fledgling company, so when he tipped off his superiors that my dad was taking courses to become a nuclear medicine technician or some other chemistry-based researcher, they listened. And then they approached him to start up their lab. He declined, knowing he would have to drop out of school to take the job. But they kept asking, and he eventually accepted—after cleaning up at poker during the company Christmas party and having a heart-to-heart with the owner.

My father had been at Hammond for a few years when my grandfather decided to retire, in the early eighties. On his last day, the owner of the company decided to give my grandfather a twenty-foot fishing boat, with a strong inboard Mercury engine. The significance of this gift cannot be overstated. My grandfather and father were true outdoorsmen. There is a news article about them catching the biggest walleye in Michigan in 1971. My grandpa caught fish even bigger than that one a few times, though, and let them go because he didn't want the hoopla. That was my grandpa.

When the time came for my grandfather to receive this gift, in front of the whole company, my father stayed in the lab, cleaning glassware, during the entire ceremony. This type of gesture was too new to my family. The owner came to my father: "Pete, don't you want to see your dad's send-off?" My father kept scrubbing the glassware under the running water with tears in his eyes—knowing what that boat would mean to a man who spent so much of his life fishing the streams and shores of Lake Huron.

"I love you, man," was all my dad could choke out, while tending to his duties, not wanting others to see he was crying. That gesture, that gift, cemented my father's loyalty to the company. Every ounce of effort and dedication and resolve he had—his natural genius—was focused toward Hammond's success—for four decades. That commitment helped create an industry. It put me through college and helped me go to medical school. And it gave my brother a second chance at life. Now it was doing the same for me.

This was the legacy that rested on my shoulders. I had spent a lot of my life trying to prove to my dad that I was worthy, that I was my own man and could take on the world myself. But now, once again, I was leaning on him for help. And he was ultimately my boss.

I called the lab manager on the Sunday before I started. DJ—I had known him since 1987, when I was in eighth grade. He was a childhood hero of mine. He'd been hired as the research effort was expanding at Hammond, and he was a ringer for their softball team, which competed favorably in the men's league at Softball City in Sterling Heights, Michigan in the late eighties. The guy was a dangerous lefty pull hitter—providing a steady diet of screaming line drives to opposing fielders—on top of a great glove and arm and all the bravado and booming voice that made for a valuable beer league player. "Be you! Be you!" he would yell from the dugout at critical moments in a game.

I would go watch them play, and afterwards, he was always cool to me. "What's up, big guy!" he would say to me. He made everyone feel cool, even an awkward eighth grader like me. And, Jesus, could he put beers away—they just made him more outgoing. His lingo was tight and macho, but there was always genuine warmth behind it. Everybody loved this guy. He and his Eastern Michigan University roommate (who also worked at Hammond) went to my wedding and performed their dance routine to The Gap Band's "You Dropped a Bomb on Me," which they had perfected in their college days. I was glad that a connection from my past was going to be the bridge to my immediate future.

"Hey, D, it's Chris here."

"What's up, guy? You doing all right?"

"Yeah. Just thought I'd give you a call, you know, before I get started," I said nervously. "It's been a while. A lot has happened. As I am sure you know."

"Yeah, I know. I talked to all the women who work in the lab, and everyone is on board." He paused for a moment. "So, seriously, are you doing all right?"

"My prison time was OK," I assured him. "You wanna know something crazy?"

"What?"

"You know George Willette?"

"Yeah?"

"Well, he was my cellmate at Elkton."

"What?! Are you effing kidding me?"

"Yeah—George. I started telling him about the kind of work I would be doing and the chemicals we use, and he completely flipped out and started naming people at Hammond Kentucky. Hammond was his biggest account. He knew you."

"Dude. You—no way. We wondered what in the hell happened to him. All of a sudden he stopped showing up. Just disappeared... We used to get Reds tickets from him all the time."

"Yeah, well, he was my cellmate. Can you believe that?"

"No freakin' way. He was a good guy."

"Yeah. He got into the same trouble as me."

"Oh man."

"Yeah. Small world, eh?"

"Yeah. No joke." He got a bit more reflective. "Well, if you were with him, that place couldn't have been too bad. I was thinking you got all jacked up and destroyed in there."

"No, it wasn't horrible. And he was a great cellmate," I assured him. Then I changed tack, "So what time do we start? Do I need to dress up, or is a polo and jeans OK?" I asked, a bit worried that I had only one dress shirt, and it had been pitted out from my medical board hearing. I had a few polo shirts that I'd acquired from the halfway house's goodwill offerings for their employment program.

"We start at seven a.m. It's a lot easier trafficwise. Jeans and polo is fine, man. We are low key. You know that."

"OK."

"Dude, I am so glad to hear it went OK and that you were with Willette. That makes me feel a lot better, man. You sound good."

"Yeah, I am. I am the healthiest I have ever been. I have been waiting for this. I can't believe it is actually starting tomorrow."

"It'll be good, bro. It will be good. See you in the morning."

And so, on August 10th, 2015, I showed up to Hammond Industries with my metaphorical hat in my hand. I was in a stupor. I knew how humiliated my father was by having to make a place for me at the facility (even though the owner offered me that safe landing). I did not know what kind of reception I would get from my co-workers, who would know *all* about me and who wouldn't, and what would be said. It was all beyond unnerving. I felt sick knowing there might be people who would consider me chomo scum of the earth but would not say it to my face for fear of retribution because of who my father was—and would secretly and deeply resent it. I feared insincere friendliness, whispers and utterings behind my back, becoming a dirty joke that everyone was in on. I could create a huge problem for everyone, a morale killer, made worse by my legacy on the line going all the way back to my grandfather.

My stomach churned the moment I stepped into the vestibule and smelled the familiar odor of methyl-ethyl ketone and butanol. It brought me back to school days, when my parents had just one car and we would pick up my dad up in the afternoon and his clothes would fill the blue station wagon with the strong stench of organic solvents.

The first person I met in the lab was Tim. He was a consummate intellectual chemist, with a dark and warped sense of humor. On the dry erase board, he'd written the following equation:

$$\sqrt{(-\text{shit})^2}$$

I pointed at it and said, "Hey, does that mean 'shit just got real'?"

"You're the first person who has gotten that right away!" He smiled and nodded his head. "I think I am going to like you," he added wistfully while squinting his eyes. He had over fifteen years of experience. and his fund of knowledge and intuition bordered on genius.

There was Marsha, an older woman who was sweet toward me from the beginning. She put her arm around me within the first few days, saying, "I am glad you are here and am looking forward to what a fresh set of eyes can do to help."

There was Sarah, an absolutely adorable young woman in her early thirties, a mother of small children, and the analytical chemist of the group. She was a tiny Greek spark plug with a trendy hairstyle: a buzzed crop on the left side and a thick mop of black hair laid over to the right, covering scars from a sulfuric acid burn left by a previous job. Multiply pierced ears and tattoos further showcased her rebellious side, while her huge, round, bright eyes conveyed warmth and welcome. She always kept her gaze on me from across the lab, even when she thought I wasn't looking. Maybe I was something of a curiosity. I knew she knew my history, but she always made time to talk to me. Her nickname was Squirrel, and it was fitting, with her tiny, fastidious mannerisms, but she was no lightweight. In a company of mostly men, she ruled the roost and didn't put up with any crap.

There was Alexei, from Belarus, near Minsk. He was soft-spoken and burly, like a quintessential Eastern European wrestler. Around the lab they called him The Russian, and later joked about him being one of Putin's spies, coming to rig the 2016 presidential election. Like many people from other countries, he regarded what I'd done and all the mess it created for me as a colossal waste of time and energy. Eastern European countries have real problems and do not have the luxury of inventing them, he once conveyed to me.

"You are going to be with Chuck," DJ told me in his office. "He is a smart-as-hell kid. I pulled him in from production to work in research a few weeks ago. He doesn't have much formal training in science, but the kid's got skills. He just doesn't know it." Chuck was exactly the kind of person I admired: naturally gifted, without the benefit of wealth and privilege to gain advantage, one of those diamonds in the rough my dad always told me to look for. Even in this age of prerequisites and paper-based qualifications, stories like his persisted at Hammond. "You guys are going to be working on a big project to improve one of our coatings and try knock one of our competitors out of a market. You know chemistry; you know how to run experiments. You need to teach him the ropes."

"OK. I will," I responded.

Chuck was a tall, lanky kid, twenty-six years old. He was a huge college football fan, especially Notre Dame. He loved hip-hop and was an incredible athlete, very deft of foot. He and his girlfriend had just had a baby, and life suddenly had gotten real for him. Previously, he'd been considered a slacker, but he was too cool to let go then. Now he had direction and purpose, and people at work had taken notice in his maturation. Now he knew how to do everything at the company, from driving and loading forklifts to running quality control tests on the finished products. He was the ultimate utility man. And I am sure he was wondering what in the hell he was going to do with a forty-something year-old retread who wore glasses. I must have seemed like a middle-aged buffoon to him. Fortunately, opportunities to prove my worth presented themselves. Chuck liked to pipe music through his workstation, and my suggestions and knowledge of underground hip-hop, instrumental trip-hop, and late eighties rap impressed him. Pop-culture references and knowledge of sports helped, too.

Of course, it wasn't just Chuck I needed to prove myself to. And luck was on my side there, too. On the fourth day I was at Hammond, after weeks with no rain a brush fire erupted in the pine bushes in the front of the facility, and I jumped into action and used a fire extinguisher to douse the blaze, stopping it in its tracks. My clothes and hair smelled like a campfire for a few days, but I got a lot of high-fives. A few weeks later, in the company softball game (after going three for three and having a lot of RBI), I made a diving catch to end the game. I was swarmed by the whole team like we had just won the World Series or something.

At that point, I think I'd earned my Hammond street cred. I was not just a hanger-on who was going to sit there with his daddy as his protector and benefactor. He definitely would not have stood for that anyway. He viewed my presence there as a favor and debt he owed to the company for creating a position for his wayward son. He was opposed to me staying with the company for too long and implored me to return to medicine, even if it meant going to China or Zimbabwe. At every turn he told the Hammond brass this was only a temporary arrangement. Nonetheless, I made it clear that I was going to put my physical safety at risk for the sake of all things related to the company. I played that softball game without health insurance (and told others my concern) and shrugged off a potential torn Achilles tendon—something that happened to one of the guys in the previous year's game. I drove to work in my crappy silver Neon without health insurance for ninety days, and if a truck trespassed into my lane, I mentally told the driver of the errant truck, *If you hit my car, you better kill me—because I don't have the money to pay for an ICU admission. You better just end it and not mess around!*

Whether it was protecting the property (I'd be damned if the place burned while I was there) or selling out for a silly play in a game that meant nothing and was already won, I was balls to the wall and all in. Despite my offense and my past, I got to show that I am a normal guy and a gamer, not an awkward social outcast.

So Chuck, among others, knew I was not messing around, and eventually he looked me up online. *Why is this old guy suddenly here, with all of his chemistry knowledge and Microsoft Excel skills, at Hammond Kentucky, of all places?* And at some point, after a few months, I felt comfortable enough and had enough beers in me to text him one night.

"Hey, Man, there is a lot about me you may not know. Or do know. There is a lot more to the story."

He replied: "I wondered when you would bring this up. Don't worry, Brother. I don't judge. It's all good. People make mistakes and do weird shit sometimes. You are good with me."

I gave him my book. It turned out his girlfriend's brother was on the sex offender registry. He had sex with a fifteen-year-old when he was nineteen. So Chuck was already dubious of the whole social policy. My new support network and family at Hammond was cemented during those critical first few months. It was unconditional.

Chapter 14

"Every parting gives a foretaste of death, every reunion a hint of resurrection."

—ARTHUR SCHOPENHAUER

I DROVE PAST my old home in Upper Arlington. The contractors, who'd bought the house for cash, had already made their mark on it. Blowing out the attic was something Susan and I always wanted to do. I was happy to see that progress on the structure. The expansive front lawn, where I used to crawl on my hands and knees with my kids on my back like a slow-roving elephant, was empty in the crisp late-August sun. I had not seen the place since I left almost a year before. And as I turned the corner, hoping my old neighbors would not see me, I saw the travesty. The entire backyard had been replaced by more house. They'd blown out the back, erased the patio we had put in, and made the backyard a sliver of what it once was. Susan and I had vowed to keep the original home's footprint and only expand upward, but the contractors had turned the home into a McMansion—eliminating all its historic luster. A large backyard was a rarity in Old Arlington, and the new construction had destroyed that feature of our old home—the feature that made us buy the home in 2009. It was depressing.

As I turned the corner, I saw Susan's stepmother, out for a walk.

I slowed the car and rolled down the window.

"Janet?" I asked through the window.

"Chris?!" she exclaimed.

"Hey! Good to see you!" she opened the door of my piece of crap Neon and got in.

"Wow! Here you are! I just wanted to go for a walk," she explained. "I didn't expect to see you already!"

"Yeah, I got in a little early and thought I would check out the old neighborhood."

I drove on, around the block.

"It's weird seeing all this again. It's like a whole lifetime ago."

"It is."

"Yeah. I'm not thrilled with what they are doing to the house."

"I know, me neither. But that is what sells these days."

"I know." I waited a bit, putting the car in neutral at the stoplight. "I can't believe we lived in that house. In this neighborhood. It's just all so foreign to me now. Like I don't belong here."

"That was a chapter in your life," she helpfully mentioned. "But that has closed. You have a new one coming up."

"I know. But this was a good one."

"But were you happy? Were you happy living here?"

"No."

"Then it wasn't the right thing for you, was it?" Janet was someone who could jump right into life's difficult conversations and realizations as quickly as she could suggest alternative driving routes to avoid construction or what type of shortening she uses when baking cookies.

"It's not just me. The kids." I added. "It was all theirs, too."

"But not for you," she stood by her position, "You are where you need to be now. And so is everyone else."

"Maybe."

"You will find a new path. A healthier one. You are smart and have worked hard. And—look at you—you look great!"

"Yeah. Prison was good for my health. Much better for me than being a doctor," I joked. This observation had become my go-to when discussing prison with people for that awkward first time.

"Oh, stop!" she said. "You have two kids who are beyond excited to see their dad today. That's all that matters today. Not these fancy houses."

"Maybe."

We drove to the condo where Susan and my children had relocated, just about a half mile north of our old house, closer to their school. I had not seen them in 250 days. For 90 days I'd lived six miles from them but never saw them, my contact limited to a weekly Sunday night call. It was August 29, 2015. Susan had gone to see her brother in Chicago. It was my father-in-law who insisted that I see the kids this weekend. It would have been too difficult for Susan to see my face; she had been dreading my return since my release.

"Daddy!" When the door opened, the kids swarmed and hugged me. It was one of the best greetings I have ever had. My son patted my belly, "Whoa, you are not fat anymore!" He pondered for a bit, "Can we still call you Fatty Daddy?"

"Yes," I said matter-of-factly, "you can still call me Fatty Daddy, or Fatty for short." There was some giggling between them. They were quick to give me the tour of the condo: their own rooms, their playroom with a skylight, Mom's room, which I dared not to step in.

Despite the new furniture, it held the ghost of our former home. Items were heaped, not yet unpacked from the move and downsize. Clothes and papers in piles awaited organization in the corners of rooms. Walking through the kitchen was like walking through a museum of the prehistory of my life, complete with relics and artifacts of days gone by. The plates from which we'd eaten meals as mere students of law and medicine in Chicago, the glasses we drank beverages from in the punishing heat of Houston, the coffeemaker that kept us caffeinated during the long hours of my OSU gig and through the stress of my house arrest. Even the forks and knives had stories behind them. Yet these objects were no longer part of my daily life. They served a new master now, a single mother under a new circumstance, and they mocked me for my insignificance. Even the books on the shelves, some a carryover from my college days, were there to remind me that I was no longer part of the operation.

"Hey, Chris," my father-in-law said, as he gave me a long hug. He had wanted me to see the kids much sooner but understood the perils of a visit to the halfway house.

To reconnect, my kids and I fell back on some of our old standbys: Legos, dinosaurs, Nerf dart guns (which abruptly ceased after my son took a dart in the eye), silly things on YouTube. They always liked Peter Gabriel's *Sledgehammer* video (calling it "the fruit face one"), Herbie Hancock's *Rockit* ("the robot legs one"), and *Three Stooges* episodes.

Through it all, no matter what we were doing, I could not stop looking at them. They already looked older than when I saw them last. When they caught me staring (more than once), they would ask, "What?!"

"Nothing," I said, smiling. It hurt to see them, the strain in their faces. The move, my absence, their knowing I'd got in some kind of trouble and was not a doctor anymore, it added up to a heaviness we all were aware of. But no one wanted to talk about the invisible elephant in the room, not on the first visit.

Every half hour or so, my son asked about the time: "What time is it? How many hours have you been here? How many more hours will you stay?" I stumbled on these answers. Our dissolution decree stated that I could visit the kids once a month for four hours with supervision. This was a far stricter condition than my federal supervised release restriction, which ensured that all my parental rights were intact. According to that document, they could stay with me, we could go camping, I could drive them to school, I could go to their sporting events and performances, I could pretty much do anything with them.

But Susan was having none of it. Her only goal was protecting the children. From her point of view, I had a target on my back, and she wanted to limit any possibility of blowback toward me from the community that the kids might witness. Even had she allowed it, there was no way I would show up at any of their events. I could only too easily imagine the stares, the whispers. It was just too soon for me to be out and about in that neighborhood again. And she didn't believe that I had changed (the drinking, short temper, etc.), which is not surprising, given how little we spoke to each other since I had left. All I could do was make these short visits the best they could be and enjoy my time with the kids.

My father-in-law overheard my son's questions and watched me struggle. When I stepped into the kitchen to get a glass of water, he put his hand on my shoulder. Looked me in the eye, he said, "Chris, you can stay here as long as you want. I am in charge today," he nodded. "And I already talked to your PO. We can go out to eat or take the kids to the Lego Store. Just enjoy this day."

"OK," I could barely speak. "Thank you," I muttered through tight, burning vocal chords. For what he had done for me through all of this, I will always be grateful.

Walking through the Lego Store was terrifying. I had agoraphobia. I felt like I wore a huge sandwich board that said SEX OFFENDER/CHILD PREDATOR. Walking among the children there was like navigating a mine field. Even more frightening was the sea of adult faces—the parents that I feared would recognize me and alert the authorities. I imagined the news vans screeching to a halt outside as the store emptied in hysteria. I tried to avoid eye contact at all costs. My stomach was in knots and hands were sticky with sweat, yet I had to keep that smile on my face and engage with my kids while we checked out the Lego Millennium Falcon or the Lego Friends Sunshine Ranch set. I wanted to spend as much time with them there, for their sake, but I also wanted nothing more than to get the hell out of there. I told the kids they could each get a set to build when we got home. And when I went to pay for it, about $50, my father-in-law insisted on paying instead, of course. When we stepped outside the store, it was as if I had held my breath the entire time, and I could finally exhale for the first time in forty minutes.

We ended the day with dinner at the Buffalo Wild Wings near the old neighborhood. As I walked into the dining area, I scanned the room for any recognizable faces. I didn't trust the hostess, whose service industry–mandated smile made me think she recognized me. I could barely eat, but still managed to make my kids laugh with some silliness. I've always been able to be funny and charming on the outside while my insides are collapsing. A particularly useful skill in that moment.

We'd driven separately to the restaurant. I took my car while the kids rode in the backseat of my soon-to-be-ex-in-laws SUV, so we had to say our goodbyes in the BW3's waiting area. I tried my hand at a claw crane game and won a futuristic toy soldier for my son on the first attempt. I had never won anything on those machines in my life. I tried a few more times to get an MP3 player for my daughter, but the more valuable prize required greater precision in crane maneuvering, so it was to no avail after almost $10 worth of effort. "It's OK, Daddy. I saw you trying hard," she assured me.

When I hugged them goodbye, I held them close for a long time. "We love you, Daddy," they said.

"I love you guys, too. So much," I choked out. "I miss you already." I'd told myself I would keep it together that day, for them. But then I looked up from my embrace and saw the red, tear-filled eyes of my in-laws, and the heavy smiles on their faces. *Oh shit. Now it's coming. Floodgates. Damn it!* It's difficult for kids to see their parents cry. Crying is the purview of childhood, the currency of children's communication. When adults do it, it's unsettling to kids.

I'd promised Susan I wouldn't let it get weird, but they looked very concerned when they pulled back from our embrace. My face was giving the game away. "We had a good day, Daddy," already trying to talk me off the ledge.

"I know. We did." I remained stoic, but my eyes were watery. "OK you guys. I need to get on the road before it gets dark." I said gruffly, trying to bring the sense of routine into the interaction. "And you get to hang out more with Grandma and Grandpa!" I said encouragingly. "I will see you guys again soon. I just live down in Cincinnati—I am always a car ride away." My in-laws gave me a very brief hug, knowing I was on the verge and that they needed to get away quickly, while the pleasantness and smoothness of the day remained somewhat intact. Fortunately, a light rain began to fall, which served as cover for their expedited retreat.

As I sat in my car, I looked over, and both of their faces were plastered against the SUV's rear window, staring at me with looks of concern and sadness. I kept nodding, smiling and waving at them and mouthing the words *I am OK, I am OK, I love you, I love you.* To which they meekly waved back. As the car drove off, they changed windows to continue watching me, as if using every last second of opportunity to see me with their own eyes, their small faces getting smaller as the vehicle receded.

The moment the SUV turned out of sight, I erupted into uncontrollable sobbing. My sleeve was quickly drenched in tears and snot, but it all just kept coming out. I yelled undecipherable words at the top of my lungs in my closed car, oblivious to what any passersby might hear. The last time I cried like this I was holding our Boston terrier as she was euthanized in my arms.

I was seeing the full extent of my failure as a man and father right up close. The cramped living space my children now lived in, with an ungodly high rent coming at the end of each month. The sense of loss and disappointment in their faces, which they bravely tried to hide from me. So many of the opportunities in life—ones I had worked hard to ensure they would have, ones I could never have dreamed of having when I was a kid—were now all gone because I'd bankrupted our family. But probably the hardest thing for me to see that day was the loss of time with them. That was all gone too. I'd been given a brief glimpse of happiness, which was then snatched away, as many other good things in my life had been.

I will never be part of their everyday lives again. I will not watch them grow up or help them do so. I won't be there for general advice, to tell them how to handle a bully, to use my math and science knowledge to help them with their homework, to teach them how to throw a curveball. I won't go to parent-teacher conferences, I will not watch their games from the stands and see them look over their shoulder to make sure I saw the good play they made. I won't help coach their teams. I will just visit every once in a while, like a grandparent who lives far away.

I felt a hollow, gnawing realization that this was to be the new normal.

The car windows were opaque with condensation. My emotions had combined with the rain outside to bring the relative humidity inside to 100 percent. I cranked the defrost, and both my sobbing and visual impairment began to subside.

As I drove home, trying to wrap my head around things, I came to another realization. Perhaps my children could never have had a normal life with me. Maybe I was destined never to be a normal father. Had things not changed, I would seldom have gone to any of their events anyway. I would have been too busy with work. Or maybe I would have worked myself to death by my mid-forties. Or I would have continued to be a tyrant when I was home, and then dragged the kids through a bitter and painful divorce. If the choice was between that path and whatever this new normal was, then perhaps this was better. We'd had, at least, the fourteen months of house arrest to truly connect and bond—even if it was the only opportunity we would ever have. Maybe not being around me—whether as an emotionally broken, unpredictable father or as a social leper—will ultimately save them. Maybe this was the best possible outcome for them.

I held onto the reassurance of this thought, that my children were being better without me. For myself, though, it was yet another hard pill to swallow, another chunk of me that life had bitten out.

Chapter 15

"In the end the Party would announce that two and two made five, and you would have to believe it."

– GEORGE ORWELL, *1984*

WITH MY MOVE from Columbus to Cincinnati, my supervision was transferred between the corresponding offices within the Southern Ohio District. My new probation officer gave me some time to settle into Hammond and recover from my medical board hearing before making his first house visit. It was part of the supervision protocol that he make at least one unannounced visit to my place of residence per quarter. So after I spent a day at work in mid-August, the doorbell rang and the dogs barked incessantly, as they did in response to anything outside the usual pattern. Over the clatter of canine claws and the pounding of human feet on the floor above me, I could hear Eleanor both greeting the visitor and admonishing the dogs for their "rudeness." I had become accustomed to the cadence but could not discern any words. After a brief period of quiet overhead, Eleanor's voice boomed down the stairwell to my apartment, "Chris, there is someone here to see you!" I knew who it was. There was only one person who would ever come to see me unannounced.

As in any legal-type situation, my first thought was that he would have his handcuffs out and a gun drawn, but it was nothing like that. In the foyer upstairs, my new probation officer stood silhouetted by the sun shining through the tall windows, which created beams of light, illuminating the dust and haze of the home. A seemingly angelic visitation from a PO. "Chris?" he said, extending his hand.

"Yes," I reached out to shake it, "Thomas—err, Mr. McCutcheon."

"You can call me Tom." (I always addressed him as Mr. McCutcheon nonetheless, in emails, texts, and in person.) He was in his late forties. His hair was flecked with gray, and trendy sunglasses sat atop his head, partially submerged in his spiked mop. His skin was suntanned ruddy in the way that redheads and other fair-skinned people can get by the end of the summer. The guy definitely worked out. He was shorter than me but very imposing. Even if he hadn't been in charge of my life, I wouldn't mess with this guy. He wore one of those thin cotton T-shirts, almost form-fitting, that draped well on his frame. His trapezius emerged from the collar to his neck with bulbous authority. His biceps balled up when he moved his arms. Thick forearms and hands extended and conveyed his physical strength. He had a reassuring smile, though, as he sensed my uneasiness.

"Well, I will let you two talk," Eleanor said, and quickly departed.

"Do you want to head down to where I actually live?" I asked nervously, laughing a bit.

"Sure."

I showed him the layout of the six hundred square feet of living space I had recently acquired. As we went into each room—living/bedroom/TV, kitchen/dining, bathroom, two closets—I watched him make mental notes. Maybe he was considering the places I could hide contraband or evidence of any future illegal activity, like a hidden meth lab or something. Eventually, we sat down at the table. Since it was his first visit, the ground rules were once again laid out for me.

"I know you have heard some of this from Ms. Evans, but we have to go over it again. Plus, it's a little different, now that you are out and not in the halfway house."

"I hear you."

"So as part of the conditions of your release, you are not allowed to be alone with children without my knowledge and approval and other adults present—with the exception of your own children. But if you are going to be with them, in areas where children congregate, you will need to be with another adult."

"All right."

"You are not to use any Internet-capable device, unless it has Federal Probation Office–approved monitoring software installed on it. You can have a laptop or five smart phones—but they all would have to be monitored at $30 per month per device."

"OK."

"And I know you mentioned to me that you will be doing some kind of consulting work, with a doctor in China?"

"Yes. A radiation oncologist in Shanghai. I would be doing some editing and research advice, you know, clinical operations insight and stuff."

"Well, you may want to get on that sooner rather than later, so here is the information for the monitoring company that is contracted with us," he said as he handed the paperwork across the table.

"OK, I will get on this."

"And just so you know, you are not allowed to run or own a business. So I would recommend classifying this as contract work, and you can use a 1099 form to claim it on your taxes."

"OK."

"And you are not allowed to view any form of pornography or other sexually explicit media."

"I know."

"But it's more than that. You are not permitted to view certain things in order to curb your arousal pattern. And it can go beyond pornography. I am supervising a guy who is still quite sexually attracted to children, and even seeing kids on a cereal box is enough to make him masturbate. So he needs to be watched closely." *Jesus, I was lumped in with* this *guy?* He moved on.

"For now, you are within your sixty-day period since your release from custody, where you cannot leave the Southern Ohio District. After that period, you will need to fill out a travel request form—I will provide you a copy when the time comes—that I will have to review and approve. Your travel into other jurisdictions will need to be approved by the receiving probation office, too. From what I can tell you, if it's work related or to see immediate family, it usually gets approved, but each district is different when it comes to personal travel or vacations."

"OK."

"And we need to talk about your mental health aftercare." I'd been waiting for this. He began to thumb through more papers. "So the court has mandated, here in your J&C (Judgment and Commitment), that you receive mental health treatment for your sex offense—"

"I have already. I went through cognitive behavioral therapy for my PTSD. And sexual abuse therapy. It was all out of pocket—" I could feel the tension in my voice getting more acute.

"It's good that you did that. That is not being discounted here. I know you had a very good therapist, but she was not contracted by the federal government for sex offenses. She was not specialized in sex offender treatment." I cringed at that. *Sex offender treatment*. All I could think of was the program at Elkton, where people came out diagnosed and branded things they weren't. Where they were routinely dressed down and humiliated and called monsters. And in my mind it meant that I, too, was considered a cereal-box masturbator by association.

I was just not up for picking at the old scabs and going through therapy again. It was exhausting and painful work when I went through all my issues during the pretrial period. I'd just started working. I was still reeling from my medical board tribunal. I was emotionally exhausted from recent life transitions. And I felt that going along with this would itself be an admission of something that just wasn't true—an agreement to be classified as something that I am not, a false confession like those of the Salem "witches" or waterboarded "terrorists."

"Look," I protested, "I am not a pedophile. I am not into kids. I took a lie detector that proved it. So what's the point now? Why did I go through all that therapy if I just have to do it again?" I was definitely more confrontational than when I'd been in the halfway house. I am sure my fatigue lowered my guard and impaired my better judgment.

"I know you aren't. I know most of you guys aren't pedophiles," he calmly stated, as if to disarm me. It was the first time I'd heard something like that from a member of the system since my judge had said it at my sentencing. "Most of you guys get pretrial therapy or counseling. Most of you guys also take lie detectors that prove you are not contact offenders or pedophiles. You are not unique there. But you committed a serious offense. You crossed a lot of boundaries, and you need to figure out how you arrived to that, to where you did what you did."

"But I addressed it already," I said defeatedly. "I just want to move on." He looked at me, quiet. Maybe he wasn't expecting this kind of defiance.

"I can file a motion with the court to ensure that the treatment you receive will specifically be sex offender treatment. According, to your judge's sentencing orders, you are to receive mental health aftercare at the discretion of the probation officer. But I can firm up this clarification. You are a sex offender, are you not? You committed a sex offense?"

"Yes." I already knew this was a battle I was not going to win.

"Well, you need sex offender treatment, then. Right?"

I sighed. "All right." There was a long pause as he shuffled through his papers some more. The air became thick; I felt the weight of the house on me in my basement. "Well, will I still get PTSD counseling—some kind of maintenance therapy or something? Or am I going to be told I am an evil person the whole time?"

He was both annoyed and confused by this statement. "Where are you getting this from?" he asked, squinting his eyes and shaking his head.

"No offense, but the stuff I heard about the sex offender treatment program at Elkton was pretty horrendous—like bordering on professionally irresponsible horrendous. A bunch of myth propagation."

"I have a guy in mind for you who I think you will really like. He is on top of the literature, the studies, and the data. He has a very sophisticated view of this issue. He knows what the score is. And he specializes in PTSD and other trauma-related mental health problems on top of it." I nodded reluctantly. "Like I said, I think you will like him." His concern was genuine, not a phony front of a ham-handed mandate. "A lot of you guys are against it at first. It's not easy to confront your past behaviors. But after a while, you see the value in it. Then, after a while, a lot of you don't want to leave when it is time to move on."

My face betrayed my feelings. I was not buying it. (I am sure this is why, despite my agreement to enter the program, he filed a motion anyway to ensure my compliance. I already seemed defiant in his eyes, and he was not going to put up with my crap.) "Give him a chance. You need to do this anyway. This is not a choice. Just give him a chance. If it's not working out, then you can try someone else. I don't want you to do anything that you won't find to be helpful to you. But I am quite sure this will be a helpful experience for you. And it's only $25 a month. I know you paid a pretty penny for your previous therapy."

"OK." I did feel better after his assurances.

"And, speaking of lie detectors, you will need to take regular polygraphs."

"Really?" I had not seen polygraphs on any of my paperwork from the court documents. But in the state of Ohio and in many other federal districts, routine polygraphs are part of sex offender supervision.

"Well, yes," he said, somewhat struck that this was news to me. "Otherwise, it's all just lip service." I nodded. "It's like if you had a drug offense, you would need to take a urine drug screen, to make sure you were not using again. The polygraph is the equivalent test for sex offenders. To make sure you are complying with your conditions of supervised release. For example, one of the questions will be, 'Have you ever lied to your probation officer?' or 'Have you viewed pornography?' and so forth."

"All right." I signed the papers to consent for the sex offender treatment program and release of mental health information to the probation office and the consent to polygraph testing. And he left, after we'd talked for almost two hours, just getting to know each other, so that he had a clearer picture of my previous life and my current one.

The sex offender treatment program was every Thursday night. Group would start between five-fifteen and five-thirty and last an hour and a half. Every other Thursday I would stay for an hour of individual counseling after group. It was designed for all kinds of sex offenders. Contact, noncontact, and everyone in between. Since 80 percent of all federal cases are nonproduction/noncontact child pornography offenders, the majority of the group consisted of these types of offenders.

Aaron was the youngest in the group (I was second youngest), in his early thirties, and not surprisingly his path to darkness was the most like mine. It was trauma-based, as are the majority of these cases where the defendant is under fifty. He was bullied throughout his life. He was routinely beaten at and on his way to and from school. Highlights included getting his head and hands slammed in locker doors, having a brick thrown at his head (which left a dent and scar on his scalp), being tied to a tree and stabbed repeatedly with a large tree branch fashioned and sharpened into a spear (which left scars on his torso). He never told his parents out of embarrassment and shame. He spent most of his life depressed, anxious, and terrified of people, and stayed indoors whenever he could.

Often, he turned to pornography to numb himself, escape, and keep his mind off of killing himself. When someone from a chat room sent him several child pornography images, they intensified the numbing effects. When this person was busted, the authorities traced his emails to Aaron and arrested him. He was given five years' probation. The sex offender treatment he received consisted of being told that viewing child pornography was wrong and that he was wrong, while not really addressing why he did it. Four years into his probation, he slipped back into depression, became suicidal, and reoffended. He then spent five years in prison.

Jerry was a once highly successful salesman, a man in his late fifties who just got bored with his life. He had affinity for the female body, regardless of age, and started viewing child pornography. In some ways, it reminded him of his youth and adolescent curiosity. It was like he went back in time. He became fixated on high school and junior high age girls. When he was that age, he'd been incredibly awkward and never really interacted with girls. He felt like he was getting to see what he hadn't then, only this time he was armed with a computer and the know-how that came with age.

Lawrence was a high-numbers guy—like tens of thousands if not hundreds of thousands of files. He was part of an online club that bonded over trading files. It made him feel like he belonged to something, and doing something illegal was a thrill in itself. He said he felt he could be whoever he wanted online. It was an escape for him. He was in a dead marriage, and his wife filed for divorce the day after their home was raided by the FBI. He was charged with distribution and spent over six years in prison. Ironically, he and his ex-wife have gotten along much better since the divorce, and she played a key role in getting him back on his feet.

Tony was a former police officer, and David was a fund-raiser for a nonprofit. They were classic porn addicts who had worked their way through entire different genres and fetishes of porn, eventually getting more and more extreme to satisfy the diminishing returns of their drug of choice. Their wives left them and, humiliated and bitter, put up as many barriers as possible to keep them from seeing their children.

Like those of most nonproduction/noncontact offenders, these cases were not born out of a true sexual pull toward children or a progression toward the sexual assault of children but an assortment of complicated mental health issues. The sexual nature of the content was more a coincidental by-product than the goal.

The non–child pornography cases were academically interesting as well.

Arnold was an auditor for Hamilton County. He was caught masturbating in his cubicle at work. When he first described himself to the group, he said, "You know the movie, *40-Year-Old Virgin*? Well, I am the sixty-year-old virgin." He was more than socially awkward; I would venture to guess he had a touch of schizotypal personality disorder or was on the autism spectrum. He viewed all women as evil, cold, and unapproachable, but found them arousing, thus his urge to masturbate, regardless of the setting. He had some bizarre predilections, like dressing up in chain-mail and other "medieval" suits of armor (that he made himself)—complete with a long sword and shield—and walking around his neighborhood or a local mall. He had an intensely negative relationship with his sister, who sounded like she had borderline personality disorder. It also sounded like his interactions with women had been a constant stream of rejection—which devolved into avoidance and self-sabotage. He did care greatly for his mother, perhaps the only positive female figure in his life, but one that also kept him in a state of arrested development.

He was harmless, avoidant of people and relationships as he was.

He was the only nonfederal case. His behavior was a state or county misdemeanor (he did not have to enroll on the sex offender registry) and was voluntarily taking the class to help get his record expunged. From what I could tell, he really wanted to stop his urges. They troubled him, and he knew his behavior was not normal.

Stanley was an older guy, in his late sixties. He was a pilot who'd gotten into the habit of meeting with prostitutes when he flew into different cities. It was his way of escaping his life for a while. He'd picked up this habit during his first marriage, to the daughter of a wealthy banker in their small town. She had numerous affairs—often with men he knew—and boasted about them to him openly. He sought out prostitutes to counter the humiliation he felt. Then it became his way of coping with all the negative feelings in his life that he suppressed.

He typically found these women in Craigslist's personals section. One day, he got a message from someone, a very attractive girl who in her picture looked to be young, in her early twenties. When he asked her age, she said fifteen. He told her he was not interested, that she was too young. But the messages kept coming over the next few weeks. Finally, out of curiosity (what kind of a fifteen-year-old would be interested in an old man in his sixties?) and weakness (she *was* attractive, and this was a new, exciting kind of thing for him) he decided to meet her, crossing the Ohio River from Kentucky into Cincinnati.

Upon arriving at the movie theater where they planned to meet, he was swarmed by the police. He had actually been talking to an agent of law enforcement, posing as the girl. Crossing state lines made it a federal case of importuning a minor. He spent six years in prison. His attorney wanted to fight the case, arguing entrapment, but he didn't want to pursue it. He realized that his decision making was getting more and more unhealthy, and this was proof to him that he had spiraled too far into darkness. (A man his age should not be meeting a fifteen-year-old girl for *anything*, much less sex, he thought.) He was relieved to have been caught. Each encounter had made him feel more empty afterward. Despite all this, his second wife stood by him and stayed with him throughout his entire ordeal. They became much closer because of it when she learned his life's story.

It was Jermaine who was the most unique among the group, and the most troubling—but not for the reasons one would assume. He was the only black guy in the group, in his late fifties, but looked my age. He ate well, exercised regularly, and took great care of himself.

He'd grown up in the projects of Chicago. Through middle school, he said, he was an all-A student, and I could tell he wasn't bullshitting. His natural intelligence shone through when he talked in group about politics and current events, and he was very articulate and compelling in his speech and musings. Right before high school started, his father left the family. Also around that time, his mother was murdered. He became a ward of the state and bounced around among various foster families. But his real family eventually became the gang that ruled his neighborhood. He entered the path of a career criminal: guns, drugs, robberies, car theft. He had been shot at and had shot at people. He had been stabbed a couple of times, too. He had a pretty impressive rap sheet and spent a lot of time in prison in his early adulthood. But the one charge that cost him the most was his sex offense.

In 1997, he got a hotel room with his girlfriend. They'd had sex for the first time a few days before, and it was clear that the same thing was going to happen again. When it became apparent that neither of them had brought condoms, she put on the brakes. He got frustrated and grabbed at her breasts and crotch, playfully (in his mind at least), saying, *c'mon, baby*, and the like. She stormed off, and he assumed she was grabbing some condoms from a nearby convenience store. When there was a knock at the door, he opened it, expecting her, but it was the police. According to Jermaine, she had become infuriated with him at being pawed and had told the police.

He spent two years in an Illinois state prison for sexual assault. He wondered if his criminal career and many other things that he did for which he did *not* get caught factored into the conviction and sentencing. Still, she had not intended to get him into so much trouble and was devastated herself. They remained a couple throughout his incarceration. She sent him money for his commissary and visited and wrote him all the time. She always apologized. And he always assured her that she had nothing to be sorry about, that he was in the wrong. And during that time—his third or fourth stint in prison by then—he realized he needed to change his life if he did not want to die in prison.

When he got out, he kept his nose clean. He did three years' probation and completed the ten years on the sex offender registry required by the State of Illinois, all the while trying to avoid his gang-affiliated past. He wanted a fresh start, to get away from the grip of his old neighborhood, and came to Cincinnati to live with distant relatives and begin his new life.

Now Jermaine is a good-looking, well-spoken man, who never had problems meeting women. And in short time he acquired a few new girlfriends. One of them caught wind that she was not the only one and was not happy about it. When he broke off the relationship, she tried to frame him for stealing her jewelry. The case was quickly thrown out, but the county court, when doing his background check, realized that he had been a registered sex offender in Illinois. It turned out that for the same offense Ohio required fifteen years on the registry—something Jermaine was not made aware of when he moved. He thought that when he was done with his punishment in Illinois his punishment was done. But states aren't the same. Still, the county judge waived the requirement anyway (he would have had only another year or two on the Ohio registry, had he correctly self-reported on time) and said he was free to go, saying that Jermaine had served his time and fulfilled his post-conviction requirements.

But when he walked out of the courtroom, federal authorities apprehended him. He was charged with a Class D felony—violating interstate commerce by failing to register with the Ohio/Hamilton County sex offender registry—and sentenced to five years in prison (longer than he'd received for any of his more violent or destructive crimes). He was also required to be on the Ohio registry for the rest of his life. To top it off, on his registry paperwork after his release it said that he sexually assaulted a minor, despite the fact that the intimate partner he'd groped almost twenty years before was thirty-eight years old at the time. In other words, the registry itself manufactured a new sex crime, and the additional costs exacted on his life (not to mention taxpayer dollars) were staggering.

This was the group of guys I spent most of my Thursday nights with after my release from custody. They were good guys. They were not dangerous, sex-crazed, heavy-breathing, fire-hydrant-humping, hiding-in-the-bushes animals. They did not defend or minimize their actions. They were men who were atoning and trying to figure out what led them to their choices and actions. They were just trying to pick up the pieces after their lives were shattered, in a world that didn't really want them around. And during the check-in portion of the group meetings, when each member of the group summarized his week's events, the struggles they shared were profound. Guys would get a job through a temp agency and do great work. Then when it came time to consider a permanent hire, they would be let go because of their record. More specifically, had they run drugs or guns or robbed a liquor store, they would have been fine—but a sex crime was a deal breaker. Companies did not want their name besmirched by association.

Hearing of their problems finding housing was painful for me. It was difficult for guys who did not have a family member nearby to give them a place to stay. Several were relegated to living in the derelict apartment complexes that were the only ones that accepted sex offenders, near gutter bars, pawn shops, and the hangouts of street prostitutes. My probation officer once told me he had four sex offenders coming out of prison who had nowhere to go. They were abandoned by their friends and families. Homeless shelters do not accept sex offenders, even those guilty of public urination or having sex with a sixteen-year-old when they were eighteen. And registrants who lived in their car or an alley have to report to the sheriff's office every day.

Even when a registrant is blessed enough to land a home with a sympathetic landlord (as I was) or family member to take them in (in a sufficiently open-minded neighborhood), that goodwill can get lost quickly when it starts to hit people's pocketbooks. According to a heavily cited article in *American Economic Review*, the value of a home adjacent to one with a sex offender living in it drops by an average of 12 percent and becomes difficult to sell. Homes within a tenth of a mile drop in value by an average of 4 percent. This sets up the next wave of backlash, in the form of understandable anger in reaction to an artificial depreciation of what is most people's largest financial asset, which can create a whole new level of resentment.

The societal distrust and animosity that went with the label was incongruous in the context of the guys I met in this group. But they lacked someone like Eleanor in their lives who would quell the dust clouds stirred up when someone new learned of my presence in their sacred neighborhood. An obligatory, reactionary panic ensued about once every eight months, and Eleanor sorted it out each time. But not for these guys. For them, it was a punch in the mouth at nearly every turn.

At each group session we had a main theme to discuss: lingering versus looking, attraction versus arousal, the Offending Cycle, women, intimacy, hiding desires. The program was clearly heavily geared toward contact offenders. It felt like much of the group counseling had been clumsily retrofitted to apply to people like me, who were, ironically, the majority. The average time spent in the program was twenty-four months, the first fifteen of which were very difficult for me, though. The program had to cover all the reasons and psychological underpinnings of why the person had committed his offense—and it had to include all severities of offenses.

The individual sessions were good, in that they helped me navigate the day-to-day as I was trying to rebuild myself and deal with the specter of probation and being on the registry. My counselor, Frank, was as outstanding as my probation officer promised.

But there were many times on my drive home from group when I felt like I was being gaslighted. I was furious, thinking that my mind was being manipulated—like I was being fed the reasons the system wanted me to have for my offense. I was questioning and doubting myself rather than focusing on my own reasons for my actions. It was as if my greatest fear about the program were coming true. After group, I would turn off my car radio and talk and argue (sometimes loudly) with myself on the twenty-five-mile drive from Price Hill to the Eastgate Area of Cincinnati, to make sure I wasn't losing my sanity. I am sure folks in adjacent cars who observed me talking to myself would have had differing opinions regarding said sanity, but venting helped me. It also helped that I started seeing Rachel again when I went to Columbus. She was the therapist who had treated me for PTSD and sexual abuse counseling before I went to Elkton. Seeing her undid much of the damage and confusion that the program was causing me at the time.

Despite the philosophical concerns I had with the group sessions, I have to say that being present at a table filled with guys who were facing the same stigmas and problems that I was facing at the time was invaluable to me. The support and feedback we gave each other, as we shared advice and our experiences, helped us navigate through a world that was pitted against us. I developed a rapid and strong kinship with these good men. A 'Brotherhood in Registry,' if you will.

But, as I would learn, since the group portion of the program has to cover a lot of ground over its twenty-four-month cycle, it can take a while to get around to the things that matter for a given individual. I happened to join the group at a point where many of the issues that pertained to me had just recently been covered. So it took about fifteen months before we got to trauma, anxiety, repression/suppression, life-stress, and personal crises. When we did, it showed me that there were far more layers to the onion than I'd ever imagined.

Shortly after I started the sex offender treatment program, I had to take my first probation polygraph. I'd started the program late, relative to my release, and my first polygraph was scheduled for March 3, 2016. The comparison of the polygraph to a drug test is overly simplistic. If one has ingested opioids or cocaine, unequivocal chemicals (products of drug metabolism) with distinct chemical structures, will show up in the urine. That is pretty straight forward and objective. The polygraph, however, measures a variety of physiological changes (heart rate, blood pressure, skin perspiration, breathing rate, etc.) that occur under interrogation. An increase in any of these metrics after a specific question is deemed to be indicative of deception—meaning it does not actually detect lies. True lie detection is only possible when the truth is known and the person under examination is asked questions about that truth.

I was especially worried about this exam. People with PTSD and anxiety are known to generate false positives. My final medical board hearing was coming up in six days (in which the fate of my license was to be determined), and my mother's double mastectomy for a recently diagnosed breast cancer was scheduled to occur two days after that. My nerves were already completely shot.

This was not going to be like the previous voice-stress analysis I'd undergone in September of 2013. Then, my attorneys had limited the exam to just three questions and specified that I could stop the interview at any time. For this exam, I was under the jurisdiction of the federal government, with no legal representation or constitutional rights. This time, they could ask me *anything*. Not just about current actions—or even past actions before my criminal case—but about my thoughts, too. And there was no recourse. Though a part of me welcomed this as another opportunity to make it clear that I was not a monster, pedophile, or sexual deviant, the stress I was under on top of the exam itself gave me pause for concern.

I had to take a half day of vacation time from work and pay $200 cash for the exam. Interestingly, the office of the polygrapher was only a few miles south of where I lived, in a complex I drove by every day going to and from work.

It was a cold, wet, gray early-March day. Weak, wet snow still clung to blades of grass but had disappeared from concrete and asphalt, though wetness remained on those surfaces. The polygrapher was a chipper individual, at least. He gave me a warm welcome when I arrived and brought me into his tiny office with its wood-paneled walls hung with certificates, skin-thin blue carpet, and yellow-stained drop ceiling.

"You might as well sit down in the hot seat," he said jokingly. "You have probably heard all kinds of things about polygraphs being pseudoscience and whatnot." He had thick gray hair and an equally thick matching mustache on his broad face. "Well, in the right hands, it is very good at detecting dishonesty. Like upper 90 percents good," he said while sifting through my file. "You know, my son is a doctor. Went to University of Indiana," he said proudly, but without arrogance. "He told me this was all a bunch of mumbo jumbo, until I tested him and his friends. Well, I made a believer out of him." He paused again and looked at his paperwork. "And you are a doctor, too. Yes. I remember when your case came out—in Columbus, right?"

"Yeah."

"Given the line of work that I do and the guys that I examine, I always have an ear out for those stories." He continued laying out his paperwork. "How long are you on paper?"

"Five years."

"Eh, it will go by before you know it. Just keep your nose clean and get past this," he said, trying to be encouraging. "You know my son did medicine overseas. He said they are dying for American-trained physicians to help them."

"Yeah, I have thought of that. I don't think I can be a doc in the U.S. anymore. Not even sure I would want to fight that uphill battle."

"Five years is a blink. And, from my experience, most of the guys in your situation aren't what everyone thinks. So you can move on. Start over. Go somewhere warm," He laughed. Then his face got more serious. "Well, we should get started. Your counselor and probation officer—by the way, you could not have asked for better guys. Frank and Tom are top-notch guys. I have seen some officers make people's lives hell or try to beat them down. But not these guys. They get it. They know who to focus on. They know who is dangerous and who isn't. We are stuck having to do this, so we do it. But they really know the full story."

"Yeah, they have treated me pretty well."

"So they have given me a list of the questions they want me to ask," he said pulling a larger, legal-size piece of paper from the pile. "But, before we get to that, I will have to strap you in." He wasn't kidding. When he was done I had wires all over me. A cap over my fingertip (to measure sweat and pulse), a blood-pressure cuff around my arm, a double strap across my chest (to monitor breathing, I imagined), and a few other electrodes. The hot seat suddenly became scalding. To say this all felt invasive is an understatement. I was fully expecting a metal bowl with a skein of wires attached to it to be placed on top of my head, after contact points on my scalp, temples, and forehead were dabbed with a brine-laden sponge. I was hooked up to a machine that looked like something out of a 1960s psychological testing documentary, the leads already oscillating and indicating my keenly heightened body metrics. We had gone through some of the questions before, during the pretest interview, but once the exam officially started, I could hear my pulse coursing past my eardrums.

He fired away at his questions. This time, they got to ask everything:

> "Is your name Christopher Pelloski?" Yes.
> "Do you live in Ohio?" Yes.
> "Do you live in Kentucky?" No.
> "Do you work in Kentucky?" Yes.

These were followed by a few more neutral yes-or-no questions. Then came the big ones:

> "Have you ever paid for sex?" No.
>
> "Do you think of children when you masturbate?" No.
>
> "Have you ever had inappropriate sexual contact with anyone under the age of eighteen?" No.
>
> "Do you have deviant sexual thoughts about children?" No.
>
> "Have you been around children while unsupervised by other adults since you have been on probation?" No.
>
> "Have you used any illicit drugs since being on probation?" No.
>
> "Have you been forthright about your alcohol consumption?" Yes.

This last question was a tough one to answer because it was just after the holidays, after Thanksgiving, Christmas, and the Super Bowl. He had asked me about a typical week's consumption, but I did drink it up with my family on these occasions. He definitely took a little more time watching the leads after I answered this. I didn't want to go down the whole alcohol route again. My PTSD was in full crisis during my downward spiral, and heavy drinking was part of my symptomology. My defense attorneys wanted to make alcohol abuse a mitigating factor to my offense, to lighten the sentence. I was sent to Alcoholics Anonymous and barred from consuming alcohol during my house arrest. After further exploration, I was eventually deemed not addicted to alcohol but was self-medicating my PTSD symptoms. Still, I'd hated being improperly labeled, and over time I began to become hypersensitive to it. So I began to worry a bit. But he then continued.

> "Have you ever forced yourself upon someone in a sexual manner or committed unwanted sexual contact on anyone?" No.
>
> "Have you possessed or viewed any form of pornography since you have been on probation?" No.
>
> "Have you ever left the Southern Ohio District without permission since you have been on probation?" No.
>
> "Have you ever used an unmonitored, Internet-capable device since you have been on probation?" No.
>
> "Have you been to a massage parlor or looked for ads on Craigslist to meet for sex?" No.
>
> "Is there anything you have not told me that you would not want your probation officer to know?" No.
>
> "Have you ever lied to your probation officer?" No.
>
> "Have you been truthful with every question asked today?" Yes.

After this last question he said, "This completes the exam." He wrote a few more notes on the graph paper that had all of my biologic data on it, which at this point was several yards long, and tore it out of the machine. "I will probably see you in about a year." I later learned from some of the guys in my group counseling that this was code for having passed. As he removed all the contraption's leads and cuffs from my body, I felt as if it reinflated to its normal form after being crushed by the enormity of the experience.

I took these exams several times during probation. A lot of these questions were asked repeatedly, as if I *now* would suddenly develop a sexual affinity towards children. It was utterly invasive; I had no privacy. In the preliminary interviews, I was asked if I was dating anyone and how many people I had sex with. It was humiliating and, really, none of the federal government's god-damned business. All they needed to know was if I was complying with the conditions of my supervision and not doing anything illegal. Instead, it was turned into a voyeuristic confessional. The tests made me reluctant to meet new people or date. I didn't want to get their names dragged into government files because of their affiliation with me. It was like being violated in a whole new way. How having sex with one—or ten—consenting women over the age of thirty-five would have anything to do with viewing children being sexually abused online is beyond me.

I passed the polygraph that day and every time after. I always passed. But I wasn't allowed to have copies of the reports (despite paying $200 for them) because they were deemed "proprietary." Having passed these kinds of questions would certainly help someone in my position dispel misconceptions, one would think. I should have been allowed to carry these reports with me at all times and be able to provide them to anyone who doubts my harmlessness.

But this didn't happen. Further, nothing changed when I passed. I was still on probation—with all of its restrictions, like it had to be all or nothing. I was still considered dangerous and on a list of other people considered dangerous—even though no one ever spelled out to me what I was in danger of doing. Did they think I would tackle someone and take their unmonitored laptop to watch pornography? Or did they think I would molest a kid? Based on what evidence? Not only my own case but population-based research on my offender demographic showed it clearly was not an issue. Yet I still was not allowed to be around children, and this made me hesitant to leave my basement apartment (*What if a kid walks into a public bathroom and I am the only adult in there?*)—which intensified my loneliness and isolation until they were unbearable at times. Would those who viewed ISIS decapitation videos not be permitted to be around other people's necks without supervision? Of course, isolation and lack of intimacy are big risk factors for many sex offenses (according to the same authorities who create these punitive policies), but never mind *that* catch-22.

I still had to ask permission to travel. But given that my offense was computer-based, what difference did it make if I was in Cincinnati or San Francisco to the risk of me reoffending? There are unmonitored computers in every part of the country and porn on cable channels and pay-per-view in hotels. What difference would it make if I was in a different federal district? It just didn't make sense. And for the rest of my life, I am going to operate under the assumption that my computer is monitored anyway. I don't need to be on probation to reconcile that reality. Hell, I think we all should just assume that Big Brother is watching us online. He is. Ain't that right, Snowden?

I also saw a disturbing inconsistency in the weighting of polygraph results. A failed polygraph, or just an answer that could be interpreted as deceptive, could be used to send me back to prison or ratchet up my restrictions. But a passed test counted, apparently, for nothing. Even when it was confirmed, again and again, by the feds' own examinations, that I did not have a sexual affinity for children and would never lay a sinister hand on another human being (of any age), the system continued to treat me like a contact offender or a fragile pornography addict on the brink of reoffending. As if just one look at a *Sports Illustrated* swimsuit issue would flip some kind of switch that would have me watching six-year-olds being forcibly sodomized before you knew it—the same way it's assumed a sip of beer would have a recovering drug addict injecting black tar heroin a few minutes later.

Nowhere in my extensive neuropsychiatric evaluations and sexual abuse/PTSD therapy was I ever given the diagnosis of "pornography addiction." Yet I was treated as if I were a violent, contact sexual offender, when I wasn't. Just like I was given the label of alcoholic, when I wasn't. This shitshow creates a whole new set of problems and stressors for those already suffering. I felt stuck, running in place, on this obligatory treadmill.

Chapter 16

"Sometimes you climb out of bed in the morning and you think, I'm not going to make it, but you laugh inside remembering all the times you've felt that way"

—CHARLES BUKOWSKI, "GAMBLERS ALL"

THE UNIVERSE HAD once again made February 2nd a pivotal day for me. It was the date of our divorce/dissolution hearing. I actually laughed out loud when I opened the envelope from the Franklin County Family Court and saw "Feb 2, 2016" in bold print. It's now a date when I brace myself for personal catastrophe.

I stayed the night at my friend John's. John was the fabrication specialist from my old lab at Ohio State, who had built, by hand, the devices we used to irradiate anesthetized mice for our research. He was the one who gave me Kleenex at my sentencing hearing. He'd emailed me while I was at Elkton and visited me a couple of times at the halfway house. He was another person who had been in my corner since day one. Since I would be returning from a Hammond meeting in Detroit the day before the hearing, I asked if I could stay at his place, near Columbus, so that I didn't have a long drive that morning.

I had met his wife a few times, and she felt comfortable around me as well. Over time, I would stay with them often since visits with my children, getting back into therapy with Rachel, and working with attorneys who hired me as a consultant on medical malpractice cases frequently brought me back to Columbus. They adopted me, like a son or brother, and were devout Christians who gave me the benefit of forgiveness and helped me seek redemption. They would often send me little cards with appropriate scriptures or care packages with some food, knowing that 80 percent of the meals I ate in my basement apartment consisted of honey, peanut butter, and cold whole milk. Where Qui had been my guardian angel during my stay at Elkton and the halfway house afterward, John and his wife gradually assumed this responsibility after my release from custody.

"God, I am so tired of this blue suit," I quipped that morning. "I wore it for the plea, the sentencing, the medical board examination, and now my divorce."

"Maybe we should burn it," John joked, "like a ceremony or something." Our shared deadpan humor and love of puns and sight gags always made us comfortable with each other. He'd helped me get my office set up when I first arrived at OSU. I had a model of the brain that I used to show patients where I would aim the radiation, and it had been packed toward the top of one of the boxes. Opening the box, I pointed to it and said, "Good thing I remembered to bring my brain here," and we'd been cool ever since, at work and through the aftermath after my case went public.

"Maybe," I responded, "but I still will need it for my medical board decision hearing. Why mess with my streak of good luck now?"

Interestingly, after a few staff members who wanted me burned at the stake when my story broke in 2013 had caught wind that John and I remained close, his position at OSU (after 37 years of service) was suddenly terminated under extremely murky circumstances and without due process. Kind of makes you wonder, doesn't it? And John, being the good man he is, would not let me feel horribly guilty for the possible collateral damage I may have caused him. But deep down, he was devastated.

February and March of 2016 were hellacious months for me. The divorce hearing that day was just the first ordeal. During these months, the court-mandated sex offender treatment program began in earnest, which was followed closely by my first probation polygraph, while the medical board's final decision about my license was upcoming. And this time frame was to be capped off by my mom's planned double mastectomy. It was a steady stream of gut punches and a whole platter of shit sandwiches. After nearly eight months of finding a new rhythm and having finally hit a flat, predictable patch, I was facing a new round of upheavals.

When I arrived at the family court level of the Franklin County Courthouse, I saw Susan already sitting in the waiting area. She was dressed smartly in a business skirt and matching jacket. She had taken a job at a law firm a few blocks away as a paralegal but planned to take the Ohio bar exam. We did our small talk. I noticed the case schedule, with the names, courtrooms, and status of each posted on various flat screens throughout the waiting room. "Jesus, it looks like a damn airport, with all the flight arrival and departure information on those screens," I said, laughing and pointing.

"Yeah. My lawyer said a lot of dissolutions are happening today, so things should run quickly." I saw our names on the screen listed as "On Time," even though several cases were still ahead of us. I looked over my shoulder across the waiting room and saw several other couples having hushed conversations like the one Susan and I were having—smiles, some laughter, and the same postures Susan and I held, heads tilted toward each other. Dissolutions were nonconfrontational endings of a marriage, as opposed to the stereotypical picture of divorce, with the soon-to-be exes at each other's throats.

I didn't have the energy—or money—to be confrontational. I was so wracked with guilt for the trouble I'd caused that I was focused solely on keeping my kids from having to move again. I also needed to save money to pay the attorney fees for my medical board hearing; I was already knee deep in a repayment plan. So I wasn't about to hire yet another attorney. Psychologically and situationally, I was bent over a barrel. Numbly, I signed the dissolution decree, and with it signed away all proceeds from the sale of our home and cars, gave away what was left of the retirement account, and assumed all the credit card debt accumulated during our marriage, to the tune of (in total opportunity cost) about $170,000. I also agreed to pay double the court-calculated monthly child support payments, which was possible only because I was keeping my medical school loans in forbearance, while the interest on those debts was capitalized, adding to the principal that would eventually need to be paid off. I also was required to make extra payments toward a $100,000 debt, a reimbursement of sorts to Susan, for the legal fees that my criminal and medical board cases had pulled from our previous nest egg, now ravaged. Lastly, she was to remain the primary beneficiary on any of my insurance policies, present and future ones.

My masochism was in full flower: I accepted and even encouraged my continued punishment, it seemed. If someone had put a contract in front of me that gave away both my kidneys, I would have signed it as well, with nary a whimper. Although Susan said she could not support me as a wife anymore, my level of continued financial support was certainly husband-like with this comprehensive financial leveling. Even though we decided it was best to end the marriage, I felt a sense of responsibility to continue my level of financial support (despite resigning myself to a pauper's monthly budget), because I still struggled with a paralyzing remorse for what I had put Susan and the kids through the past few years.

The process itself was brief—a few yes-no questions and some signing of papers, and it was done. It was a far cry from our wedding ceremony and the $50,000–$60,000 reception that followed, which our college friends declared the best party they ever attended. We were given a few minutes to ourselves in a small room off the courtroom. It was awkward but expected. "Well, I guess we gave it our best try—it just wasn't in the cards," I perfunctorily said, to break the silence, half expecting an eye roll or punch in the mouth for summing up over eighteen years so dismissively.

"Yeah, we did," Susan offered, and we embraced briefly and platonically. Our respective suit jackets bunched up in the shoulders and made ruffling sounds in the otherwise silent room.

On the elevator going down, I continued the light chatter. "So, um—uh, I will come up this weekend and see you and the kids. Saturday?" exaggerating the everything-is-cool tone in my voice.

Susan laughed, perhaps also working not to let what just happened sink in. "Yes. Saturday is wide open, so come up when you can. We can think of something to do with the kids."

"OK. Good."

When we got to the street, I turned to her. "Do you want to grab a beer or something? I feel like that was pretty unceremonious." We needed some kind of closure to the day, I thought.

"Believe me, I totally want a beer right now. But I have to get back to work," she said, sounding a little disappointed. "And I don't think having beer on my breath would go over well with my employers," she chuckled.

"Yeah. I should probably be heading back to Cincy anyway. To beat rush-hour traffic," I assured her.

"OK. Well—see you in about five days then, yes?"

"Yes." And with one more awkward nod, she was off. When she'd turned the corner at the end of the block, I turned around and walked to where I was parked in a nearby garage. And just like that, in the same detached, businesslike manner that had governed most of our marriage, it was done.

Eventually, the time came to face the music from the State of Ohio Medical Board. The hearing examiner had recommended a permanent revocation of my license. This hearing was my last chance to plead my case. Five-minute arguments were to be made before the board made its final, official decision. I was already pretty well spent from the events that had occurred within the month.

When my case first went public, it created a massive wave of panic and the worst assumptions were made about me. Of course, when the facts were later clarified, they were not plastered all over the TV news and newspaper headlines the way the original revelation had been. It was more of a back-page, well below-the-fold type of information dissemination. So that bell was never really unrung. Further, after my sentencing, there were many pissed off people who felt that I got off easy because I was a fancy, rich, perverted doctor. I am sure they missed the back-page clarifications or chose not to believe them anyway. So this was the public backdrop for my medical board hearing on March 9, 2016, back in the same building as before. This was the hill I had to climb.

The Ohio Medical Board has been criticized in the past for its punitive approach to physicians with mental health issues. That approach is partially rooted in the Michael Swango debacle, in which OSU allowed the subpar medical student and active serial killer into its surgical residency program. He went on to kill patients in the 1980s and 1990s. Since then, the board would see to it that all physicians in Ohio would be free of any undesirable qualities. As a result, many physicians (in Ohio and other states) conceal their mental health problems and refrain from seeking help—just as I had done—and go it alone, while their personal lives and physical health suffer. Infallibility is a must, so appearances must be maintained.

My final medical board hearing was a continuation of the previous narrative about me. It had been seven months since my cross-examination in August, which had been just days after my release from the halfway house. The hiatus gave Hoyer false hope: *If they were taking this long, maybe they were really looking at the evidence and testimony*. I was not holding my breath. I would not allow myself to cling to such a flimsy raft. Nothing had been rational thus far—why would I think things would change? A federal judge had had his hand forced by social policies. Why would I fare any better this time—even after serving the penalty that my judge said was exorbitant as he handed it to me?

Still, I went through the motions in preparation for this exercise. My initial statement draft was defiant—but that message was eventually toned down. I might as well be gracious in my inevitable defeat and go down with a shred of dignity. And at that point, I really didn't care anymore.

To the chagrin of all involved, all three local news networks would be present and have their cameras rolling during the entire hearing. The board sat at a wooden wall of desks at the front of the bizarrely darkened auditorium; a galley of pews occupied the back. It looked like a courtroom that was undergoing a rolling brownout. My attorney spoke first. Her main point was that the board had previously returned the licenses of physicians with mental health or addiction issues after corrective action and therapy were completed. She mentioned that my mental health issue had never affected patient care, and that I had already served my penalty for one of the symptoms of my poor mental health.

Then it was my turn to speak:

> I cannot fully explain my behavior so that one with a healthy mind could understand. I know this, because now that I am much healthier, I cannot understand it either. I felt compelled to step into that world because just being there brought me back to some very dark times in my life.
>
> But regardless of the reason, it was a very harmful activity—for everyone—and inexcusable.
>
> The things I viewed were indeed disturbing. The file names and content were disgusting. And the salacious details are going to be brought up, yet again, to paint the picture that those were things that I liked or wanted to do.
>
> So let me be very clear here: While everything that I saw was disturbing, I never have nor never would want to do those things, to anyone—yet some of those things were done to me when I was a little boy.

The body language of the board couldn't have been any clearer. I was distracted by one of the member's facial expression, which looked as if he were either trying to understand Mandarin spoken with a bad speech impediment or strain with constipation. Few looked me in the eye. The fix was in. I pressed on anyway.

> I have addressed the reasons why I did what I did. I was justly punished and rightly publicly shamed for my actions. I have since done everything that I can to try to right all of the wrongs, including voluntarily placing my license on indefinite suspension for almost three years.
>
> I think about just how much our society has already invested into me and how much time and energy it took for me to acquire the skills and experience that I have. And it is agonizing, knowing that my actions have jeopardized all of it.

> But I have also come to realize that, had things not changed, these gifts would have been permanently lost anyway, because I was on a path to an early death. Because I was not well and not taking care of myself.
>
> Because I did not respect those skills that I was given—because I did not respect the profession of medicine. All because I did not respect myself.
>
> But I am now the healthiest I have ever been in my life. I am finally comfortable in my own skin. And I can treat thousands of cancer patients for another twenty to twenty-five years, and help so many get through such difficult times, as well as—if not better than—I did before.
>
> I have essentially lost everything that I have worked for so far in my life—deservedly so. But I know I have so much good left in me to give. I am asking for forgiveness, but if that is not possible at this moment, then at least a chance for redemption.

When I returned to the galley benches, an attorney representing another medical miscreant leaned over to me and put his hand on my shoulder. "That was well put. You really couldn't say any more." In all honesty, I could have flashed the board a set of double rods and said, *You all can go fuck yourselves. So let's wrap up this bitch, so I can get on the road to Detroit and be with my mom.* The outcome would have been the same.

Then it was good ole' Aaron G. Carpenter, Esquire's turn, and true to form, he prattled on with insufferable sanctimony. I really couldn't focus on what he was saying (I already heard it before from him); I was only focused on my mom at that point.

What was very unsettling, and probably the only words that I really caught while I sat there was Carpenter saying that my children were in the next room when I viewed what I viewed online. It was interesting he would say that, as if he had the floor plan to my home and had studied it and used the viewing time stamps to calculate the likely whereabouts of my home's inhabitants, which seemed somewhat voyeuristic on his part. In reality though, I was always on the opposite side of the house when I entered that eerie bubble of dissociation. Invariably, several rooms and hallways separated me from any other human beings when I viewed.

It troubled me to no end that this piece of shit would mention my children at all, at a public hearing of all places. Remembering how he trembled back in August, lips quivering and his balding head becoming visibly sweaty with excitement while he rattled off the disgusting details of the media that I viewed, I became nauseated again, just as I had then. It was like he couldn't contain himself.

When it was the board's turn to talk, it was as if they had not read any of the hundreds of pages of documents we submitted as evidence. They quoted incorrect information taken from the initial news reports generated after my arraignment in July 2013. One of the members said, "It was a good thing he was caught before he could harm or molest anyone," which entirely ignored the data on this offense, Dr. Kimmel's testimony, and the findings and the results of my investigation, including the voice-stress test. He basically parroted misinformation (that my offense is an indicator of impending child molestation), when he had the chance to speak rationally on the subject. But when three news networks cameras are on you, I suppose you have to toe the party line, no matter how false the message may be.

There was no mention by the Board of my first book either; the same one I busted my ass to get out quickly so that they could read it and know what really happened. The same book which had its veracity confirmed by the detective who investigated me and the forensic psychologist who evaluated me. *All* of the evidence was ignored.

The death blow, though, came from the psychiatrist on the board. And it really was a head scratcher. He opined that since I made the moral decision to view children being sexually abused, even if it was the result of a mental illness, I did not have the moral character to be a physician who treats patients, as this action was unforgivable. This statement was interesting because impaired physicians who make the "moral decision" to show up to work intoxicated and consequently miss a diagnosis, amputate the wrong appendage, or incorrectly fill out a prescription, because they have a problem with addiction (thus mental illness) *is,* apparently, forgivable. Historically, as Hoyer pointed out, those physicians *do* get their licenses back after they get treatment.

One way to read this is that I would have been better off (or of higher moral character) had I shown up to work high on Percocet and blasted someone's brain with sixty Gray (a unit of radiation dose) in one shot (thus killing them). I would have gotten a free pass, due to my opioid addiction. Instead, I committed a passive act in my own home (which did not affect patient care) as a symptom of a different mental illness. I suppose I chose the wrong mental illness with the wrong maladaptive coping mechanism, at least for the State of Ohio. Of course, none of the mouth-breathing "journalists" covering the proceedings picked up on that obvious inconsistency. They were too busy reveling in the denouement of my downfall.

The board unanimously voted to revoke my license—no dissenting opinion or even much discussion. Their marching orders were followed to a tee. No one was going to risk being branded a pedophile sympathizer with the news cameras rolling.

As I was leaving, a few reporters approached me for comment before I made it to the elevators. One of them, some little guy from Channel 10, asked me, "Dr. Pelloski, what have you learned from this?" I was taken aback by this banal question, asked as if the proceedings had occurred in a vacuum. *What do you mean what have I learned from this? I wrote a god-damned book about what I learned from this. What have* you *learned from this? And if you did your damned job, you would have taken this opportunity to educate others, and there wouldn't be reliance on my book-writing to inform the public about what actually happened. If you did your job, I wouldn't have to do it for you.* Maybe he heard the thoughts going through my head, or just caught the daggers from my eyes, because he fell back a bit.

But I bit my tongue and, looking down at the tiny man, simply said, "When you lose the public's trust, it's a difficult thing to get back. I respect the medical board's decision on this matter."

It was a difficult thing to say to an agent of the very apparatus that paints everyone as a caricature with its stupidity, laziness, ratings lust and penchant for clickbait—all of which contribute to the problem.

But I said it nonetheless. Not caring to be a doctor anymore probably made it much easier to say, "I have no further comments."

I don't know if justice was further served, despite my already having served my penalty. I don't know if society is somehow safer now with my knowledge, skills, and experience discarded with such oblivious ignorance and indifference. In any case, it was clearly a *great* day for cancer. One of its formidable opponents had been removed from the field of battle.

Texts rolled in from friends, family, and colleagues on the drive up to Detroit:

> So sorry to hear, man.
> Why did they take so long to decide?
> Cowards.
> What a waste.
> What will you do now?
> Thinking of you today.

And so forth.

When I finally arrived at my parents' home, my mom greeted me with a big hug at the door. "Oh, honey, I am so sorry." It was the kind of hug I'd dreaded when I was little after injuring myself or getting my feelings hurt. I would tell myself I would not start crying like a little girl (to maintain my continued proper socialization into the working-class ethos), but I was too numb and preoccupied when she comforted me anyway. I did not break down. I was more worried about my mom: how she was handling the news and what was on her horizon. Her eyes were puffy.

"It's alright, Ma—I kinda knew it was coming."

"But they spent so much time on it. I thought they would give you a chance."

"It's a tall order, you know, to take a stand like *that*. On something like *that*, when you have all those cameras on you."

"The news was there?"

"Yeah, all the local stations."

"Jeez."

"It's fine, Mom. It's fine. I know I have told you, I don't miss it. It's been almost three years now, and today just really isn't beating me up. If I really wanted to go back, I'd be livid, or sick to my stomach. But it's almost like a relief. The decision was made for me."

"I know. But you were so good at it. You helped a lot of people."

"I was—I did. But at this point, it's really not my loss anymore. Yeah, I messed up, but I wasn't right in the head. I just think of the millions of dollars society dumped into me, and it's all gone now. Their resource, that they created: That is what's gone now. It's not me who is punished; it's everyone else now. And I did everything asked of me. It's not on me anymore. I don't know what else I could do."

We moved to the living room and sat across from each other on two opposing couches. I already had a bottle of Bell's Two Hearted Ale in my hand. My sleeves were pulled up, my tie unknotted but still snaked around my collar, and my shirttails flopped over my belt. I looked like a drunken businessman waiting his turn to rock Robert Palmer's "Addicted to Love" at a late-night karaoke bar.

"It was a shit show, Mom," I said, followed by a sip of Kalamazoo's finest brew. "They said stuff that wasn't true. They made false assumptions. It was if they had spent seven or so months—I have to think they were really considering it—and then someone came in at the very end and said, *No freaking way*. So they did this song and dance and went along with it." I pondered a bit more. "What really bothers me is that what they said today could have been said years ago, without all this time in between. And saved me a lot of money. It was like no thought went into it." I could tell my mom was starting to get upset. "But if they don't want or need my skills and training, then what's the point?"

"Still, all that schooling—"

"I know. But I was *miserable* the whole time. It was like trying to get a square peg to fit in a round hole." She nodded, mist accumulating in her eyes. "You told me I looked like I aged ten years that first year of medical school when you first visited me." She nodded, reluctantly. I changed my tone. "Let me put it this way: I think I will enjoy complaining about *why* I was told I could not be a doctor again—the decision process, you know—far more than I would enjoy actually *being* a doctor again." I laughed toward the end to help ease some of the heaviness. "I mean seriously, Mom. I was going to drop at some point. I'd probably would have been dead by now, if things hadn't changed."

"I know, honey," she acquiesced. "I have never seen you this happy before—on the inside. I know you are happy. I can see it in your eyes."

"Yeah. I do really like what I am doing now. I get to use all of the science I ever learned, all over again. And I absolutely love the peeps I work with," I said, with a reflective grin on my face. "And I do enough consulting on the side, so it's not like my medical knowledge is going *totally* unused. I still get to discover new things, write about my findings, and teach again. That was the part I liked the most anyway. All those skills I learned, I am still using. Just differently now."

"Life is too short to do something you don't like. I don't care how much money you make." From a conversational standpoint, she had swung over to acceptance and support of my new lot in life. So, true to form, I took up her previous position in the delicate dance of vacillating contrarian viewpoints that characterized how my family processed difficult issues or decisions. By the end of a debate, one party would be arguing *for* the very thing that they'd attacked in the beginning, with equal vehemence.

"I don't know. Maybe it wouldn't have been so bad if almost every one of my patients was not going to die soon," trying to assure her, albeit in a morbid way. "People would tell me, I wish you were my doctor, and I would tell them, Uh, no you don't. That means you only have six months to live!" We both laughed a bit more. "I don't know, maybe not doing only brain tumors or treating kids that needed radiation—it might have been easier. Maybe if I'd mixed in a breast cancer, Hodgkin's, or prostate cancer case, it wouldn't have been so bad."

As soon as the words left my lips, I cringed.

"Hey! I am getting both of these chopped off tomorrow because of fucking breast cancer!" she said, cupping her breasts and feigning indignation.

"Yes," I acknowledged. "I know, Ma. Breast cancer is not easy. But, you know, glioblastoma, like, kills you dead, pretty quickly. I don't think this is going to do you in like—" I gestured toward her and pointed to my head, to contrast her breast cancer with the lethal brain tumor I used to research.

"I know. I'm just giving you crap," she said, smiling. Mom is a nurse. Nurses have the best gallows humor of all.

I was glad to change the subject, despite the new one's darkness. Easy subjects were never our forte. "So how are you doing with all of this?"

"It is what it is." She got more serious. "It needs to be done. This cancer needs to get the hell out of me. And, truth be told, they,"—motioning to her breasts again, "have caused me a lot of problems. Back pain, grooves in my shoulder from my bra straps. I am done with it. It will be a nice change. I will be rid of them." Her voice became light again. "And then, with some reconstruction, I can have normal-sized boobs for once. I will be a whole new woman!" We both laughed again, briefly, and then went back to stewing silently as I sipped from the bottle.

"I love you, Mom. And you are going to do just fine."

"I know. It's going to suck for a while, but then it will be over," she said heavily. Then she added, softly, "I love you, too, honey."

I was so grateful that my mom was the first person I saw after my final board hearing. More importantly, though, I was glad that I could be there for her. I knew she was scared beneath her glib, cavalier attitude (a strategy I learned from her). Had things not changed, I would have been too busy and consumed by my own work to be there truly *with* her. Present. I would have done the cold, clinically detached calculus in my head—average survival rate and expected complications for a low-risk, early-stage breast cancer—deemed hers a routine procedure with a likely favorable outcome, and sent her a superfluous card (or even text) telling her to "hang in there." I'd done the equivalent for many other family medical events and crises of equal significance. I was absent during my grandparents' stages of dying and the personal and medical calamities my brothers endured. I would have intellectualized and rationalized my absence, just as I had previously.

Instead, I got to be there with her. In the pre-op anesthesia holding area I got to hold her hand while listening to the surgeon and asking questions, without revealing my cancer-doc background. I got to sit in the waiting room with my father and brothers during the surgery, explaining what all was happening, what would happen next, and what to expect in the post-surgical recovery phase: the pathology reports, the Oncotype DX test and score interpretation, the chemotherapy options.

I drove from Cincinnati to Detroit for every one of my mom's four chemotherapy administrations, which were given every three weeks, just to be there, to make her laugh or get her Gatorade and crackers, to relieve my dad from helping her change position. (When he first saw the surgical scars across her chest and the drainage tubes for the first time, he sobbed uncontrollably.) But I got to walk my family through all of it—not as a doctor, but as an involved son and brother who knew a few things about cancer. I finally stepped up. I got to bond with my family, after my career had estranged me from them for so many years. It was an incredible life event that would never have come to pass had not my catastrophe opened the door to the opportunity.

Chapter 17

"Except for the incarceration of persons under the criminal law and the civil commitment of mentally ill or dangerous persons, the days are long since past when whole communities of persons, such as Native Americans and Japanese-Americans may be lawfully banished from our midst."

—*DOE V. CITY OF LYNN*, SUPREME JUDICIAL COURT OF MASSACHUSETTS, NO. SJC-11822 [REGARDING THE SEX OFFENDER REGISTRY]

DRIVING HOME FROM work one day in the summer, a frantic text from Eleanor appeared on my phone as I emerged from a large dead zone in the more rural parts of northern Kentucky: "Josie is pretty shaken up right now. The police came by the house asking about you. Please get home as soon as you can and talk to her."

Things had finally been quiet for a while. I had reached peace, or at least acceptance, with the probation-mandated therapy and had no polygraph coming up. I'd become used to the calls from the Clermont County Sheriff's Office every six months reminding me to reregister as a sex offender or face a new felony charge, and the letters from the Kentucky State Police that arrived every ninety days to confirm that all the information they had on me was correct—with "Sex Offender Department" in bold print in the return address. Eventually, I'd got used to all of this. And Eleanor took it upon herself to make sure I got out of the basement every once in a while. Because of her connections and the kindness of her heart, I got to see musicals at the Aronoff, watch live stand-up comedy shows, view plays, go to the symphony and attend art shows. This helped me feel normal again, especially in those early months.

But new things with new people still brought palpable fear in my throat. I had forgotten—briefly—how it felt to experience constant surprises. But that feeling returned quickly with that text. It's that same shot of adrenaline and fear you get when you pass a highway patrol car on the side of a freeway going fifteen miles per hour over the speed limit and then see that car behind you when you look in the rearview mirror.

Josie and her husband were new tenants; they had only lived upstairs in Eleanor's house for a few weeks when the police came. I hadn't really talked with them much, and I wasn't certain how much they knew about me. The drive was grueling that day—every traffic slowdown felt like an eternity. I both wanted to get home instantly and also never to arrive. But, eventually I arrived.

I turned the key in the front door and slowly opened it. Atypically, I was not greeted by the incessant barking of Eleanor's dogs, which meant they must be outside, which meant that someone else was there, either on the main floor or in the backyard.

"Hello?" I said, quietly hoping there would be no reply.

"I'm in the kitchen, Chris." Damn it, it was going to start now.

Josie was in her mid-to-late fifties and showed signs of hard living and smoking. Her voice had that signature rasp that always seemed ready to pitch into a coughing spell. She had the stellate wrinkles around her lips from years of puckering around cigarettes while being exposed to the oxidative blue vapor they produced. She was a tiny woman, but wiry and tough as nails. She'd worked the midnight shift in Ikea's shipping and receiving department for over a decade. Her skin was permanently tanned and weathered, with varicose veins here and there on her legs (suggesting a life of hard living), and scars on her forearms from when, serving as a military nurse, she had pulled survivors and victims from the rubble of the Beirut barracks bombing in 1983. A white woman from rural Michigan, she had been married to a black man for most of her adult life—which certainly wasn't easy, given the times she grew up in. They had recently been forced out of their apartment of ten years, so the owners could sell it. She knew difficult times, and its marks were bored into her body and countenance.

"Hey. I got a text from Eleanor. I am really—"

"Now before you say anything, I just want you to know that I know you are a good man. Eleanor has had nothing but good things to say about you. I know you have been here for about a year, and I know you got in trouble." She paused after the tone was established and just looked at me for a bit from across the kitchen island, intensely. Then she turned and looked out the window over the sink at where the dogs were lying in the grass, basking in the sun—three little islands in a vast green sea, oblivious, and carefree. Their faces radiated contentment as they picked up the scents on the soft breeze.

"So what happened?" I finally asked.

She took a deep breath without turning. "The doorbell rang," she said, shaking her head. "I look out and see a police car in the driveway. I don't like cops. They make me nervous. So already I don't like this, you know." She turned around to look at me again.

"Yeah. I know the feeling."

"So he asks me if Christopher Pelloski lives here," she continued. "You and I really haven't met, and I don't know your last name. Well, I didn't before." She gave a nervous smile, which quickly faded. "I told him, I know a Chris lives here, in the basement, but I don't know his last name." Then her jaw tightened a bit. "He then tells me that I better not be perjuring myself. That I could get in trouble for not cooperating with authorities and all that." She shook her head again, slowly. "So of course I get real scared, you know. I have no idea what is going on, and I don't want to get you in trouble. So I am really scared."

"Jesus. I am sorry—"

"So then he pulls out a picture of you and points to it and asks if this is the Chris that lives here. I usually see you in your glasses and you didn't have glasses in this picture, but it kind of looks like you, so

I panicked and said, 'Yes, there is a Chris that lives here that looks like that guy in the picture.'" She became anxious again. "I'm sorry. I didn't know what to do—"

"No, no, you did the right thing. I bet it was the checkup for the sex offender registry, to make sure I actually live here." She slowly nodded her understanding, seemingly relieved that I wasn't upset with her, and perhaps also that her assumption was correct. "Of course, he could have just asked my probation officer to verify, but, none of the parties talk to each other," I said, to show I was annoyed with the system, not Josie. "They came out last fall, too, and were a bit rude to Eleanor then."

"Yeah. This guy was a real prick about it," she continued. "After I said that was probably you, he gives me this big, fake, almost evil shit-eating grin—after threatening me with perjury, you know—and says, 'Well you tell "this Chris" to call us when he gets home.' Then he just walks away, gets into his squad car, and *slooooowly* pulls out of the driveway and *slooooowly* drives away—I could see all the neighbors looking out their windows or gawking from their front yards—like he was putting on some big show. I just closed the door, disgusted."

I just nodded and sighed and let my shoulders slump. That was what it was: residential verification of my sex offender registration.

"I know what you are going through," she told me. She turned to look out the window again, as if she might be envious of the dogs' obliviousness to the human goings-on indoors. "The same shit happened to my brother." She took another deep breath, gearing up to tell a story that had probably haunted her for a long time. I knew that presentation well by then.

"His daughter, my niece, was murdered, and they never figured out who did it. But my brother suspected that her husband did it. We all did. The guy was a violent, manipulative piece of shit—a low-life, you know. So he caught wind that the family suspected him, especially my brother, and he put their four-year-old daughter up to claiming that my brother, her grandfather, touched her inappropriately. It was complete bullshit. We all saw through it. I know my brother. I grew up with him. He would never harm anyone, and there was nothing in his fifty-plus years that ever gave me a worry or concern. And we had a few 'handsy' men in the extended family. So it's not like we were clueless. My brother was not one of them."

"Jesus."

"It was obvious that little girl was put up to it. Even the attorneys saw through it. But, that low-life kept pushing for a trial. God-damned sociopath, using his daughter to frame someone. The evidence was so flimsy, but the judge was up for reelection that year. So my brother was found guilty—but got less than a year—which says that judge had serious doubts. But it didn't matter. He spent his time in prison, fearing for his life, since, you know, he was a 'child molester.' He lost everything. When he got out, it took him forever to find a place to live. It took him forever to find a place that would hire him. It just destroyed his life. That piece of shit killed this man's daughter and made his life a butt of endless jokes. And do you know what my brother is most worried about?"

"No." I was too shocked to say anything else.

"He is worried about his granddaughter who, once she becomes old enough, realizes that she was used to put away her grandfather and ruin his life. He is worried about what that is going to do to her. That's the kind of good man he is."

I just shook my head.

"That is why I am not surprised that you are who you are and are being treated this way."

"Well, they are going to treat me how they want. But that is not cool how they treated *you*. Threatening you. That is horseshit. I am so sorry for this."

"Well, like I said, I know who you are. I know who my brother is, and as far as I am concerned, you have my utmost support." Once again, I had the right person by my side at the right time. I worried when those blessings would end, but right then I thanked Josie profusely and told her that her brother was lucky to have a sister like her.

The existence of the sex offender registry is predicated on the belief that all sex offenders have a high rate of recidivism and reoffense. The registry is believed to help communities and law enforcement keep track of these offenders—for the sake of public safety. The classic argument given is that if someone gets raped, law enforcement can quickly look up where sex offenders live nearby and expedite their investigative efforts, since they know right where these local, likely suspects live. However, this rarely ever happens, for a couple of reasons. First, most victims are raped or assaulted by someone they know—not the stranger in a ski mask hiding in the bushes. Second, those on the sex offender registry include people who got caught taking a drunken leak in a park or alley, married couples who got caught having sex in a public place, people slightly over the age of consent who had consensual sex with a slightly younger significant other, and people who looked at illegal pornography—not exactly the likeliest of potential rapists. But the biggest reason that the registry is ineffective is because the assumption that sex offenders are at a high risk for reoffending is pure bullshit.

That assumption stems from a 1986 article in *Psychology Today* written by Robert Longo. In the article, Longo stated categorically that, "Most untreated sex offenders released from prison go on to commit more offenses . . . Indeed, as many as 80 percent do." This "fact" was a "best guess" assertion based on his limited experience working as a rehabilitation counselor in the Oregon prison system; he presented no data to back up the claim. Further, the article was not scientifically peer reviewed but was rather more of an opinion piece in a popular psychology magazine. Yet, this nugget of "data" was picked up by Barbara Schwartz, a psychologist who incorporated it into a 1988 Department of Justice (DOJ) handbook. Years later, in an interview for *Untouchable*, a 2016 documentary about sex offenders, Schwartz essentially admitted to her fabrication: "I couldn't find any information on sex offenders' recidivism rates . . . so basically I just made up a model." Among the six references that "supported" her declaration were a dictionary and Longo's *Psychology Today* article. Schwartz admitted to "making a bunch of guesses."

To Longo's and Schwartz's credit, both are now appalled to know that their best guesses became the foundation for the harsh sex offense policies that are now in place (according to a 2017 article by Jacob Sullum)—policies that ignore all the social-science research that has been done since the 1980s. Schwartz has called it "deliberate indifference."

This DOJ handbook was later cited by Solicitor General Ted Olson, who passed this information on to Supreme Court Justice Anthony

Kennedy. Justice Kennedy mentioned the "80 percent recidivism" rate claim in the 2002 *McKune v. Lile* decision, which upheld a mandatory prison therapy program for sex offenders, and in the 2003 *Smith v. Doe* case, which upheld the retroactive application of Alaska's registration requirements for sex offenders. As of 2015, this false finding has been repeated in 91 judicial opinions and briefs filed in 101 cases, reinforcing the misconception. And once a Supreme Court justice says that something is real—even when it isn't—it might as well be. And this happens almost overnight. This one incorrect assertion is the basis for all the harsh sex offender laws that have been recently enacted, including exorbitant prison sentences and the registry.

Longo's article is eerily reminiscent of a letter to the editor in a 1980 issue of *The New England Journal of Medicine* (Jane Porter and Hershel Jick, M.D., "Addiction Rare in Patients Treated with Narcotics"), which declared that there was only a 1 percent likelihood of patients becoming addicted to opioids after short-term use. This five-sentence paragraph, which was also not peer-reviewed, went on to be cited in the literature hundreds of times, and, taken out of context, was used by Purdue Pharma to assert the safety of OxyContin, leading to a massive increase in prescriptions for the drug and ushering in America's current opioid epidemic.

These two examples demonstrate what can happen when an unquestioned authority—the highest court in the land and one of the world's most prestigious medical journals—is a source of dubious information. The first example has given us a program that costs taxpayers billions of dollars annually to enforce, with no demonstrated safety benefit, and creates a subclass of citizens with severely violated constitutional rights, as the punishment continues in perpetuity after they have served their penalties. With the second example, we currently have three million opioid and heroin addicts, with more than half a million dead from drug overdoses between 2000 and 2015. Ninety-one Americans die from these drugs every day now.

The reality is that numerous social-science and criminology studies, at the state, federal, and international level, have consistently determined that the recidivism rate for sex offenders is very low. According to a meta-analysis in the *Journal of Interpersonal Violence* published in 2014, which examined the histories of 7,740 sex offenders, the recidivism rate for low-risk offenders (nonviolent, noncontact, etc.) is 1 to 5 percent after release from incarceration/probation, and it stays at that rate, even past ten years. High-risk offenders (rapists, molesters, etc.) have an actual recidivism rate of 22% within the first five years of release, and that falls to about the five percent range after ten years. So the rate of even the worst-of-the-worst sex offenders is still a far cry from the erroneous 80 percent claim. These numbers are dwarfed by the recidivism rates for just about every other crime except murder—even more so when one considers that included in these figures are technical violations and nonsexual crimes, much like Jermaine's failure to reregister with Ohio when he moved from Illinois. What this boils down to is that the trail of victims that sex offenders are purported to leave simply does not exist. But our society is made to think there is, and confirmation bias ensures that we continue to believe it. New draconian policies continue to be crafted and reform efforts continue to be thwarted based upon this widely accepted falsehood.

The way the news media covers sex offenders is geared toward fear mongering, rather than providing information. Whole segments of local news shows are dedicated to sex offenders: who haven't registered, who just moved in, who was spotted where, etc. They never say how the person ended up on that list. *A public urinator just moved into your neighborhood* just doesn't have the punch of *You have a sex offender next door! Protect the children!!* The label has taken on a life of its own that is, in many cases, far worse than the inciting offense. In other words, the public urinator is assigned the same threat level as a serial rapist. As one of my former clinical instructors said, "If everything is important, then nothing is important."

Sex offender status can also be misleadingly portrayed. The Ohio-based website entry for me states that my offense was sexually motivated. This is so inaccurate as to be libelous. It was traumatically motivated—yet that evidence is ignored. To make matters worse, it states that my victim was a six-year-old female not known to me, which makes it sound to the casual reader like I was a stranger who picked some random child to molest. I know this because, when I began to rent from Eleanor, some of her friends expressed concern to her that she was renting to "someone who molested a six-year-old."

It's incredible that a strict liability crime (meaning the act itself is the crime, regardless of motive) should have so much weight given to the motive, in terms of the reaction towards it and the social policies that govern it, when in so many cases, the assumed motive is incorrect and retroactively ascribed. And having a police car parked in the driveway of a home where a sex offender lives doesn't really help clear the air either. That show of force may just be part of a routine residence verification, but it can easily rile up nosy neighbors and scared soccer moms who may wonder *What did he do now?* given the high-recidivism myth, making the tasks of re-assimilating and staying under the radar damn near impossible for a registrant.

I suppose people can't fathom any reason, other than evil, why someone would choose to do something disturbing. That is because the emotionally driven decisions made by an unhealthy mind do not make sense to a mentally healthy person. Why do people continue to shoot up heroin when they know their family is suffering because of this behavior? Why do people drive drunk when they know it is dangerous and risk getting pulled over? Why do people continue to gamble even after losing all their children's college funds? Are they evil? The answer is much more complex. But for many, it is easier to write people off and dehumanize them, because of their illogical or repugnant behavior, than it is to consider all the factors at play.

This most likely stems from a skepticism about mental health that, compared to most Western societies, may be uniquely American. A 2015 article by Kathleen Weldon from the *Huffington Post* cited data showing that 30 to 50 percent of Americans view depression and other mental illnesses as a sign of personal or emotional weakness, and that one in five Americans felt that seeking help or taking medication for a mental health condition is a sign of "character weakness." It harkens to that old school adage, "It's all in your head." Which is, ironically, true—just as COPD is all in your lungs.

Let's take a minute to compare two things that I know something about: cancer treatment and the judicial system. During the evolution of an FDA-approved anti-cancer drug, it undergoes rigorous scientific vetting at the concept, laboratory, animal study, and human/clinical trial levels. It can take ten to twenty years before a drug goes from an idea to becoming part of the standard-of-care treatment. At each stage, the mechanism of drug action, efficacy against disease, and toxicity is closely monitored. By the time the drug is ready for clinical use, an entire peer-reviewed body of literature has been generated that is backed by a mountain of data. It is approved only after enormous population-based studies (sometimes requiring thousands of patients) have shown the desired results.

The way some of our laws are written is the polar opposite. Sometimes an event is so horrific that the disgust and outrage initiate a legislative process to make sure that such a thing could never happen again, and to give a sense of closure and empowerment to the victims or their families. In these cases, often the law is named after the victim. In these types of laws, the data consists of a single point. The sample size is $n = 1$. And from this $n = 1$, laws that affect thousands are created that have huge societal costs (in dollars and suffering) and other unintended consequences.

If this approach were applied to anti-cancer drug development, we might have a situation where a desperate medical oncologist is willing to try anything to save his patient, Megan, from a rapidly progressing acute myelogenous leukemia. He reaches for an experimental drug that a grad student is using on frog epithelial cells in a petri dish in the basement laboratory of his facility. He administers it to Megan, and miraculously, she is completely cured of her leukemia. So with this $n = 1$, the oncologist pushes forward his new drug, Megan's Drug, and in this scenario he is able to mandate that *all* cancer patients be given this drug—because cancer is horrible and kills people and it should be prevented from killing people at all costs. And so Megan's Drug is given to every cancer patient. But what happens? It has no effect on solid tumors, like lung or prostate cancer. It has only a modest effect on sarcomas. And the kicker is that it only works on certain leukemias. It also turns out that patients who get this new miracle drug have an almost 50 percent mortality rate due to liver and kidney failure. The effort to stop all cancers has resulted in tens of thousands of prematurely dead cancer patients.

Of course, this scenario would never happen in the field of oncology because that is not how anti-cancer drugs are developed. An oncologist who proposed treating *all* cancer patients with the new drug based on an $n = 1$ test population would get laughed off the podium at medical conferences. Yet, this is exactly how our legislative process works. Very little large population-based, social-science studies go into our lawmaking, and most especially, not to our sex offense laws. About the only thing our two-party political system can agree on is to ratchet up the punitive measures against sex offenders because it's an easy way to make it look like they are doing something. Everyone feels safer, and the taxpayers who are left footing the bill for these measures don't say boo about it.

Now, the knee-jerk response to this criticism is typically, *Well, if it can prevent one bad thing from happening, then it is worth all the hassle and cost.* But that's *not* how it works. It may feel good to say that, but it's *not* worth the cost. First, we cannot prevent every bad thing from happening—no matter how much we do. Second, the logic is inherently flawed. An extension of this thinking would mandate that everyone be locked up for life because one or more of them might commit a crime. You cannot erase the liberties of the many to prevent the bad behavior of the few and still expect to have a functioning society—whether it concerns convicts or free people.

There are many instances where the laws of the land were made to placate the unsubstantiated fears and beliefs of the masses. Japanese Americans were put in concentration camps (I refuse to call them internment camps—they were concentrated, into a camp, after all), because Anglo Americans feared that each individual Japanese American had a direct line of communication to Emperor Hirohito during World War II. The myths surrounding sex offenders are no different.

In contrast to the United States, much of Western Europe actually uses data and social science to help guide their policies. As a result, those countries have much lower crime rates, shorter incarceration times, spend less money on their prison systems, and have a fraction of the recidivism rates as we do in the States. It's because they use the same approach to create their laws as the one that led to platinum-based chemotherapy being used in cervical, lung, and head and neck cancers, rather than the disastrous Megan's Drug scenario.

From the perspective of an offender, the messy, unsupported by evidence, and hyperbolic punitiveness of these laws impedes the process of atonement. If I got my hand chopped off for stealing an apple, rather than focusing on the harm that I generated against the agricultural and fruit distributor industry (by cutting into their bottom line and impeding business growth opportunities), I would be preoccupied with the fact that I was missing a hand. Further, all the incorrect assumptions linked with the offense—that you want to molest children, that you are sexually attracted to children, that you are a monster—make it almost impossible to speak in your own defense. Any alternate explanation can seem like minimizing what you did. And the situation is made even more difficult when some segments of the population call you a child molester while other, more libertarian-leaning people feel like you did nothing wrong since you just looked at a record of something that had already happened (as one normally does when, say, watching TV news). Some people want you hung from a tree, beaten with a baseball bat, castrated, or thrown in prison for life. Meanwhile, other civilized democratic societies in Europe view the same offense as a misdemeanor and mandate counseling—end of story. With such a wide spectrum of reaction toward this offense, it's nearly impossible to come to grips with a constantly moving moral target and know exactly for what I am to atone.

It's seems to confuse some people that I can simultaneously be both critical of the policies that govern my offense and feel remorse for my offense. As if speaking out against the policies are in some way minimizing or excusing what I did. That is a simplistic assessment. These people are insisting upon an all-or-nothing, black-white explanation, but such a reductive perspective can never provide full—or productive—answers. For me to accept the blanket condemnation, to agree to wear the Monster label, would be for me to endorse and perpetuate a system that is entirely wrong in its basic assumptions, and ultimately counterproductive to society.

Chapter 18

"Nearly all men can stand adversity, but if you want to test a man's character, give him power."

—ABRAHAM LINCOLN

ONE SUNNY SUNDAY afternoon I was returning home from a jog and had just reached the front door when I heard the screech of tires from the T intersection two houses down. I turned in time to see two pickup trucks collide in an explosion of sound and debris. The speed they'd been traveling was way too fast for that street.

I always hated that intersection. It sits at the top of a fairly steep hill, creating a blind spot in both directions, especially for those turning onto the road. The sun hung low in the sky, behind the hill, and based on how the two trucks had collided, I deduced that one of them was turning left, its driver not seeing the other truck coming up the hill, possibly with the sun in his eyes. The other driver was probably unable to see the turning truck at the crest of the hill, and was certainly speeding. I had frequently seen collision debris at that intersection. None of this was surprising to me.

The sound of the explosion echoed through the neighborhood, and people who were already outside ran toward the scene. Those who lived in houses close to the intersection came out and started calling 911. The driver of the oncoming truck got out and asked people to call an ambulance and see if the occupants of the other vehicle were OK. He stumbled as he walked across the road and then fell to the ground. A few people gathered around him, obviously not knowing what to do. A young woman exited the passenger side, dazed and crying. The driver of the turning truck, which had been T-boned in the accident, was motionless and slumped forward, his inert body being held up by the shoulder restraint. "There are injuries!" someone yelled into their mobile phone. Others shouted in panic and confusion: "Are you OK?" "Who else is in the car?"

I stepped off the porch, and began to walk toward the intersection, but then I started seeing the faces of neighbors whom I'd never talked to over the year-plus I'd lived in the neighborhood taking quick glances toward me. What was I going to do? If I started doing a neuro exam on crash victims, or started palpating their abdomens to identify internal bleeding, I was going to out myself as someone with medical training. I would have to give statements to police and paramedics and put my name to them. What if the neighbors who had previously been quiet suddenly started wondering why someone like me is living in the basement of one of their neighborhood's homes, sparking a new uproar? Would I get into trouble for practicing without a license? How would someone feel if they later learned the guy who was probing their belly was a registered sex offender?

I stopped in my tracks. *To hell with it*. It was too disheartening that I had to run through this mental checklist of considerations before using my medical expertise and training to help people. I made an about face and returned to the porch. As I turned the key in the door, I could hear the scene building over my shoulder—more shouts and traffic backing up behind the collision.

I went downstairs, texted my probation officer that I returned from my run (I had to let him know when I left and when I arrived home, because I ran through a park, a place where children congregate), took a shower, poured milk over a bowl of Frosted Mini-Wheats, and watched the Lions beat the Vikings in overtime, all the while trying not to think about what was happening not a hundred yards away from where I sat stuffing my face and watching NFL football. As I did, a realization crept in. I had gone from being someone who was willing to buck the rules and regulations—to risk getting in trouble with prison authorities and losing good time or getting sent to the SHU— to help a convict who was just having a seizure, to being someone who turned his back on a real medical emergency involving unincarcerated taxpayers who had real worth and value by society's standards. It's incredible what being broken down does for one's apathy and cynicism. I'd put my own interests above the immediate, physical needs of others. It was a bitter pill to swallow, but I took the low road nonetheless.

My drift away from medicine and the tenets of the Hippocratic Oath had, of course, begun much earlier—even before the decision was made for me by the Medical Board of Ohio. But this was the first time I'd been confronted with a choice. And I chose not to help—for the first time ever. Making that decision was both eerily easy and shameful, in equal parts. At least society was safer, though.

But I didn't turn my back on all humanity, I just chose to serve a smaller subset: the humans of Hammond Industries, who had shown *me* humanity. Rather than serving the whole population—everyone being at risk of acquiring one cancer or another—I chose a tribe: the handful of people who'd taken me in, and let me be who I was, and slowly came to accept me without judgment. Who didn't think I was a dangerous monster. Who looked beyond the headlines and assumptions and actually got to know me. In time, I became part of their family.

Hammond's culture of acceptance has a long history. I was not just there because of my surname. A lot of guys with a checkered past had worked there. One of the guys in production had served time as a result of his struggle with drug addiction a few years back. He was such a valued worker that his job was there for him when he got out. When he had a heart attack while at work, followed by triple bypass surgery the next day, management scrambled to figure out a new position for him when he returned, since he would have physical activity restrictions post-surgery. I only learned about his record talking with four other co-workers after he was driven off in the ambulance. In just that group of five, three of us had done some kind of time. It is rare, these days, for a company to look beyond the background check and see the value of the person and offer a shot at redemption. The incident only deepened my appreciation for Hammond's very humanistic approach to its employees.

Over time, my skills returned—all that scientific knowledge I had amassed and all the practical knowledge about how to manage a laboratory and people, to develop research programs, to effectively communicate complex issues to a mixed audience, to teach and mentor, to organize operations. These were the parts of my old professional life that I missed the most. Hammond provided me with an environment where they could be reanimated, after being dormant for years.

It didn't matter that it was a new field for me. In some ways, I felt that not knowing everything and having little experience was a way for the universe to keep me grounded and humble. I was no longer an expert who knew all the answers—and that was finally OK with me. I could talk openly about my ignorance, not try to conceal it as I did when I was a cancer expert, when I wasn't allowed to not know something.

The scientific process and the path to discoveries was the same. And the way private, industrial research worked was much better suited to my approach and personality as well. In the academic oncology field, research efforts lived and died by federal grants. Oftentimes you spent months writing a grant proposal, asking a question you already knew the answer to, in hopes that you would be among the 5 percent who got funded. And you wouldn't find out for six months or more after you submitted it. The term for this art form was *grantsmanship*, and it was the only way your lab got funded and thus the way the people in your lab put food on their tables. But it was also why the war against cancer saw such infinitesimal gains, much like the World War I trench warfare. There was little room for risk or groundbreaking discoveries.

Private industrial research moves much faster. I am sure some of this has to do with the fact that human biomedical research needs to be checked by regulations to ensure direct patient safety. But in the realm of physical/technological science, if you have an idea or a gut feeling, with a little preliminary data the game could change almost instantaneously. I liked that aspect of it. A lot of my scientific hunches regarding cancer had proved to be correct, but they were only actualized by others, years—if not decades—after I made my postulations. That work moved at a snail's pace.

At Hammond, I was given charge of using a technology called electrochemical impedance spectroscopy (EIS) to measure how our anticorrosion coatings did their jobs. For decades, the EIS field had shied away from using the technology with zinc-rich coatings, saying it couldn't be done. Engineers and grad students lamented many a fruitless effort with this class of paint. But words like *It can't be done—we have tried and it doesn't work* were always music to my ears. I heard the same thing in the radiobiology field, when I was told that large numbers of mice could not receive the same numbers of radiation treatments as humans do, because the mice die from the repeated anesthesia. It had been tried for decades. But I created a system for doing so in under two years, enabling us to ask and answer a lot of cancer therapeutic questions in a short time using an actual living system, not just cells growing in a dish. I missed that kind of intellectual challenge and the opportunity to rise to the occasion. But that all came back. And so did I.

With EIS, I could break down the voltage potential and impedance changes over the duration of an environmental exposure and quantify them. The way zinc-rich coatings work is that the zinc pigment in the paint oxidizes first. This gives the coating a white appearance, but it spares the iron in the steel from rusting and weakening for a long time. This is particularly important if the coated part is an axel on a car or a strut on a bridge. When those items fail the result can be catastrophic.

The proprietary method I developed was a game changer. Where previously it had been necessary to evaluate almost three months of exposure to saltwater spray to determine which coating showed rust first, my method allowed for much more rapid screening of candidate paints and faster feedback on the use of the raw materials that went into them. For paint formulators who had been in the business for ten, twenty, or thirty years, the new method gave them a whole new way to look at what their products did. It also delivered much more functional information, rather than just determining how long it took before the coated steel would start rusting under the paint.

But for me, on a personal level, it solidified my importance to the research efforts of the company. I, indeed, brought a fresh set of eyes to the company. I was not just riding on my dad's coattails. This method is now used in the development of all of Hammond's coatings, and the competitive advantage it confers may be immeasurable. I made that happen—and quickly. Once my techniques showed some promise, I suggested we get a $100,000 package of equipment and instruments to expand our throughput. It arrived at our facility within a week—no futile grant writing or six-month wait needed.

When I arrived at the Kentucky facility of Hammond, it was essentially cut off from the main facility and headquarters in Detroit. It had long been in decline and was at its nadir. Although DJ had done a great job as the research manager for about fifteen years, over the last five or so he had begun to look past his role there and toward the next phase of his life. There had been bad blood between DJ and some of the people who worked there and with some others in Detroit.

Things changed after I had been there for about a year. Much to my father's chagrin (he was still hoping I would return to medicine), I was tapped to assume the role of lab manager due to my experience in leading programs. I was paired with Tim, the chemist and formulator, who had almost twenty years of experience. We were to act together as the co-research directors. I worried he would be insulted by my having been put in that position, that it was all down to nepotism. But his reaction was quite the opposite. He welcomed me with, "Dude, I don't know shit about managing!" To which I replied, "Good, because I don't know shit about paint!!" We hit it off and made one hell of a team. It was as if the company gained not only a fully functional lab, but a thriving one, almost overnight. A few days after the leadership change, a double-rainbow shone majestically over Hammond. So I ran outside and snapped a picture of it. Tim and I took it as a sign of good things to come.

Perhaps a Pot of Zinc Lay at the End of this Rainbow?

Sadly though, after one more blowup, DJ was let go. And in my new position, I was the one who had to let him know. It was one of the hardest things I had to do. How do you tell one of your childhood heroes that the company where he's worked for almost thirty years has fired him? I managed; I guess I'd become well versed at delivering bad news. But after he left the room I wept. I had not cried at work since one of my pediatric patients died, many years before. But his dismissal paved the way for a true fresh start for everyone in the lab.

My laid-back, informal leadership style was especially helpful in a facility situated in Appalachia. Having my legs taken out from under me had diminished the uppity Yankeeness of my more northerly roots. I slipped back into teacher/mentor mode, but combined that with goofing off with the folks in the lab. We'd often throw a Blitzball back and forth to each other, throwing curves, sliders, and forkballs while discussing projects or addressing production problems. Or we'd go outside and throw a football around for a breather. Self-deprecation and silliness went a long way toward getting people to believe in themselves and go beyond merely doing what they'd been told to do. And this in turn allowed us to achieve more than we'd thought possible.

Our productivity soared once Tim and I took charge of research operations, which made the Hammond Brass in Detroit ecstatic. And I saw, for the first time, that I did not need to submerge myself in work to get results. I had some balance in my life. I'd always thought I needed to get myself in a maniacal state to achieve, but I learned I didn't need to do that. And my co-workers, who knew all about me—previous and current life—were there if I started getting too tunnel-visioned or kept my foot on the gas for too long. I was told not to stay late or come in on weekends. They looked out for me; they recognized my propensity to work too hard and told me to knock it off if it flared up.

But one of the greatest things my position afforded me was the chance to work more closely with my father. We would design experiments together and discuss them over the phone in the office or when I visited my parents in Michigan. (Mom would frequently roll her eyes when we got going, but she followed that with a warm smile, seeing that he and I were working and healing together.) He was a bottomless fountain of practical and theoretical knowledge. Every time I talked to him, I learned something new. From the ambient temperatures and humidity of an application facility and how that affects the way paint flows off of a part to polymerization reactions of a resin and additives, he just knew it all. And he was proud of how quickly I learned and of the work that I did for the company he'd dedicated his life to.

I also got to see firsthand the stress he had lived under for all the years I was growing up. I got to see why he was sometimes distraught when he came home and would vent. All the research questions, troubleshooting, and the eleventh-hour miracles had come directly from him. He was not exaggerating when he said millions of dollars and hundreds of people's jobs were on the line when he made final decisions. I got to live in the world he'd created. Every experimental protocol, every QA form—the whole system—was his creation. I could recognize his voice and fingerprints in each step of the product-development process. In many ways, I got to walk through his mind and realize just what an incredible natural genius he really is. The founder's original vision coupled with my father's scientific and organizational aptitude—starting with just some test tubes in a makeshift lab—truly created an entire niche industry, and along the way built a house that provided a livelihood to so many people. I was honored to be part of that. I felt like I had finally come back home, as a scientist.

Over time, my father became more accepting of my being part of the company. After Tim and I turned things around at the Kentucky facility, and after I gave presentations to Ford and Chrysler engineers, who walked away duly impressed, he came to see the value of my participation in the company he'd helped build. Despite his obligatory objections, I think he was proud that the same company he helped build stepped in to rescue me.

I still had an avenue to use my medical knowledge, as well. Through my consulting work on the side, I was helping guide the research efforts of a radiation oncologist in Shanghai. Economically, China had grown very quickly over the last several decades and had developed the modern medical infrastructure that it had been lacking. But experience and know-how were still needed. That was where I was able to help, with the multidisciplinary approach I had learned at MD Anderson. There were a few instances where I got to design clinical trials for glioblastoma that I could have only dreamed of doing if I were still a doctor in the United States. I was also functioning as an editor-in-chief for several radiation oncology journals. The advice I was able to give in publications, in addition to accepting and rejecting the works was another way I could still keep my hand in the oncology field.

In addition, several times I was called upon to weigh in and decipher events in medical malpractice cases conducted by attorneys in Columbus, who knew I had the skills to do so. I was able to take hundreds of pages of medical records and distill them into the critical threads of events and decisions. In some ways, I was a neutral medical arbiter in determining whether a case was worth pursuing or if the correct decisions had been made but the outcome was determined nevertheless by horrible, unpreventable bad luck. It saved all parties involved a lot of time and energy. My consulting work certainly kept me financially solvent as I was getting back on my feet.

The bottom line is that I was truly given a second chance. I was allowed to lead and innovate and use everything that I'd learned—not just the acquired science and management skillsets but the knowledge and insight needed to handle myself, emotionally, while trying to accomplish so many things. Eventually, I became as busy as I once was, but I did not have to work myself to death to get results. I knew, by watching my weight and being mindful of my fatigue, when I needed to take my foot off the accelerator and go do something fun or mindless—or at least something not work. I wasn't weighed down by narcissism, either. I wasn't projecting arrogance all the while being fearful I could not measure up. I measured up just fine. I had gifts. They weren't destroyed or lost by what happened to me. I was fully aware of the value of these gifts and no longer took them for granted this time around. I was going to preserve and respect them, as I hadn't before—and myself in the process.

I suppose I truly had to lose everything to finally appreciate what I had.

Chapter 19

"The first step to improvement, whether mental, moral, or religious, is to know ourselves—our weaknesses, errors, deficiencies, and sins, that, by divine grace, we may overcome and turn from them all."

"Right actions for the future are the best apologies for wrong ones in the past."

—TRYON EDWARDS

WHILE REINVENTING MYSELF PROFESSIONALLY, I was also able to peel back a few more layers of the onion when it came to my psychological makeup and what lay beneath my offense. Much to my chagrin, I had to admit that my probation officer was right about the sex offender treatment program. It did help me. Once I shed my distrust of the legislative overtones and one-size-fits-all reality that comes with a federal program that must accommodate *all* sex offenders, and once the topics of trauma, PTSD, and anxiety became the focus, I began to look a little deeper into myself. In the individual sessions, Frank definitely tailored his approach to each guy. His insights and perspective on my particular case were invaluable. Even having had a year of sexual abuse/PTSD counseling and more than eighteen months of the program, I was able to gain a whole new view of myself once I hit the homestretch of the program.

While I did not have a true porn addiction—no more than I was a true alcoholic—I had abused pornography much as I had abused alcohol. They were more related than I'd originally thought. Just like alcohol has a time and place (parties, celebrations, toasts, holidays with the family, going out with friends, etc.), pornography also has a time and a place (an outlet for horniness, a component of a couple's foreplay, a stimulant for producing semen samples in a fertility clinic, etc.). These are frivolous freedoms any free-thinking adult who appreciates both the first and twenty-first amendments to the Constitution can enjoy. What they should not be are coping mechanisms or ways to escape life's difficulties.

My use of alcohol was very straightforward. It was a form of self-medication, to turn off the high-alert status that my PTSD conferred upon me. It was a way to get out from under myself and make the fear and anxiety go away. I was a happy drunk—the life of the party who made everyone laugh. The use of alcohol in PTSD for this purpose is heavily researched and well documented. Interestingly, now if I drink too much, I go to dark places, feel the losses I have incurred, and anger bubbles to the surface, suggesting the impact the chemical has upon me has fundamentally changed. So, I don't drink to excess these days.

My relationship with pornography was much more nuanced. It turns out that as we develop during childhood, neural networks within our limbic system are being built that govern emotions and responses to events. Meaning that there is a unique, complex brain circuit with millions of nerve connections, neurotransmitters, and hormones for each emotion of the human experience: anger, love, fear, happiness, sadness, disappointment, etc. All have a cellular, molecular, and structural signature. After a normal, healthy childhood developmental process, these patterns are appropriately called upon to fire by the brain in response to events encountered later in the adult life.

My development was anything but normal. First off, I had the PTSD-susceptibility trait, meaning that I was born with my head on a swivel and already had an exaggerated fear/anxiety response. At the same time my parent's marriage was at a crossroads (with frequent and explosive fighting and a separation—which was traumatic enough for any kid to endure), I was sexually abused by several adults. Also, in that post–sexual revolution period, *Playboy* and *Penthouse* issues were ubiquitous in all households during my youth, which compounded my early exposure to sexual themes.

So basically, I had plenty of reasons for my fear and anxiety to be off the charts, all the while I was being sexualized and seeing sexual material that, collectively, barely made any sense to me at all at such a young age. The end result was that my fear/anxiety neural network had blended circuits and co-developed with my sexually themed neural network. My limbic system had no chance of separating these two very different human emotions without extensive therapy and reprogramming. I am certain that this phenomenon significantly contributed to the offending behavior of my fellow inmates at Elkton, who'd also experienced trauma and coincident early sexualization during their own tumultuous childhoods. The saturation of porn in today's Internet-based world (which makes *Playboy* and *Penthouse* look quite tame in comparison) is particularly concerning for the next generation of children who will be prematurely exposed to this content while encountering coincident life stressors during their development—suggesting this problem is only going to get worse and more common in the future.

Just as my mandated abstinence from alcohol made me reevaluate the role of alcohol in my life, my mandated abstinence from pornography put me through the same mental exercise. As I reflected, I recalled there were numerous times when I was not particularly horny, but was instead stressed, scared, exhausted, and generally out of my mind, and reacted by going to look at the ocean of pornography that had become abundantly available online. Watching consenting adults engage in sexual activity has nothing to do with trying to make a grant deadline or owing a massive tax debt. But in my mind, it did. I had subconsciously connected looking at sexually oriented material with periods of extreme fear and anxiety. It makes obvious sense to me now, just as I can clearly see the link between my alcohol use and PTSD. But throughout most of my life, I was blind to this connection. "The Program," the federal sex offender treatment program that I had distrusted and railed against, showed me this.

The revisiting of PTSD was also very illuminating and showed me that there is always a new insight to be gained, even regarding an old subject that you feel you have mastered. There is the concept called the Window of Tolerance. This is the healthy point of balance, where the world and the emotional responses to it are manageable. It is characterized by calmness with an arsenal of healthy coping mechanisms to deal with life stressors and other bumps in the road.

The Hyperarousal Zone is the hypervigilant state of a PTSD crisis. It's when the shit is really hitting the fan. You are on edge, fearful, combative/argumentative, paranoid. Emotionally and cognitively, things are highly dysregulated. Many times a week, I self-medicated with excess alcohol consumption or viewed legal pornography. These maladaptive coping mechanisms were the slow and subtle ways to shift me back into the Window of Tolerance. Alcohol created a false happiness when it was really the removal of stress and anxiety. Pornography provided a sense of familiarity with its association to stress and anxiety. When I overdid it, I shifted past this optimal emotional arousal zone and into the Hypoarousal Zone. This zone is characterized by emotional numbness, the reduction of cognitive processing and activity. It was where I could escape in my own mind and shut down. It is the yin to the PTSD crisis' yang of hypervigilance.

However, when times were especially bad for me, when my PTSD/existential crises were at their greatest severity, watching young children being raped, obviously in pain, and crying was a quick, if jarring, way to achieve an almost instant shift from being deep within the Hyperarousal Zone to deep within the Hypoarousal Zone—completely bypassing the Window of Tolerance. Viewing child pornography was a highly effective shortcut from a state of overwhelming fear/anxiety to extreme numbness. This was dissociation. This emotional-balancing behavior is what drove my repetition compulsion to reexperience my own sexual abuse, because that connection to my past guaranteed my mind's complete shutdown. It was also why my formal diagnosis of PTSD was given the modifier, "with dissociative features." Of course, the guilt and shame I felt afterward and the images I saw only added to my ongoing stress levels, making things worse in the long run.

That was not the end of it. I also realized that I had a very deep-seated streak of self-sabotage within me. It is a piece of psychological baggage that commonly comes with being a victim of abuse. One thinks they are not worthy of anything good. Despite all the hard work that I did, the sacrifice of my twenties to the field of medicine, the hours on end that I worked, a part of me felt like I didn't deserve any of the success I had, that I was a fraud. I had a raging case of imposter syndrome (Also known as *impostor phenomenon, fraud syndrome,* or the *impostor experience,* it is a concept describing individuals who are marked by an inability to internalize their accomplishments and a persistent fear of being exposed as a fraud. The term was coined in 1978 by clinical psychologists Pauline R. Clance and Suzanne A. Imes.) So the risk-taking behavior, the lack of respect for all I had been given and acquired—all of it—occurred because I never felt I deserved anything good in life—so why would I do anything to protect it? Despite putting in all that time and energy, sleepless nights, and masochistic dedication, I still felt like I was playing with house money.

The thing that normal, healthy people can't understand is why I wouldn't work to preserve my investment. Why would I throw it all away? The answer is that, in my broken mind, it wasn't mine to begin with. So it was almost a logical conclusion that I didn't care for or respect it. That is why I chose to do something illegal, something appearing stupid to the normal person, when I had so much to lose. This is also why meting out harsh punishments for crimes that are secondary to emotional or mental illness fail to deter others from committing them. The unhealthy mind does not rationally weigh the consequences of the illicit act—no matter how educated and informed it is.

My therapist, Frank, asked me to list and rank the factors that led to my offense, as part of my relapse prevention plan (something all participants in the federal sex offender treatment program must develop upon completion of the program). Repetition compulsion accounted for about 60 percent of my emotional undoing. A vicious cycle ensued, since seeing children being sexually abused stirred up more flashbacks of my own and generated new guilt. These feelings were intensified by treating children with cancer and reading about horrible atrocities committed against children. It all kind of reinforced in my mind that the world is, indeed, a dangerous place for children. About 20 percent was due to conflating viewing explicit sexual imagery with extreme stress and fear. There was plenty of that going on during my downward spiral. The last 20 percent was my self-sabotage streak, a symptom of my imposter syndrome. The more successful I became (I was on a meteoric trajectory professionally and financially), the stronger this tendency became. My mom, a few of my friends and even the forensic psychologist, Dr. Kimmel, have postulated that I wanted to get caught, that I am smart enough that if I was really into child pornography, I would have figured out a way to avoid detection and gone on the dark web or something. But I didn't, I put myself right out there so that the authorities could easily see me, with my status in the community making me an irresistible target for law enforcement and prosecutors. I am now certain that a part of me did this on purpose.

All of these factors combined to make a perfect storm, such that viewing child pornography became the smart-bomb of all maladaptive coping mechanisms, as it effectively hit upon each emotional scar and pathologic tendency that my mind had within it at the time.

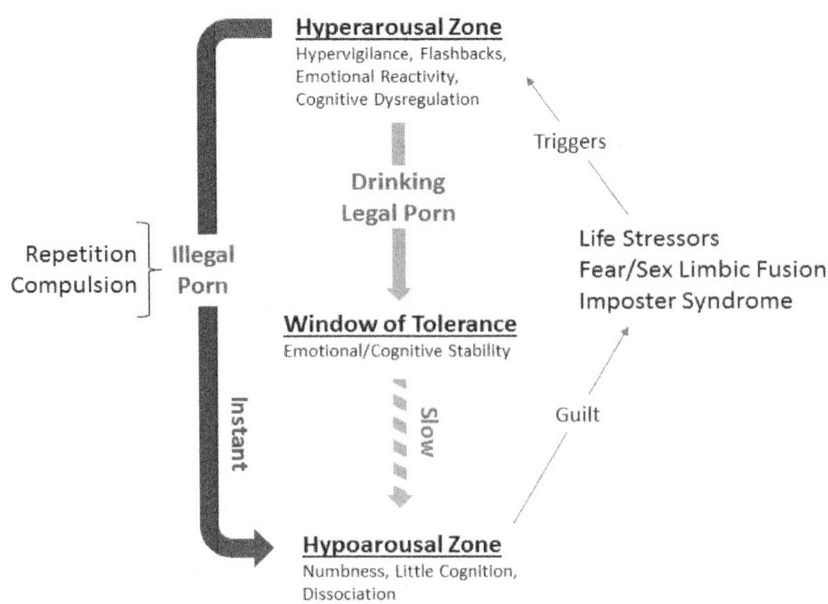

Psychological Schematic Of The Perfect Storm

My other takeaway from performing this exercise is that I can no longer say I have it all figured out. PTSD did play a role, yet I was previously convinced that it was the *only* thing going on. When I completed my first book, I felt like, *OK, that's done. Time to move on.* But it's not that simple. From now on I need to keep my mind open and my head on a swivel—not for imagined impending doom—but for being aware of my feelings and working to interpret them quickly. I can no longer stuff them down, ignore them and just press on with work and other things to keep from dealing with them. And while these latest revelations are indeed a much deeper insight into how I behaved compared to what I previously thought, I'm not "dropping the mic" and declaring victory. It's not that kind of self-discovery. It's a harbinger and reminder that there may be even more to learn about myself in the future.

I completed the federal sex offender treatment program on January 18, 2018, when I had my last follow-up visit with Frank. I was in the program for twenty-four months. I have to admit, here was where "the system" actually got it right—but this was *all* that was needed, really. That's how it would have been handled in Europe: counseling and a warning. I am not sure what purpose was served by the news vans and helicopters, scaring the hell out of people, putting me and other harmless people in prison (for years in many cases), or depriving the public of one very good cancer doctor and researcher. I suppose it was for news ratings, the projecting of others' fears and insecurities, the illusion that the world and its children were being saved through false heroism, and making those in the prison business richer at the expense of taxpayers.

Did I deserve to spend time in prison? I think it did me some good. It helped to break me down, strip off a few layers of narcissism, and allowed me to take a self-inventory and truly rebuild from the inside out. (But why was I on the hook for four years while others got eight, ten, or sixteen years for the same crime?) Maybe prison was good for me because, yes, I did need a time out, but my time there did not run much longer than the six-month period that seemed to be useful for otherwise nonviolent, non–career criminal inmates. I was also fortunate to have a good deal of support and to know I had a good job waiting for me when I got out. My experience was very different than that of the typical U.S. prisoner. It's more on par with a prisoner in Finland—hence the overall favorable assessment of my incarceration. For a lot of these other guys, though, prison (and the sex offender registry after) were the worst thing that could have happened to them. These harsh penalties made a bad situation worse and compounded it with new sets of problems for them.

Is the world at large better because of how these offenders are treated? More specifically, did my spectacle of a case set an example and deter others from doing the same thing? Are there now fewer files available online for others to see since the last time I ventured into the dark world of that peer-to-peer network on July 8, 2013?

One of the best things about this country is its capacity to change. Plenty of venerable institutions ("science," religion, politics, etc.) in the past have used fear, misinformation, and hidden agendas under the guise of authority to justify and enable destructive policies such as those perpetuating race and sex discrimination. The effectiveness of this strategy exposes the vulnerability of the American public and inspires contemporary tactics like "fake news" and Russian misinformation campaigns, which appear to sway opinion and even elections. But eventually the judiciary catches on and corrects the legislative wrongs (often via landmark rulings) of the other two branches of government. I certainly hope they keep hammering away at these crazy practices that currently dictate my life, as my judge has a record of doing. All the data and evidence are there—someone just needs to have the stones to trumpet them.

Federal judges are the best hope for this because of their lifetime appointments. Changes will not come from any political office that requires a vote from the public. In the current social climate, the slightest hint of reversing or lessening the severity of any form of punishment or post-incarceration supervision of sex offenders is career suicide for elected officials. Being branded as sympathetic to all those "dangerous perverts" is not a good look.

There is a bigger paradigm shift that needs to happen as well: We need to stop criminalizing mental illness and marginalizing the mentally ill. Perhaps we should look to the other side of the Atlantic Ocean for further guidance. I know we, as a society, are capable of doing so. Look at alcoholism. Previously, it was viewed as a character flaw, a choice made by a lesser person for the express purpose of embarrassing themselves and their families. People kept it a big dark secret. Now we call it a disease and have an entire industry and subculture based on its therapy. People openly talk about their recovery from alcohol in books and on talk shows. You can even show up in the operating room drunk, cut the wrong leg off, and get your medical license back—after the disease is treated and under control.

When I first got out, people who I had not heard from during my house arrest and incarceration started getting back in touch once I had access to regular email for the first time in nearly two years. Many had read my first book, and that was their impetus to reach out: former classmates, teachers, patients, and distant relatives who had been kept in the dark for quite a while. The support was incredible.

Very early on, I received the following email from a high school classmate who had moved in the same circles I did, but we were never really close. Yet he pretty much dissected my life after reading the book, and in so doing provided me a roadmap for what to do with all of this mess. I hadn't read his email for quite a while, but after completing the program and getting back on my feet, I had a deeper understanding of what he was saying.

> Hey Chris,
>
> I read your book. This next statement seems a little weak but I genuinely mean it: sorry you had to go through all of that hell, both as a child and as an adult.
>
> Before I got to the end of the book, I had pretty much come to the same conclusion you did in your final chapter, which was the childhood trauma may have been awful, but it did make you driven, it helped you become the intelligent, striving, scientific force you are today. Maybe the universe (I'm not one to believe in fate or destiny,

really) but maybe the universe had to torture you in your youth to ignite your real talents. Then, in turn, it took the shit legal mess to go back and fix what it damaged in making you, so that you could be a talent without burning out before your time—kind of a two-fold smelting process that, unfortunately, was hell to live through (and you were never given the choice of whether you wanted to do it or not) but it created a good man with a lot of skill, talent, energy, education and intelligence.

And obviously, as awful as it was, it didn't shatter your capability to love and empathize. Because if it had, I don't think your wife and children and parents and in-laws and vast number of friends would have stayed with you. At your core you were always a pure and good person, the "smelting process" was really just there to make you an immense talent.

Whatever, I'm sure you already had all those thoughts with your own metaphors to explain it, as did those around you. Coming from me, a sort of distant friend or acquaintance, it all sounds a little trite, but I just wanted you to know, some of us never really doubted you were a decent guy.

I think the book was obviously good for you and your mental healing, but more than that, it was an excellent look into the criminalization of these kinds of sex crimes (what you did, I personally wouldn't even classify AS a sex crime; I don't know what I'd call it, exactly, but you personally didn't commit a crime of sex). I think the information you detailed about PTSD and about how the laws work with the kind of case you went through is very important to get out there, important that people know.

I also think you had a rather scathing review of the Academic Medical Field, and that too, needs to come out. No institution—government, educational, corporate—should have the power to cajole, threaten, or ma-

> nipulate people into feeling they must turn their back on someone to protect their career. Unfortunately, I know that this happens in academia all over, not just in the medical schools and sports departments.
>
> You taught me some good information with your book, and I thank you for that. I really hope you are able to get back into the medical field and put your talents to use. I would love it if you were treating people again. I would love it if you were doing research again. Just don't try and do it all at the sake of your family. I think it is perfectly fine for you to let go a bit, not be a 100 percent in all areas, and take the time to enjoy being a dad and husband and a man on earth. I'm just one anonymous person, but you proved your worth to me back in high school just by being a nice guy.

My previous life's path was not the right one for me. It's like I was shot out of a cannon and never had time to stop and think about anything. I was always traveling at maximum velocity toward an elusive apex. I just didn't know there was any other way. Danger and failure were always just around the corner. There was no time to savor victory or learn from defeat. Defeat existed solely to be thwarted. At some point in my mid-thirties the projectile began to lose momentum—it could no longer maintain the upward trajectory—and I fell. Gravity won, and it was a steep and rapid personal descent.

A sad irony is that, without viewing child pornography, I would have never known for sure that I was sexually abused. Without getting caught, my life never would have got the time-out I needed to be able to connect the dots and see the effects the abuse had on me. Had I not had the opportunity to explain the emotions that viewing child pornography evoked, I would not have recognized the dissociation I was experiencing—a phenomenon that, once observed, would lead to my PTSD diagnosis. This intervention happened just as the cannon ball's plummet was accelerating.

How much worse would it have gotten? Would I have beaten my wife in front of my children? Would I have progressed from "Yelly Daddy" to "Punchy Daddy"? Would I have snapped and beat the crap out of someone at work? Would my mental condition have eroded so much that I started treating patients improperly so that either I did not give them a chance to cure their cancer or permanently harmed them with radiation? Would I have gotten completely hammered one night and driven my car through a crowd or killed other drivers? Would I have committed suicide or killed myself through overwork?

Any of those things could easily have happened if not for this intervention. And while my criminal act was deplorable, it pales in comparison to the direct harm I could have wreaked upon others through these alternate endings. That is probably why I did not kill myself. If I had been responsible for the death of people because I was drunk, or had physically hurt my wife or children, or let a patient die or paralyzed them, I probably would have offed myself. I don't think I could have ever forgiven myself for any of those outcomes.

To add a further layer of irony, from a public perspective, I would have been forgiven much more readily for beating my wife or plowing my car through a crowd or harming a patient while under the influence of alcohol. Yet I was figuratively burned at the stake for looking at something to process my trauma.

That said, despite the much greater humiliation and stigmatization, I would not change the defining events that led to my intervention. I am grateful that my offense was a passive one and not one in which someone was killed or maimed. Although disturbing and harmful in its own way, it was perhaps the least of the inevitable catastrophes that were awaiting me. And I can live with that, even if others can't get over what I did. I've done all that I can to make amends and better myself. The rest is out of my hands.

There is no going back to how I was. It would be like a butterfly turning back into a caterpillar again. Once a threshold moment has happened, things can never be how they were. But the silver linings abound.

Had this intervention not happened, I would never have spent the time that I did with my children during my house arrest, establishing the strong love-based relationship that I have with them now. My ex and I would not have had the clarity and courage to recognize and finally give each other permission to leave our difficult marriage. I would not have had the opportunity to reunite with my parents and brothers—who were essentially estranged by my maniacal, all-consuming, and ultimately empty ambition—and repair our relationships. I got to see and experience up close my father working in his field and understand the pressures he'd faced when I was growing up. I got to see the world he created, and I was able to step in and help hold the fort (and the people in it) that he helped build. I got to be there for my mom when she was being treated for breast cancer, when the old me would have been too busy to invest emotionally in her battle.

I also got to see just how important and permanent being a good parent is, even when your children are all grown up. My parents stepped up and were there for me, at a time when I needed them most. I got to feel the full power of unconditional love. And that gives me hope for the future with my own children. Sure, I will miss out on a lot of soccer games now, but I will always be their father, and they, too, will need my love and guidance in navigating their adult lives—which can be just as traumatic and challenging as childhood, if not more so.

I got to see what true mercy and forgiveness is, as well. I met so many great people along the way, guardian angels who were there to guide me through: George and Leonard, Russo, and even Jon, who taught me a lot about myself while at Elkton. Qui, who visited me every two weeks and spent hundreds of hours of her time to get my book published. John and his wife, who took me in as a member of their own family. My PO, Tom, and my counselor, Frank, who let me know they understood, even though they worked within the framework of a broken system. They were there to genuinely help me, not merely police me.

I finally had time to read books that expanded my knowledge of humanity, religion, and our collective history. Had things not changed, I would have missed all of these facets of life, the richness that was always around me but went undiscovered in my pursuit of the next big thing.

Frank once told me that I was in the top 0.1 percent of the guys he has worked with coming out of the prison system, with regard to the rapidity of my recovery. But I shouldn't be the exceptional outlier. My experience shouldn't be reserved for MDs from top-tier medical schools who have a job waiting at a company that is unique in the way it readily welcomes less-than-perfect people with open arms—that also happened to be one founded by their father. It shouldn't have depended on the luck of coming across Eleanor, who gave me shelter and defended her decision to frightened neighbors. It shouldn't have required liquidating my life savings (something many do not have to begin with) to ensure I had adequate legal representation to prevent me from being buried by harsh sex offender laws.

I was blessed. Most in my situation are not. But had any of us lived in Finland or Germany, none would need this series of miracles, lucky breaks, and other advantages to get back on his feet. We would have paid our dues (without the sensational dog-and-pony show and life-crushing penalties), received the counseling we needed and then reentered a society that was open to giving us a second chance. That understood not only were we rehabilitated but that we would work extra hard to truly take advantage of getting another shot at life. But that is not how it works in the States, where the majority calls itself Christian, but doesn't behave like it.

The source of my stress is no longer internal. It's all external. It's all the shit that came attached with my offense. And, of course, this is yet another irony. When I was so horribly emotionally dysregulated that I was killing myself, everyone was cool with that, because they didn't know what was all going on with me. Now that I've finally got my shit together, I am considered dangerous and can't be a doctor anymore. Only *now* am I unfit. How does this make any sense? But I try not to dwell on that too much—though I confess, it continues to eat me up from time to time. (I am allowed to be *both* sorry for what I did and upset about what happened to me.) I have come to the conclusion that it is much easier to deal with living under social policies that have no rational or scientific basis than it is to have one half of your brain trying to eat the other half. One has at least some sort of chance at true happiness with the former.

I have led an interesting life. I have learned so much—things that cannot be forgotten. I have seen and experienced the *human experience* from many angles and perspectives. I was educated at some of the world's greatest medical facilities. I helped save thousands of lives, and powerlessly watched many die. But I was also educated (with equal depth and intensity) in a prison, in a halfway house, and by sitting with social workers and psychologists and gaining an insight into myself and others.

As my friend said in his thoughtful email, this "smelting process" forged an innovative mind that is full of knowledge and skill, because it put a fire inside me to hammer out the best from my raw materials, my natural abilities. Regardless of its source, I have garnered a rich experience. I have shaken off the negative aspects of this process and learned to work to repair the damage that was done, along the way gaining a sense of awareness and humanism that I never had before. Having done all of that, I am primarily left with the good it created for me. I am now able to practice emotional jujitsu, whereby one uses the opponent's force (or life adversity, in this metaphor) to counter the attack, rather than relying only on one's own strength to oppose it.

To put it simply, I am happier now than I was before. And that is saying a lot. Before, I was a topflight radiation oncologist, trained at the best place in the world, who was earning half a million dollars a year. Now I am a felon and a registered sex offender and I live in, as Eleanor puts it, an old lady's basement. I have an unflattering picture of me posted on the public sex offender registry's website, complete with my address. On the surface, these circumstances are well beyond downfall—they look like a free fall into an abyss, by any usual measure. But under that surface is a sad commentary on who I was before. I have learned, the hard way, that all the money and prestige and accomplishments in the world mean shit if you hate yourself, if you are miserable. And I got to understand this before I go toes up, before I lie in my death-bed, lonely and bitter, and realize that life got the best of me because I fell prey to self-deception and delusions. Inner peace and meaningful relationships with others are the only things that matter.

That is what you get to take with you when you cross over. That's the real legacy you leave behind. All the rest is just bullshit.

I am just getting started with my new life. Only this time, psychologically speaking, I no longer have one hand tied behind my back.

I am not afraid all the time anymore.

Afterward

IT'S BEEN ABOUT a year since I completed the primary writing for this book, and I am well into the second half of my life. My new life. I met an amazing woman who loves me, clearly unconditionally. She met me when I was completely broke, was burdened with stigmatizing labels, and had zero game. We now live on a farm in Northern Kentucky (in the heart of 'das HaterLand' of all places!) and enjoy each day we have together as if it were our last. This city slicker as taken quite a shine to feeding chickens, learning basic carpentry, and using his hands to work the land. It's yet another unanticipated twist in the tortuous path my life has taken. How we met—completely happenstance in a Steak 'n Shake parking lot during lunch break at Hammond—makes me wonder if a higher power was at play. For that I am beyond grateful.

I am still on probation. I am still on the sex offender registry, and still no one has explained to me why that is—outside of the patent answer that it's the law. I am not sure how many passed polygraphs are needed to declare someone safe and warrant their removal from a list of unsafe people. But I have to think that at some point common sense will prevail in this country. Until then, I will just keep my nose clean and ride out probation.

I also look forward to my children getting older and learning more about what all happened to their dad. I look forward to having a more significant impact on their day-to-day lives again. I think those days are coming, too.

I finally have a chance for true happiness in my life. I just need a little more bullshit and a few more dust clouds to subside to fully enjoy it.

It's, as they say, a process.

Glossary

BOP: The Federal Bureau of Prisons (BOP) is a United States federal law enforcement agency. A subdivision of the U.S. Department of Justice, the BOP is responsible for the administration of the federal prison system.

Commissary: A store within a correctional facility, from which inmates may purchase products such as hygiene items, snacks, writing instruments, etc. It is generally prohibited for inmates to trade items purchased on commissary. However, certain items tend to be used as currency. Cigarettes were a classic medium of exchange, but in the wake of federal prison tobacco bans, postage stamps have become a more common currency item.

Diesel Therapy: A purported form of punishment in which prisoners are shackled and then transported for days or weeks on buses (the origin of "Diesel" in the term) or on planes (Con-Air) to multiple facilities across the country.

FCI: Federal Correctional Institutions (FCIs) are medium- and low-security facilities, which have strengthened perimeters (often double fences with electronic detection systems) and is mostly cell-type housing. Called "Up the Hill" at Elkton, given its topographical location.

FSL: Federal Satellite Low (FSLs) are low-security facilities, often adjacent to higher security facilities, which have dormitory housing, a relatively low staff-to-inmate ratio, and limited perimeter fencing with unrestricted inmate movement. The FSL was called "Down the Hill" at Elkton, based on its relationship to its corresponding FCI. Sex offenders were not permitted to be in true federal prison camps, which have no fences, due to their perceived security threat. Even non-violent/non-contact, computer-based offenders.

Good Time: Under United States federal law, prisoners serving more than one year in prison get 54 days a year of 'Good Time' on the anniversary of each year they serve plus the pro rata 'Good Time' applied to a partial year served at the end of their sentence, at the rate of 54 days per year. It encourages good behavior during incarceration, as it can be revoked with rule infractions. This is what made my 12-months and a day sentence significant. That extra day qualified me for 'Good Time.'

J&C: Judgment and Commitment. This is the form that states the defendant's plea, a jury's verdict or the court's findings, the adjudication, and the sentence imposed by the court, including the conditions of supervised release.

SHU: In the US Federal Prison system, solitary confinement is known as the Special Housing Unit (SHU), pronounced like "shoe."

Selected Bibliography

From Peer Reviewed Journals:

Hanson, Harris, Helmus, Thornton. 2014. "High-risk sex offenders may not be high risk forever." *J Interpers Violence*, 29 (15):2792-813.

Seto, Hanson, Babchishin. 2011. "Contact sexual offending by men with online sexual offenses." *Sex Abuse.* 23(1):124-45.

Linden, Leigh, and Jonah E. Rockoff. 2008. "Estimates of the Impact of Crime Risk on Property Values from Megan's Laws." *American Economic Review*, 98 (3): 1103-27.

van der Kolk. 1989. "The compulsion to repeat the trauma. Re-enactment, revictimization, and masochism." *Psychiatr Clin North Am.* 12(2):389-411.

Porter, Jick. 1980. "Addiction rare in patients treated with narcotics." *N Engl J Med.* 302:123-123.

Articles by Jacob Sullum and Elizabeth Nolan Brown, Reason:

http://reason.com/blog/2018/05/30/eighteen-is-old-enough-for-war-but-not-s

http://reason.com/blog/2018/04/11/court-says-relying-on-fake-recidivism-nu

http://reason.com/blog/2017/09/18/dick-pic-makes-teenager-guilty-of-sexual

http://reason.com/blog/2017/09/14/im-appalled-says-source-of-pseudo-statis

http://reason.com/blog/2017/05/31/house-overwhelmingly-supports-bill-subje

http://reason.com/blog/2017/03/08/justice-kennedys-trump-esque-claim-about

http://reason.com/archives/2017/03/15/sex-and-kids

http://reason.com/blog/2016/09/30/judge-dismisses-challenge-to-special-sex

Pertinent Newspaper Articles:

https://www.cleveland.com/courtjustice/index.ssf/2015/02/cleveland_federal_judge_hands.html

http://www.dispatch.com/content/stories/local/2014/07/11/Pediatric-oncologist-sentenced-to-1-year-in-prison.html

Made in the USA
Coppell, TX
08 January 2023

10668087R00164